IMAGINING
AFGHANISTAN

Global Fiction and Film of the 9/11 Wars

Comparative Cultural Studies

Ari Ofengenden, Series Editor

The series examines how cultural practices, especially contemporary creative media, both shape and themselves are shaped by current global developments such as the digitization of culture, virtual reality, global interconnectedness, increased people flows, transhumanism, environmental degradation, and new forms of subjectivities. We aim to publish manuscripts that cross disciplines and national borders in order to provide deep insights into these issues.

IMAGINING AFGHANISTAN

Global Fiction and Film of the 9/11 Wars

Alla Ivanchikova

Purdue University Press
West Lafayette, Indiana

Cataloging-in-Publication data is on file with the Library of Congress.

Paper: 978-1-55753-846-8
ePDF: 978-1-61249-581-1
ePub: 978-1-61249-580-4

Cover image: Courtesy of David Gill (www.shot2bits.com).

To my parents

Contents

Acknowledgments

I am deeply grateful to family members, friends, and colleagues for their ongoing support during the entire time I have been working on this project.

The cover image shows graffiti painted inside the ruins of the Russian Cultural Center by an Afghan artist named Shamsia Hassani. The words on the ravaged brick read, "The water will come back to the dried river, but what about the dead fish." The photo was taken in 2011 by photographer David Gill (shot2bits.com). Having been based in Kabul for seven years, Gill was the force behind many art and multimedia projects, including social documentary films *Kabul at Work* and *Afghanistan at Work*. My many thanks to these two for allowing me to use this image.

My home institution, Hobart and William Smith Colleges provided funding for trips to the archives and travel funds to disseminate my work at professional conferences. Students in my courses "Representing the 9/11 Wars" and "Imagining the Middle East" helped me grapple with many of the intellectual questions this book addresses. I am especially thankful to the Fisher Center for the Study of Gender and Justice at Hobart and William Smith Colleges that awarded me two fellowships, in 2015–16 and 2017–18. Conversations with other Fisher Center fellows, among them Marcela Romero, Robert Maclean, Elizabeth Johnson, Jennifer Cazenove, Nic Beuret, Matthew Crow, Megan Brown, and Kai Heron were invaluable and allowed me to refine the arguments for chapters two and five. I am especially grateful to Fisher Center Director Jodi Dean for her comradely support and unceasing enthusiasm for the project.

The seminar I took with Debjani Ganguly at the Institute for World Literature in Lisbon in 2015 helped me better frame some of the book's arguments. I am indebted to the works-in-progress research group colleagues for reading early versions of this work. Leah Shafer and Karen Frost-Arnold, my writing partners, made my daily writing practice a joyful experience. I thank my English Department colleagues for their support and encouragement, among them Anna Creadick, Laurence Erussard, Biman Basu, David Weiss, Grant Holly, Melanie Hamilton, Nicola Minot-Ahl, Rob Carson, Kathryn Cowles, Stephen Cope, and Alex Black. Women's studies colleagues, among them Betty Bayer, Etin Anwar, Christine Woodworth, Lara Blanchard, Charity Lofthouse, May Farnsworth, Rebecca Burditt, and Michelle Martin-Baron, provided useful feedback on early drafts. Anna Creadick, Kevin Dunn, and Chris Coffman offered valuable advice on the pragmatics of book publishing. I thank the Center for Teaching and Learning at Hobart and William Smith Colleges and Director Susan Pliner for offering writing retreats for faculty, which allowed for uninterrupted time to write at the end of each semester. Many thanks to Tina Smaldone for helping with logistical tasks. My gratitude also goes to Wendy Stoddard for teaching me the practice of meditation and mindfulness that helped me bring this project to completion.

Chapter two is derived in part from an article published in *Textual Practice* 31.1 (2017), copyright Taylor & Francis, available online: http:// www.tandfonline.com/doi/full/10.1080/0950236X.2016.1237987; an earlier version of chapter five was published in *Modern Fiction Studies* 63.2 (2017).

I thank the editorial team at Purdue University Press for their attention to detail and for bringing this project to the public. Comments by two anonymous reviewers were very valuable in making this book what it is today.

I am, of course, forever indebted to my wife, Melina Ivanchikova, who was a part of this project from its birth to completion and who made everything possible.

Introduction: Global Afghanistan

A Dim Object, a Bright Object

When photojournalist Lynsey Addario came back home to New York City in 2000, having traveled to Afghanistan still under the rule of the Taliban, she had trouble finding a venue for her photographs. She writes: "For a long time no newspaper or magazine bought them. In the year 2000 no one in New York was interested in Afghanistan" (77). At that time, Afghanistan was what object-oriented philosopher Levi R. Bryant would call a *dim object*—it emitted no light, attracted no attention, and the eyes of the world were not on it. This "dim" period lasted more or less from 1989—the year when the Soviet government made the decision to withdraw from Afghanistan (an event that marked the end of the Cold War, preceding the dissolution of the Soviet Union by two years)—to 2001, the year when the attacks on the World Trade Center in New York City shook the world. In the weeks following 9/11, as the United States was preparing to embark on Operation Enduring Freedom, the previously dim object suddenly became bright. As reporters rushed into Jalalabad, Kabul, Kandahar, and Herat, media outlets around the world were flooded with images of Afghanistan and its people.

What started with the brief operation to remove the Taliban regime was to become the United States' longest war yet.[1] Historian Robert D. Crews estimates that more than a million American military and military support personnel have cycled through Afghanistan since 2001, not including the coalition forces or third-party nationals hired in droves by private military contracting companies.[2] This number also excludes hundreds of thousands of other foreigners—writers, historians, anthropologists, reporters, doctors, reconstruction experts, election observers, political analysts, public relations professionals, and various other advisers and humanitarians—who went in and out of Kabul and other Afghan cities during the years following the American intervention. Many were idealistic and went to Afghanistan to be a part of the collective rebuilding effort. Others were opportunistic and predatory, eager to take advantage of reconstruction money.[3] Billions of dollars have been poured into Afghanistan's reconstruction and development project—an amount that, when adjusted for inflation, exceeds the Marshall Plan for postwar Western Europe; however, this incredible influx of cash somehow failed to deliver similar results. Paradoxically, for many westerners, a stint in Afghanistan was a chance for a career break or a welcome respite from their first-world economies marked by neoliberal austerity and unemployment. "Kabul . . . is one of the few places where a bright spark just out of college can end up in a job that comes with a servant and a driver," wrote Canadian politician Michael Ignatieff in 2003.[4] These expats—some mingling and even living with the locals, and others self-segregated in the loosely knit multicultural expat scene—left their marks on Afghanistan's urban cultures, affected the economy (sometimes drastically, and usually for the worse), and were themselves transformed through this encounter, prompting a transcultural cross-pollination. The two decades following the attack on the Twin Towers will enter history textbooks as an era of the global West's intense cross-cultural encounter with Afghanistan.[5] Now is the moment to reflect upon this encounter—not just from a historical or a political perspective, but from a cultural point of view that takes stock of what transpired in this meeting of the worlds.

The brightness of Afghanistan in the years following 9/11 affected not only mass media but also other forms of cultural production, birthing an array of cultural texts set in the country. This book offers a close look into the vast cultural ecosystem—novels, films, graphic novels, memoirs, and drama—that was brought into existence by the American invasion of Afghanistan—the corpus that takes Afghanistan as its object or its setting. In the early years of the US-led war, the demand for knowledge about Afghanistan exceeded the supply; in 2007, Corinne Fowler—a pioneering scholar who provided an early overview of mass media coverage of Afghanistan—spoke of "the paucity of narratives produced in recent years. There is not as yet a sufficient body of post-Operation Enduring

Freedom narratives about Afghanistan" (215). As I am writing this, in 2019, a vast body of written and visual texts is available to anyone who has interest in stories set in Afghanistan. In fact, all it takes is a quick search on Amazon for book or film titles that feature Afghanistan, Kabul, Kandahar, or Herat in their titles to realize that Afghanistan has become a cultural franchise. As such, this corpus has its own sets of rules, laws of probability and improbability, its sets of veritable characters, its obsessions and common themes. It also has its gaps, silences, elisions, and absences that are just as important as what is present. This set of cultural texts, mostly but not exclusively Anglophone, predominantly Western- or NATO-centric, makes some things visible, just as it condemns others to invisibility; it opens some discussions while foreclosing others. These gaps and absences, just as its revelations, are the subject of the subsequent chapters.[6]

Chronology does not play a large role in this book—the chapters are organized around several thematic clusters that I outline below. Yet the three distinct "waves" of writing and screening Afghanistan in the aftermath of September 11, 2001, deserve at least a brief mention. The first wave of post-9/11 texts set in Afghanistan, published between 2001 and 2007, brought into view the humanitarian crisis in the country while replicating some of the Cold War conventions of writing about Afghanistan and even making use of British colonial imagery. Texts by European travelers Åsne Seierstad and Rory Stewart, who journeyed to Afghanistan as soon as its borders were opened to westerners by the US-led Taliban ouster, exemplify this phase, as well as its neo-imperial investments. For most foreigners who visited Afghanistan in the aftermath of 9/11 the trip was an exotic adventure of a lifetime, so claims to an extraordinary experience abound in these early works. Vestiges of this colonial mode of writing about Afghanistan persist even in some texts of the second decade of the 9/11 wars. For instance, Edward Girardet, a European American correspondent with two decades of experience in Afghanistan, evokes the British colonial era profusely in his memoir *Killing the Cranes* published in 2011, a decade after the invasion: "Working in Afghanistan was like being a character in Rudyard Kipling's *The Man Who Would Be King*" (6). Other writers of the first wave, such as early Khaled Hosseini and Atiq Rahimi, positioned Afghanistan as a generalized zone of suffering in need of Western protection and rescue. They also deployed the tropes of Soviet barbarity as a shortcut to explaining the Afghan tragedy, suggesting that communism was the sole cause of the country's undoing. By the end of the first decade of the War on Terror, however, claims to an extraordinary (and solitary) experience were no longer the rule, and the urge to portray Afghans as victims subsided. In turn, a more complex panorama of Afghanistan emerged in texts that were nuanced and multidimensional, of significant didactic and philosophical value. Exemplary of this period are Hosseini's second novel, *A Thousand Splendid Suns* (2007), Kamila Shamsie's intensely lyrical *Burnt Shadows* (2009), and Nadeem Aslam's philosophical *The Wasted Vigil* (2008)—all of which I discuss in this book.

Finally, a third wave of texts—well into the second decade of the US-led war—dramatically expands our view of Afghanistan by making visible its transnational history and transcontinental connections. No longer exoticizing the Afghan people, these more recent texts draw attention to the global problems as seen from and through Afghanistan. Portraying Afghanistan as an outlandish, medieval, isolated locale by now seems like a tiresome cliché; representations of the country's recent history have become much more nuanced, historically grounded, and self-reflective. Exemplary of this wave are novels, graphic texts, films, and memoirs that I turn to in chapters four through six. Many texts of this period do not focus on their authors' solitary experiences, but by contrast, draw attention to the humanitarian community that gathered in Afghanistan post-9/11, and in American journalist Kim Barker's words, "behaved badly" (*The Taliban Shuffle* 78). The gaze is no longer on the "exotic Afghan" but on poorly behaving, opportunity-seeking foreigners in Afghanistan—members of a new international creed produced by a combination of neoliberalism-triggered hyper-competition for diminishing resources in the global North and US militarism.

When defining the corpus of texts that comprise the object of study in this book, I propose the term "global Afghanistan cultural production" to capture the specific nature and address of these works; these texts were not written or produced by Afghans for the Afghan public but were created by foreigners for a global audience. This book is not about Afghan national literature or film produced in Dari or Pashto by Afghan authors; a reader with an interest in Afghan national literature should look elsewhere, such as to the collection of stories *Afghanistan in Ink* that provides a timely and insightful overview of Afghan national and diasporic writing. Among the authors in *Imagining Afghanistan* are American, British, French, Canadian, Norwegian, Algerian, and Pakistani cultural producers— all foreigners with their own agendas and geopolitical positioning.

A few works by Afghan-born authors are treated, such as works by Khaled Hosseini, Qais Akbar Omar, and Nelofer Pazira; however, all three are bicultural exiles residing in the United States and Canada and writing for Anglophone publics. Many of the cultural producers that comprise the global Afghanistan corpus in this book are intimately familiar with Afghanistan, having spent years there or having traveled extensively in the country. There are many texts, however, that were produced by foreigners who admit to having never been to Afghanistan; by setting their stories in Afghanistan, they engage in the act of imagining the country as befitting their own desires and agendas.[7] The texts examined here thus are windows upon Afghanistan only in a very specific sense: They are windows not onto Afghanistan and its culture, but onto the shared world of global cultural producers (mostly NATO-centric), as they capitalize on their (mostly Western) publics' appetites for cultural otherness and curiosity about a distant war.

Global Afghanistan writing and film are often in conversation with the set of works that has been referred to as "the 9/11 novels and film"[8]— cultural texts produced in response to the attacks on September 11, 2001. While there are many overlapping themes, the global Afghanistan corpus has distinct features that are often in tension with the 9/11 cultural production. In contrast to the 9/11 works with their deep investment in national trauma, memorialization, the issues of representability, and US national recovery, the texts I discuss in this book are examples of transnational cultural production insofar as they do not prioritize a single national perspective and are not focused on helping the American nation heal. In fact, while in the 9/11 texts the exceptional event of the attacks typically constitutes the affective and symbolic nerve, in the works I discuss in this book, 9/11 remains largely absent. If addressed at all, the event of the attacks is usually described indirectly and is registered from afar, as the reverberations make their way to distant places, such as Afghanistan or Pakistan, in the form of the War on Terror. Or, just as often, the attacks themselves are featured as a result of prior historical developments, in the form of an echo of a remote catastrophe—the collapse of the Afghan state. As Georgiana Banita notes in her book on the 9/11 novel, the attacks on the Twin Towers have been presented as a complete rupture from the past: "Global historical events that may have prefaced or prefigured the terrorist attacks were quickly forgotten in post-9/11 cultural discourse, while a vociferous counterdiscourse emerged around how 9/11 ushered in, seemingly out of the blue, a new transnational era" (44). By contrast, global Afghanistan works seek to inscribe optics that makes 9/11 legible as a consequence of prior historical tragedies that require commemoration.

Taken as a whole, "global Afghanistan" cultural texts exhibit a specific sensibility and flavor that are an expression of the shared historical condition in which they are situated. In the aftermath of the 9/11 attacks, this corpus registers the global, ever-expanding state of war, and conveys a sense of vulnerability and crisis, mapping the landscapes of victimhood and terror. There is a sense of global interconnectedness in all these texts as they oscillate between close-ups that reveal the violence inflicted on individual bodies caught in the mayhem of localized wars and the planetary scale that frames these acts of violence. As a corollary to registering and dramatizing the crisis of wars without end, many of these texts convey an interest in finding pathways to transnational reconciliation and peace, with Afghanistan figuring as an imagined site of such reconciliation. In sum, the texts grouped in this book register a sustained commitment to finding a language to describe what defines the post-9/11 contemporary—the era journalist Jason Burke calls "the 9/11 wars." This impulse positions the global Afghanistan corpus as a hermeneutics of the present—an effort to find the meaning of the events we collectively experience and to situate ourselves in relation to them.

Burke's term "the 9/11 wars" captures the period defined by a series of deadly conflicts in various parts of the world that followed the 9/11 attacks.[9] The 9/11 wars encompass the global War on Terror declared by George W. Bush along with its Obama-era reformulations; they also comprise the cultural wars, terrorist attacks, and low-level military conflicts in Europe, Russia, Africa, the Middle East, Southeast Asia, and the Indian subcontinent, among other places, resulting in massive, albeit distributed, loss of life, dislocation of millions, the redrawing of the borders in the Middle East, and other changes in the global configuration of power. The 9/11 wars era is seemingly the era of wars without end; dubbed a "forever war," an "everywhere war,"[10] it exhibits "a pattern of wars without objectives, exit strategies, or geographical boundaries" (Wood 71).[11] My preference for the term "the 9/11 wars," as compared to the War on Terror (Bush's strategy) and the Age of Terror (Don DeLillo's phrase), is related to its capacity to capture the broad geographical distribution of post-9/11 conflicts, affecting lives in the global North and in the global South. In contrast to these other terms, Burke's term gestures toward an era that is infinitely complex and does not easily lend itself to the East/West binaries or to the metaphors of the epic struggle between good and evil, implied in both Bush's and DeLillo's designations. Additionally, it resists the exceptionality of the United States as the prime actor (and the prime victim) of the era, drawing attention to the multiple non-US participants and casualties of these wars. Rather than being an epic struggle of good versus evil, the 9/11 wars come into view as the era of largely invisible yet persistent conflicts, with an epicenter that is constantly moving.[12] The 9/11 wars capture the ubiquity of trauma in an age when violence becomes as globalized as it is random and when military invasions, masquerading as humanitarianism, continue unabated. By bringing into visibility a distributed community of those affected by the 9/11 wars worldwide, the global Afghanistan novels, memoirs, and films mediate the complex experiences of people of multiple nationalities trapped in these wars. By examining the frames of cultural reference, images, themes, and aesthetics that emerge in these texts, this book will contribute to a richer understanding of the post-9/11 global cultural production and the place of Afghanistan in the global imaginary.

A Contested History of a Global Nation

Considered within the frame of its history, Afghanistan is a paradoxical site. Deprived of major mineral wealth (this changed recently with the world's new thirst for lithium, abundant in Afghanistan), landlocked and surrounded from all sides by three formidable mountain ranges, it nevertheless has been a locum of sustained international interest for two hundred years, culminating in the forty-year-long era of social upheaval and bloodshed fueled by external meddling and global rivalries. Its turbulent history renders the fantasy of linear progress problematic, exposing the limitations of both twentieth- and twenty-first-century developmentalisms. Its contemporary state epitomizes halted development, the ruins of its recent past mocking the dreams of Afghan modernity. Almost two decades after the US-led invasion, it remains a zone of contention for multiple militarisms, a site where the dreams for liberal democracy's reach are tested, and found wanting, as they collide with the interests of radical Islamist groups and opium producers who seek to maintain Afghanistan as their enduring base, not to mention the varied needs and demands of tribal and ethnic groups. These new rivalries are superimposed upon stark ideological and class divisions in the nation that now ranks 169/187 on the

Human Development Index.[13] And yet, as this book shows, Afghanistan's recent history is not merely a chronicle of war, but a gripping story that tells of incredible leaps forward and shocking setbacks, a history of building and dismantling, and of utopian dreaming. As such, it continues to fascinate travelers and vagabonds, humanitarians and historians, and above all, writers and readers who seek to make sense of the country's tempestuous, radical, utopian, and often violent past.

"There is a country so in the heart of the world that the world has forgotten about it," writes Tony Kushner in his play *Homebody/Kabul* (28). The image of Afghanistan in post-9/11 global writing and film is part myth, part history, part fantasy, and part collective hallucination, and the book is set to unpack its meaning. This book's title, *Imagining Afghanistan*, thus reflects the intellectual pursuit of the project: to understand how Afghanistan figures in the global imaginary and how the world, in turn, is imagined from and through this country. The interlacing of Afghanistan and "the global" is a persisting theme in all the texts discussed in this book; it is multilayered and requires an explanation. To begin with, Afghanistan is a global place quite literally; its history is intertwined with the history of the world perhaps more than any other nation-state.[14] An entire generation of refugees, exiles, migrants, and transnational militants was created as a direct result of what Oona Frawley calls "global civil war"—the war between the Soviet Union and the United States fought on Afghanistan's soil.[15] Moreover, by 1979 (the year of the Soviet intervention that marks the moment of intensification of the Cold War in the area), Afghanistan was already global—an argument I develop in chapter two. And yet, westerners continue to traffic in images of Afghan isolation and barbarity, portraying it as "a hermit kingdom"[16] or a land of medieval thinking and practices.

Furthermore, and perhaps more importantly, Afghanistan—as it emerges in post-9/11 transnational texts—is sutured to the globe on the level of symbol and image: Its tragedies and successes often metonymically stand in for the globe at large. In *Afghanistan in the Cinema*, Mark Graham writes: "Afghanistan is more than a place; it is a global situation, like all wars, a seismic catastrophe that shatters and scatters all in its wake" (114). As a synecdoche for the world—a site where global trends emerge, come to fruition, and meet their demise—Afghanistan serves as a figure for the shared experience of loss, and potentially, as a figure of redemption, an opportunity for healing from the losses suffered. Burke brings attention to Afghanistan's post-9/11 symbolic role as the measure of the Western superpowers' global reach, their capacity to impose their will upon the rest of the world, and their ability to neutralize and absorb local difference in the process of reshaping the invaded countries.[17] Afghanistan's reconstruction era, or more precisely, its failures, ultimately exposes and serves as a figure of the limits of this capacity. Afghanistan thus functions as an imagined object of cathexis of multiple, often contradictory hopes, desires, or fears—serving simultaneously as a lens for deciphering the present, imagining the future, and for reinterpreting the past (an idea that I develop further in chapters two and three).

Historian Timothy Nunan likens Afghanistan's history to a palimpsest: "Here, sediments of history lay stacked upon one another like the sheaves of the Persian, Pashto, and Turkic manuscripts Orientologists jealously poached" (19). Yet the very layered nature of Afghanistan's recent past, as well as its interlacement with the larger global history of the late Cold War era, makes this history a contested subject. The seduction to flatten these layers into a simplified image of a third-world humanitarian crisis has been great in early post-9/11 global Afghanistan texts. Critics rightfully observed that US mainstream media and White House-sponsored political rhetoric projected a version of Afghan history that was essentially diphasic: the spell of timeless, medieval oppression to be broken through a liberation from the West. This became particularly obvious in relation to women's rights and the way in which the burqa—made mandatory for all women by the Taliban regime—became a signifier of cultural barbarity requiring an intervention. In this, the West saw itself as a benevolent force, a progressive agent of world history, an altruistic humanitarian who intervenes on behalf of the oppressed. Struggles over the country's recent history and the legacy of its various parts comprise a prominent theme in global Afghanistan cultural production. Each work discussed in this book projects its own vision of this history, competing, if not violently clashing, with other visions. Although I make references to various periods in Afghanistan's recent past in various chapters of this book, it might be useful to provide a brief summary of the basic chronology of events here.

Afghanistan enters the twentieth century as a British puppet state, with a history of two Anglo-Afghan wars prompted by the British Crown's anxiety about Russian advances in Central Asia. The First Anglo-Afghan War (1839–1842) culminated in the famous ambush and slaughter of 16,000 British troops, cementing the image of Afghans as wild, brutal, and unconquerable, which, in the more recent context, led to Afghanistan's

mythologization as "the graveyard of empires."[18] During the Second
Anglo-Afghan War (1878–1880), however, the British were successful in
installing a subservient regime in Kabul, effectively gaining control of the
country. But not for long. In 1919, the British Empire, weakened by World
War I, was evicted from Kabul and Afghanistan became independent—"a
sovereign postcolonial state before it was fashionable" (Nunan, 11). Almost
coeval with the Russian Revolution, Afghanistan's independence was recognized and celebrated by Lenin and the new Soviet State, with whom
the Afghan king promptly signed a treaty of friendship. The mid-twentieth-century period of King Mohammed Zahir Shah's rule from 1933 to
1973 was marked by stability, peace, and the steady work of modernization
characterized by advances in education, infrastructure development, and
women's rights.[19] During this period, Afghanistan developed strong links
with Europe, the United States, and the USSR, with many elite members
going to universities in these countries. In 1959, female members of the
royal family went in public unveiled, encouraging modern Afghan women
to follow suit, prompting a brief veil war in Afghanistan—a religious back-
lash promptly suppressed by the monarchy committed to modernization.
The years between 1960 and 1970 saw the rise of social justice movements
that engaged in utopian dreaming and organization. Kabul University,
with its large base of first-generation students, became the epicenter of such
movements, home to both radical leftist socialist (and feminist) groups
and ultraright radical Islamist groups. Nur Muhammad Taraki (the first
socialist head of state), as well as Gulbuddin Hekmatyar (an ultraright
Islamist and later a militant known for his violence against civilians) found
their base and their audience there.

Afghanistan's history since 1973 can be likened to a video viewed in
fast-forward mode—a lot happened in a short period of time. In 1973,
the monarchy was overthrown in a coup d'état and Afghanistan became
a republic under the leadership of Mohammed Daoud Khan—the former
king's cousin. In 1978, Daud was overthrown by the socialist party of
Afghanistan, and Taraki—the party leader—became the head of state.
Forging ahead with land reform and women's education, and facing challenges to these changes in the countryside, the new socialist government
requested Soviet military support, which was denied. Following Taraki's
assassination in 1979, however, fearing the further unraveling of the
Afghan's new and unstable socialist state, USSR's head of state Leonid
Brezhnev decided to send troops to help Babrak Karmal, the leader of

the moderate socialist party wing, assume leadership. From 1979 to 1989, Afghanistan was a socialist state, its security managed by the Soviet troops who remained in Afghanistan, but who were increasingly harassed by the ever-growing groups of mujahideen[20] (jihad fighters), who received extensive Western and Saudi support. In 1989, Soviet troops withdrew, ending the era of the Soviet-Afghan War and marking the advent of civil war. Improbably, the socialist government of Afghanistan persisted even after the withdrawal of the Soviet contingent, falling in 1992 to the ultraright mujahideen forces who finally surrounded and seized Kabul. From 1992 until the arrival of the Taliban in 1996, warring factions of various radical Islamist groups destroyed the infrastructure of the country, unleashed war on civilians, and engaged in ethnic cleansing, all of which lead to the collapse of the state and massive population displacement. After fifty years of steady modernization, Afghanistan was reduced to ruins. While the arrival of the Taliban in 1996 restored a degree of law and order, it also solidified gender inequalities already in place, and did little to alleviate the poverty and breakdown of infrastructure. The US arrival in 2001 brought another change, with the creation of a fragile, unstable democracy propped up by Western money and NATO military personnel. To conclude this overview, if in 1880 Frenchman James Darmesteter could write, "The Afghans do not have a history, because anarchy has none,"[21] today a historian might observe that the Afghans, for a small nation, have a uniquely rich global history, mirroring, in many ways, the turbulent history of the twentieth century.

The Book's Key Arguments

A site in which colonial, socialist, fundamentalist, and neo-imperialist histories collide and grate against each other, Afghanistan poses representational difficulties for cultural producers. Writing or screening Afghanistan in the twenty-first century involves reckoning not only with the issues of human rights, women's rights, and transnational terror, but also brings with it contentious legacies bequeathed by the Cold War. Afghanistan, I argue throughout this project, serves as a lens through which contemporary cultural producers contend with the moral ambiguities of twenty-first-century humanitarianism, interpret the legacy of the Cold War and the defeated socialist project, recognize (or obscure) the role of the United States in the rise of transnational terror, and grapple with the long-term impact of war on both human and nonhuman ecologies. An object of desire, as much as the object to be deciphered, Afghanistan's history serves as a screen upon which fantasies of the future—images of the world to come—are projected and debated. Interpretations of Afghanistan's socialist history, its radical Islamist past, and its neoliberal present collide to lay claims upon the world that is emerging at the end of the second decade of the 9/11 wars.

This book makes three interventions. First, using Afghanistan as a case study, it offers a critique of the humanitarian imaginary—a culturally specific mode of global relationality and engagement that has become dominant in the global North after the Cold War's end. Second, the book shows an imbrication of the humanitarian narrative with post-Cold War aphasias, ranging from a virulent anti-socialist stance to Left melancholy that presents, mostly, as inconsistencies and gaps in representation. And finally, through an examination of a growing archive of writing and film that emerged in the second decade of the 9/11 wars, the book maps a way out of the humanitarian imaginary. Let me dwell on each of the three points here.

In its critique of the humanitarian imaginary, the book takes as a point of departure contemporary analyses of humanitarianism as exemplified by Joseph M. Slaughter (*Human Rights, Inc.*) and Didier Fassin (*Humanitarian Reason*), among others. While Slaughter's readings are based on a different archive—the world-spanning array of novels that came out during the 1990s human rights era—his analysis of the humanitarian narrative is useful to this project. Specifically, Slaughter views the humanitarian narrative as a literary technology that solidifies global hierarchies, "recenter[ing] the traditional subjects of history now as the subjects of benevolence, humanitarian interventionist sentimentality, and human rights" (324). Moreover, Slaughter underscores the juncture between the cultural logic of literary humanitarianism and the *Realpolitik* of imperialism, demonstrating how a human rights best seller can preempt and legitimize a real humanitarian-military intervention. My focus on Afghanistan allows me to render more concrete such critique of the humanitarian narrative by bringing into view the very specific problems and impasses that result from an adoption of the humanitarian mode for writing about Afghanistan. On the one hand, screening and writing Afghanistan after 9/11 can serve as an ultimate case study in humanitarian imaginary, exemplifying precisely the interventionist logic Slaughter critiques. On the other hand, however, Afghanistan's uniquely nonlinear history makes problematic a humanitarian reduction of its past to a biphasic formula that traces a trajectory from oppression to the subsequent access to dignity and personal development—a hallmark of the human rights best seller as described by Slaughter. When writers and filmmakers attempt such a reduction, multiple problems ensue. Afghanistan's revolutionary socialist project, albeit defeated, also poses a challenge to the liberal notion of emancipation insofar as it privileges collective, rather than individual, empowerment. This socialist past thus proves to be resistant to either cooptation or incorporation into a human rights-based mode of representation. And as such, it becomes unrepresentable.

Therefore, the second task of this book is to bring into view the multiple anti-socialist biases endemic in NATO-centric contexts and to show their imbrications with humanitarian tropes. The book argues that many prominent cultural texts, especially those published during the first decade of the 9/11 wars, are marked by an uncritical investment in anti-communism as a shortcut to explaining Afghanistan's tragedy. In these works, the ruins of Afghanistan are proffered as the ruins of communism: Sites of socialist history figure as ruined sites, meant to exemplify the violence that the socialist state, and in particular the Soviets, unleashed on bodies, buildings, and nature. In these texts, Afghan people figure almost exclusively as (albeit defiant) victims of Soviet barbarity. While most cultural theorists, since Edward Said, have been attuned to the dangers of Orientalism, they are less conscious of the long-term othering strategies that originated in the Cold War that cast socialism as an unnatural force, communists as sexual predators, and the socialist state (especially the Soviet Union) as an unflinchingly totalitarian, destructive presence in *any* region. The archive of global Afghanistan works that I put together in this book reveals that in NATO-centric contexts, anti-socialist (and by extension anti-statist) tropes are pervasive on both sides of the political spectrum, and frame both the cultural production and its reception by critics. These modes of representing *and* seeing, as I demonstrate, result in redacting indigenous Afghan Leftist history and the complete erasure of the Afghan revolutionary subject. The framework of Orientalism alone is thus not sufficient in relation to Afghanistan writing and film; postcolonial approaches are similarly insufficient insofar as postcolonial critiques reduce the socialist era in Afghanistan to the Soviet occupation, viewed as a neocolonial endeavor, similarly erasing Afghanistan's radical Leftist tradition and its revolutionary history. I thus suggest that we add to the human rights, postcolonial, and Orientalist critiques a critique of anti-socialist bias—which ranges from virulent anti-Sovietisms to forms of bias that are much more subtle, such as "Left-wing melancholy" and "capitalist realism."

"Capitalist realism"—a term introduced by Mark Fisher (2009)—captures the presence of "a widespread belief that there is no alternative to capitalism" (19), a view that presumes that alternatives to capitalism are unnatural, no longer imaginable, or always a priori doomed to failure. Afghanistan, for capitalist realists, serves as a prime example of the inevitability of socialist failure. "Left-wing melancholy" is a phrase coined by Enzo Traverso in his eponymous book that captures a similar sentiment; it refers to a sense of disorientation and loss that is a residue of the defeat suffered by the global Left at the end of the twentieth century (xiv). Both capitalist realists and Left-wing melancholics suffer the loss of utopia (the future) while haunted by memories of the past that evade understanding and mourning. History appears to them as a pile of ruins whose meaning is inexplicable and thus ungrievable: "Deprived of its horizon of expectation, the twentieth century appears to our retrospective gaze as an age of wars and genocide" (Traverso 10). Cultural producers (and critics) whose views align with these subtle forms of bias, as discussed in this book, might not reduce Afghanistan's tragedy to an image of Soviet atrocity; however, since they do not have the language to talk about Afghanistan's revolutionary past in such a way that would redeem it by remaining faithful to its emancipatory dream, they often choose to simply omit it, thus contributing to the collective work of erasure. And so, Afghan socialist modernity remains unmourned, condemned to the rubble of history.

Finally, my third intervention in this book is to suggest a way of moving beyond the horizon defined by the juncture of humanitarianism and anti-socialism. Chapters four through six move beyond critique and offer, instead, paths toward alternative imaginaries. The Afghanistan corpus of cultural texts, I argue, indexes both an endemic quality of melancholic humanitarianism as a mode of representation and a push to move beyond this imaginary. At the end of the second decade of the 9/11 wars we are witnessing, I argue, the emergence of new vocabularies and frameworks that allow writers and filmmakers to bring into view traumatic histories without succumbing to the humanitarian tropes. The humanitarian wager, I believe, is losing its appeal. New modes of representing traumatic histories include, first and foremost, a shift of attention from the suffering human figure (the traumatized survivor) to conditions and infrastructures of violence, with the intent to capture slow and distributed violence. Capturing slow or massively distributed violence requires a long-term witness or a nonhuman witness. In addition, debates over the Anthropocene, coeval with the 9/11 wars, have brought into focus deep time as a framework for thinking and action. The global Afghanistan corpus of works registers this shift: Viewing Afghanistan in deep time—as a geological object— opens up new ways of writing about human and nonhuman suffering, recovery, and resilience. Finally, many works of the second decade of the 9/11 wars stage a comedic reversal where humanitarian tropes are put on their head and the very idea of a humanitarian invasion is ridiculed. In terms of the book's trajectory, chapter three serves as a hinge as it begins a transition from critique to constructive work, from exposing the limits of humanitarianism (and anti-socialism) to considering these new modes of representation. The book thus makes an argument about the progressive disillusionment with humanitarianism as a moral framework over the two decades of US-led wars as evidenced through novels and memoirs set in Afghanistan. While we do not yet know what is coming, it is evident that the age of humanitarian reason is showing multiple fissures that might be impossible to patch.

The Trajectory of the Book

When putting together my "global Afghanistan" archive, I made a deliberate effort to include both popular works (blockbuster films and best-selling novels) and more obscure texts. The resulting array thus contains bright objects and dim objects. One may expect that bright objects tap into the dominant cultural imaginary and strengthen it, and this is often true. And, in turn, one might anticipate that obscure texts will have more freedom to challenge our belief systems, pushing the boundaries of our vision. However, for both bright and dim objects, this is not always the case. Some blockbusters undo themselves by containing unbearable tensions and contradictions, while obscure works often channel hegemonic beliefs uncritically. These difficulties notwithstanding, I believe that a combination of visual and written texts and a mix of high and low culture will offer a veritable snapshot of how Afghanistan has been imagined, and reimagined, over the span of the two decades since the fall of the Twin Towers.

Chapter one, "Humanitarian Sublime and the Politics of Pity: Writing and Screening 'Afghanistan' Circa 2001," looks at three examples of representing Afghanistan during this time period—Mohsen Makhmalbaf's film *Kandahar* (2001); Yasmina Khadra's novel *The Swallows of Kabul* (2002); and Tony Kushner's acclaimed play *Homebody/Kabul* (2002). The importance of this cluster of works, aside from providing early examples of post-9/11 cultural representations of Afghanistan, lies in its role in framing Afghanistan as a zone of immense suffering (especially women's suffering) and humanitarian crisis, which in the post-9/11 context served to give legitimacy and purpose to the US-led invasion. These works exemplify post-Cold War humanitarian imaginary by their reliance on empathetic identification with distant suffering, in their extensive medievalization of Afghanistan, and finally, in a dramatic flattening of the country's history. The chapter's key metaphor, "flat earth," draws attention to this act of leveling in which Afghanistan's deeply palimpsestic, eventful recent history is reduced to the shallow, two-dimensional chronology of the most recent crisis (the Taliban), into which western audiences then feel compelled to intervene. The chapter exposes the limitations of representing Afghanistan in a humanitarian mode and introduces the term "humanitarian sublime" to capture the deployment of humanitarian affect in response to distant suffering.

Chapter two, "Imagining the Soviets: The Faustian Bargain of Khaled Hosseini's Kabul 'Trilogy'," unveils the paradoxical place of the Afghan socialist era in the post-9/11 imaginary. As such, it sheds light on how Cold War-era biases continue to shape representations of Afghanistan's history in NATO-centric contexts in the age of the 9/11 wars. Animated by a desire to recover the image of socialist Afghanistan from its historical (and cultural) ruins, the chapter inscribes much needed ambiguity into the narrative of "ruination via the Soviets" by engaging the literary project of Afghan American writer Khaled Hosseini. By throwing Hosseini's best-selling *The Kite Runner* (a virulently anti-Soviet text) against the background of a late-Cold War novel by an American writer M. E. Hirsh, *Kabul* (1986), as well as by staging a dialogue between *The Kite Runner* and Hosseini's two subsequent novels—*A Thousand Splendid Suns* (2007) and *And the Mountains Echoed* (2013), the chapter demonstrates that Hosseini strikes a Faustian bargain that both accounts for his success and forces him into a number of representational stalemates that, as of yet, remain unaddressed by critics.

Chapter three, "Humanitarian Jihad: Unearthing the Contemporary in the Narratives of the Long 1979," argues that in the post-9/11 context, 1979 (a "dark" threshold of the contemporary), must be viewed as a genealogical point of origin that is more important than 1989 (a "bright" threshold connoting the presumed triumph of liberal democracy). The year 1979 marks a "hot" moment in the Cold War: Soviet intervention in

Afghanistan and the onset of US-led covert "Operation Cyclone" (a.k.a. the Afghan jihad)—a proxy war against the Soviets and the largest covert operation in CIA history. What were the costs of defeating what Ronald Reagan called "the Evil Empire"? How do we make visible the hidden histories of transnational terror? Nadeem Aslam's *The Wasted Vigil* (2008), Sorayya Khan's *City of Spies* (2015), and Didier Lefèvre's visual account of his journey to Afghanistan in *The Photographer* (produced with Emmanuel Guibert and Frédéric Lemercier, 2009) help us imagine our way into these CIA-orchestrated "ghost wars"—largely invisible, yet deadly.[22] Lefèvre's graphic memoir, unwittingly, offers important insights into the role that European humanitarians, such as Doctors Without Borders and European reporters (such as Lefèvre himself), played in the anti-Soviet jihad in the mountain ranges of 1980s Afghanistan. This chapter's key term, "humanitarian jihad," points to how humanitarian images—such as the famous image of the Afghan girl of the 1985 *National Geographic*—were put to use in support of the jihad against the Soviets and the Afghan socialist state. The suffering child is a signifier of crisis, but which crisis? In Lefèvre's graphic memoir, the suffering child is, unambiguously, a victim of Soviet barbarity; in Aslam's and Khan's works, the suffering child becomes a figure for US interference in the region.

Chapter four, "Witness: Modes of Writing the Disaster," discusses three texts written by South Asian writers—Kamila Shamsie's *Burnt Shadows* (2009), Qais Akbar Omar's *A Fort of Nine Towers* (2013), and Zia Haider Rahman's *In the Light of What We Know* (2014). These works conjure divergent, powerful ways of inscribing the Afghan disaster as an object of memorialization, foregrounding its key role in late twentieth-century history, and situating it as a site of convergence of multiple global forces (USSR, United States, Pakistan, and others). They provide a compelling alternative to the humanitarian mode of writing traumatic histories by constructing three modes of witness, and therefore three modes of making legible the Afghan disaster. Both Omar's and Shamsie's texts offer a long-term witness as a main device that allows them to document the crises that would enfold several generations. The focus of the long-term witness permits these writers to document the processes of slow violence and the delayed effects of war, such as mass displacement, habitat destruction, and toxicity, which take years or even decades to manifest. By contrast, Rahman's novel, through both its plot and its formal aspects, argues against the primacy of eye-witnessing. As the ontological indeterminacy at the very core of the world continuously thwarts our epistemic thrust, the disaster, Rahman's novel suggests, calls for a nonhuman witness.

Chapter five, "The Deep Time of War: Nadeem Aslam and the Aesthetics of the Geologic Turn," further maps the landscape of global Afghanistan writing (especially modes of witnessing and mediation of the catastrophe) by turning to deep memory, while further exploring the idea of a nonhuman witness. Aslam's Afghanistan-based novels exemplify the affordances of the geologic turn for writing traumatic histories in the era of the Anthropocene—the era that, paradoxically, decenters the human. Aslam's writing positions Earth (seen as a rich landscape populated by multiple species and nonliving objects) as a nonhuman witness (geo-witness) to human catastrophe—a medium of memory that registers the disaster of war at a scale that surpasses the human. Aslam's works channel species memory, insect perception, and geological inscription of the war-borne toxicities that slip into millennia-old geological strata. By bringing into focus the deep time of history's material sedimentations, Aslam dramatizes the long-term consequences of the wars waged in the region—that alter landscapes and change multispecies ecologies. Seen from the perspective of deep time, Aslam's Afghanistan is not a humanitarian scene—it emerges as a habitat of demoiselle cranes and snow leopards, a land of slow-forming gemstones and Buddhism, mapping the deep history of Eurasia, human and nonhuman.

The last chapter, "The Kabubble: The Humanitarian Community Under Scrutiny," offers an overview of writing and screening Afghanistan in the second decade of the 9/11 wars by examining French illustrator Nicolas Wild's *Kabul Disco* (a graphic novel series, 2009; 2013), journalist Kim Barker's *The Taliban Shuffle* (a memoir, 2011), and American comedian Tina Fey's 2016 blockbuster *Whiskey Tango Foxtrot* (a feature film based on Barker's memoir). These cultural texts use comedy to depict westerners' experiences in Afghanistan and index the general waning of belief in the success of US-led military interventions in the name of democratic and humanitarian aims. They bring into stark relief the limitations (and the hubris) of the humanitarian mode of representation by mocking and parodying it. These works illustrate the complicated journey from an uncritical investment in humanitarianism as an amelioration to Third World suffering to the realization of the disconnect between the global West's humanitarian agendas, and the realities of the late neoliberal moment that determine the attitudes and desires of the transnational humanitarian workers (and other expats) who partake in the financial bubble in the aftermath of the military operation. These late-arriving narratives dramatize the "Kabubble"—foreigners' Kabul—as a surreal place of transnational career-building and individual risk-taking spurred by neoliberal competition for diminishing resources in the global North.[23]

1

Humanitarian Sublime and the Politics of Pity: Writing and Screening "Afghanistan" Circa 2001

On March 5, 2016, Tina Fey's blockbuster *Whiskey Tango Foxtrot*—a film described by a *New York Times* reviewer as "Live from Kabul, It's a Feminist Comedy"[1]—premiered in US theaters. The film revealed, among other things, that during the fifteen years after the start of the US-led intervention in Afghanistan, the global West and its pundits have learned something important, although what that is may not be easy to pinpoint. For instance, Fey's film followed none of the conventions that structured representations of Afghanistan in the cultural texts that emerged in the early days of Operation Enduring Freedom, around 2001–2002. Instead of drawing attention to the cultural, religious, and moral difference (and inferiority) of the Afghan "other," as compared to the deeply sympathetic, ethical, selfless humanitarians or saviors from the West (a frequent trope in the early works), Fey's film accomplished a 180-degree reversal, subjecting the international community in post-9/11 Kabul to a scrutiny worthy of a trained cultural anthropologist. These substance-abusing, death-drive-obsessed, transnational humanitarian workers are an oddity observed and studied, akin to zoo animals, by the curious and cross-culturally competent Afghan residents of Kabul. The expats, in the film, represent a distinct breed of rather unscrupulous thrill-addicts who seek personal and career advancement as they gather in reconstruction-era Kabul—deemed "Kabubble" in the film to underscore the community's solipsism and vanity. In this savvy rendition, the Afghans are situated as the subjects rather than the objects of the gaze, marveling at, and judging in various ways, members of this humanitarian cohort, as well as lusting after them, flirting with them, manipulating them, educating them, and protecting them from various dangers.[2]

The film comes on the heels of several other cultural texts that describe the humanitarian cohort that flocked to Afghanistan in the aftermath of the US-led invasion and sought to take advantage of the billions of dollars in reconstruction money pledged by the international community. The most notable of them include French illustrator Nicolas Wild's *Kabul Disco* graphic novel series (2009–2013)—a humorous portrayal of a cross-culturally incompetent graphic designer's (presumably, the author) residency in Kabul. In similar vein, Kim Barker's memoir *The Taliban Shuffle* (2011), which served as an inspiration for Fey's film, uses comedy to portray her misadventures in the Afghan capital as she navigates her first assignment as a foreign correspondent. These self-deprecating texts deploy humor, rather than humanitarian imagery, to portray life in Kabul, and refuse to take their narrators' work too seriously—the designer in Wild's series, for instance, is not very successful, either in France or in Afghanistan. When compared to their agile, multilingual Afghan guides and fixers, members of the international cohort in these texts seem ill-adapted, lacking in skill as well as in purpose, skeptical about their role in Afghanistan but not having much going on back in their austerity-stricken home countries either. These narratives portray "Kabubble" as a theater of the absurd, where self-professed humanitarians from the global North congregate in temporary walled-off communities to compete for a piece of the pie in the transnational job market (that now includes Afghanistan). These texts thus are reflective of the later stages of the US-led war in Afghanistan; they mine the disparity between the rhetoric of humanitarianism (such as the perceived need to save Afghan women) and the harsh realities of neoliberalism that prompt Western professionals' flight to a war zone in search for job opportunities.

It is from this perspective that I will revisit, in this chapter, the early days of the War on Terror and cultural texts that emerged around 2001–2002. Quite consistently, with some variation across genres, in these early representations, Kabul figures as a humanitarian disaster: a nonspecific zone of suffering that requires an intervention from the West—a landscape of suffering so extreme that it becomes sublime. Understanding these early texts' deep investment in unequivocally benevolent humanitarianism as a mode of global engagement as well as as a mode of writing and screening traumatic histories will allow us to trace a trajectory of the global West's learning, disillusionment, and self-critique from 2001 through the second decade of the 9/11 wars.

The Onset: Operation Enduring Freedom

Corinne Fowler calls the time following the start of Operation Enduring Freedom in the fall of 2001 the period of a "scramble for knowledge on Afghanistan" pointing to the lack of public knowledge about the distant country with which the West was now at war (23). This chapter deals with the cultural texts that, while written and produced just prior to 9/11, were destined to fill the void of knowledge about Afghanistan—a country that was suddenly propelled into media hypervisibility on a global scale. While mass media offered gripping, albeit decontextualized images—of the Taliban, of ruined buildings in Kabul, of burqa-clad women, and of orphaned Afghan children begging in the streets—available literary and cinematic texts were called upon to perform a much finer task: to educate the Western audience about the country's recent history, thus making the images circulated by mass media legible. However, there was little cultural material of this sort available. Since the withdrawal of the Soviets from Afghanistan in 1989, and with the subsequent collapse of the Afghan state and the civil war that led to the rise of the Taliban in 1996, Afghanistan was a dark void, entirely outside of global attention. Feminist playwright Eve Ensler, who traveled to Afghanistan in 1999, tried to start public discussion of Afghan women's plight, but her efforts were stymied by the lack of public curiosity: "With the exception of one magazine, *Marie Claire*, I could not engender any interest in the story," Ensler complained later (36). The events of September 2001 changed everything.

Just after the attacks on the Twin Towers, two works about Afghanistan were available and thus in great demand—the film *Kandahar* by Iranian film director Mohsen Makhmalbaf and Tony Kushner's play *Homebody/Kabul*. *Kandahar* was produced in 2001 and premiered at the Cannes Film Festival in May 2001. It did not receive much attention prior to 9/11; subsequently, however, this minor flick became a runaway hit. In December 2001, a *New York Times* reviewer stated that *Kandahar* "may be the only film whose name gets more mentions than Harry Potter on CNN."[3] It was listed in *Time* magazine as one of 100 all-time movies.[4] Kushner's play *Homebody/Kabul* has a similar history. While it was written over the course of a few years (1997–2001), it premiered in New York on December 19, 2001, ten weeks after the start of the US-led military operation in Afghanistan, and in the words of one critic, "generated enormous publicity for its political topicality and the playwright's uncanny ability to anticipate history."[5] It was published as a book in 2002. Post-9/11, *Kandahar* and *Homebody/Kabul* often appeared side-by-side. In 2003, for instance, Seattle's Intiman Theater hosted a screening of *Kandahar* after staging Kushner's play.[6] Both texts thus greatly benefited from a certain kairos—a fortuitous moment of media frenzy and public curiosity sparked by a distant war. That fall, phrases such as "the battle for Kandahar" (the Taliban's stronghold) and "the fall of Kabul" were on everyone's minds. The third cultural text I engage with in this chapter—Yasmina Khadra's *The Swallows of Kabul*—was released in 2002 in French with the explicit aim of familiarizing the Western audience with the tragedy of Afghanistan. The author of the novel—a former Algerian army officer named Mohammed Moulessehoul, took a female pen name, allegedly to avoid censorship by the army. He says, in relation to *The Swallows*: "I wanted to bring a new look from a Muslim on the tragedy of Afghanistan, and to bring to it a western perspective at the same time—I have written a western tragedy, but also a book that is filled with eastern storytelling."[7]

In line with the title of this book, the makers of these cultural texts engage in the act of *imagining* Afghanistan from their particular geo-cultural perspectives. All three texts were produced in the era of Afghanistan's relative inaccessibility to foreigners. *Kandahar* was shot in its entirety outside of Afghanistan, in Iran along the Iran-Afghanistan border. Neither Kushner nor Moulessehoul (a.k.a. Khadra) traveled to Afghanistan, and thus had to defend their credibility by engaging with this question when talking to journalists: "I have never been to Afghanistan but I met a lot of journalists who worked there who told me that they read the book and said, 'I see these incidents all the time, but I never noted them,'" said Moulessehoul.[8] In turn, Kushner defended his credibility with "it's not the easiest place to get to, after all"[9] and "there was no need for me to be in the middle of a war."[10] Positioned not only as outsiders, but entirely outside the country they attempt to portray, these authors thus rely less on observation and experience than on conventions guiding representation of zones of conflict and humanitarian crisis. Specifically, they draw upon the legacy of human rights literature—a body of works that emerged in the 1990s and relied heavily on empathy—a sentimental mode of reading that depends on the reader's imaginary identification with the suffering other.[11] Aware of their role as readers' guides into unknown cultural territory, *Kandahar*, *The Swallows of Kabul*, and *Homebody/Kabul* deploy powerful, often hyperbolic images of distant suffering focusing on the long-lasting humanitarian crisis that preceded the US invasion of Afghanistan in 2001. These stories functioned, in a way, as a prequel to the liberation narrative associated with the invasion. Specifically, all three texts expose the stark poverty of 1990s Afghanistan, the plight of women, and human rights violations under Taliban rule. As such, these texts were promptly conscripted into the post-9/11 media ecology that centered on framing and justifying the US invasion of Afghanistan as a humanitarian effort. The narrative scaffolding of these three works relies on the trope of rescue—specifically, a rescue of a woman from the grips of death for which the Taliban regime is held responsible.

All three texts are NATO-centric: although Makhmalbaf, the director of *Kandahar*, is Iranian, Nelofer Pazira, who plays the lead role in *Kandahar* and on whose story the plot of the film is based, is an Afghan Canadian. In addition, as film scholar Mark Graham explains, Iranian cinema is produced for global consumption, which results in "a careful tailoring of stories and images to appeal to Western audiences' preconceived notions" (65). Such films' destination—the Western film festival circuit—means that "[a]ny politically sensitive issues that might offend Western viewers tend to be carefully excised in the cause of higher profit and greater distribution" (65).[12] Khadra is of Algerian origin; however, he resides in France and his audience for this novel was unmistakably European.[13] Kushner is an American playwright who during the 1980s supported Reagan's anti-communist intervention in Afghanistan.[14] Taken together, these three cultural texts became part of the moral assemblage that provided a context for, justified, and made legible the US-led coalition's operation in Afghanistan as an ethically necessary humanitarian endeavor—and more specifically, a mission to rescue Afghan women from the grips of an intolerable life under a repressive regime. Or as Laura Bush said, famously, "The fight against terrorism is also a fight for the rights and dignity of women."[15]

The ways in which women's rights were co-opted by the George W. Bush administration to justify the invasion of Afghanistan have been well documented by feminist critics and I will not reiterate these critiques here.[16] Instead, I will bring into the foreground what remains rather hidden in these timely and insightful critiques. Taking as a point of departure Didier Fassin's critique of humanitarian reason, I posit the three texts discussed in this chapter as acts of deployment of a humanitarian imaginary—a repertoire of images and tropes that came to define the way in which we were (and still are) invited to imagine global engagement in the aftermath of the Cold War's end. It is critical, in my view, to understand the humanitarian imaginary as a symptom and as a symbol of what Enzo Traverso calls "Left melancholia"—a sense of hopelessness and unlocalizable despair that accompanied the demise of the socialist world, experienced even by those who generally supported this demise. The focus on Afghanistan—a country that is universally referred to as "third world," but that was in fact, during its key era, a part of the second (socialist) world, provides us with a lens with which to sharpen, through localizing, our understanding of the logic and limitations of the humanitarian (or human rights) narrative as well as its imbrications with post-Cold War impasses.

I propose the term "humanitarian sublime" to designate the specific mode of representation all three texts employ. Humanitarian sublime is an act of freezing an image of suffering by removing it from the historical process that brought it on. Subtracting history from the scene sediments a timeless figure of despair that then depends on a hyperbolic mode of representation to have effect. While *Kandahar* and *The Swallows of Kabul* demonstrate a wholehearted investment in the conventions of the humanitarian narrative, creating a moral universe where the reader/viewer is invited to feel compassion toward the suffering other and outrage at the perpetrators of violence, Kushner's *Homebody/Kabul* problematizes humanitarian sentiments and offers a critique of humanitarianism as a mode of relating to distant tragedy. Yet, while exposing and critiquing the limits of "the pedagogy of pity"[17] that is a hallmark of the post-Cold War liberal empathy project, Kushner's play remains trapped inside the humanitarian imaginary, unwittingly reenacting the tropes of humanitarianism. His text can be said to suffer from a humanitarian unconscious and thus performs the same role as the other two—creating a victim and an object of humanitarian intervention. As such, all three texts illustrate the particular impasses of the post-Cold War cultural obsessions with human rights—they bring into visibility the suffering of distant others without being able to name its causes or point to solutions. They suffer paradoxical amnesias and aphasias when engaging Afghan socialist histories and thus prefer to bracket them out. They do not yet have a language in which to talk about the US role in creating the conditions in which forces such as the Taliban were able to thrive. In sum, they already are in the double-bind, or the Faustian bargain, that will become most vivid in the works of best-selling Afghan American physician-turned-writer Khaled Hosseini, which I analyze in chapter two.

Humanitarian Narrative

Operation Enduring Freedom officially began on October 7, 2001; positioned more broadly as the global War on Terror, it started as a US-led military operation to invade Afghanistan with the purpose of removing the Taliban regime, striking at the territorial base of the Al-Qaeda network, and installing a US-friendly client democracy. The invasion of Afghanistan was presented by the US government as a humanitarian act—a concerted effort to free Afghan people from the suffering and oppression they endured under the Taliban rule. This "humanitarian" war was to become a model for the many invasions and interventions of the subsequent two decades, in which military aims were made indistinguishable from humanitarian aims. Indisputably, humanitarian images disseminated in fiction and film proved useful as they played a key role in legitimizing such efforts.

As Joseph R. Slaughter points out in *Human Rights, Inc.*, the very act of reading a human rights novel can be construed as a kind of a humanitarian intervention in itself, preempting and foreshadowing a fair international order "still to come" by recognizing the rights and dignity of the characters who endure suffering (33–34). The decade preceding the 9/11 attacks can be dubbed the era of human rights (and the high point for the human rights novel) insofar as it saw a proliferation of stories that made distant suffering their central focus. Didier Fassin describes the period spanning from mid-1990s to mid-2000s as "the humanitarian moment in contemporary history" (13). It is not coincidental that human rights discourse gained traction as a moral framework in the wake of the collapse of the communist bloc. "Human rights finally triumphed in 1989," states Costas Douzinas in his critical account of what he calls "human rights imperialism" (32). Fraught with contradictions, the humanitarian imaginary as it manifests today is a distinctly post-Cold War phenomenon, ripening in the era characterized by disillusionment and the waning of equality-based projects spearheaded by socialism.[18] It is noteworthy that Richard Rorty's influential essay in praise of empathy (as a preferred mode of relating to the "other") was published in 1993—two years after the dissolution of the Soviet Union and the same year as Samuel Huntington's provocative and widely cited "The Clash of Civilizations"—an essay that foretells the coming of the era of inter-civilizational wars—was published in *Foreign Affairs*. There is a connection there, as well as a link to Francis Fukuyama's 1989 thesis about the end of history: The clash of civilizations produces suffering, but because history has ended, there is nothing that can be done about it, aside from the more fortunate ones offering humanitarian aid to (and empathizing with) the victims of suffering. After the end of history, transnational empathy replaces comradeship—a relation of solidarity in the common struggle. In the ideological vacuum spurred by the break-down of the USSR (which Odd Arne Westad calls the "empire of justice" because of its commitment to eliminating economic and social injustice) that had rivaled the United States (or the "empire of liberty"), the language of human rights promised to offer a new moral framework capable of creating vectors of connection across lines of difference.

It is commonplace now for critical thinkers to underscore that while humanitarianism has a border-defying impulse that seems to be orthogonal to the logic of the clash of civilizations, it also maintains, often explicitly, that the separations and inequalities that define the globe today are inevitable. Luc Boltanski, whose field-defining book *Distant Suffering* also appeared in print (in French) in 1993, notes that the politics of pity, which form the basis of remedial humanitarian action, involves clear lines of such separation.[19] A distant spectator becomes a witness to suffering occurring elsewhere while herself being untouched by this suffering, aside from the feeling of pity itself. This act of humanitarian spectatorship thus cuts differential lines across humanity, as it involves "observation of the *unfortunate* by those who do not share their suffering, who do not experience it directly and who, as such, may be regarded as fortunate or *lucky* people" (Boltanski, 3, emphasis in original). Similarly, Fassin, in his *Humanitarian Reason* offers a Foucauldian view of humanitarianism as a mode of affective governance. While subtended by the idea of radical equality between all humans, humanitarianism, he contends, preserves hierarchies of humanity, and instead of seeking to eliminate injustice, offers aid to merely palliate the suffering of the subjects construed as victims. Fassin writes:

in contemporary societies, where inequalities have reached an unprecedented level, humanitarianism elicits the fantasy of a global moral community that may still be viable and the expectation that solidarity may have redeeming powers. (xiii)

Unlike comradeship, it should be noted, solidarity espoused by humanitarianism is a weak, attenuated form of solidarity: humanitarians seek to remedy extreme forms of suffering (through charity) without addressing the causes of injustice (such as global economic inequality, for instance) and without destabilizing the widely criticized hierarchies of humanity.[20] Signaling the end of utopian politics, post-Cold War humanitarianism and the humanitarian imaginary that accompanies it heralds the advent of liberal "capitalist realism" that concedes that things are as they are and that there are no alternatives to the existing world order.[21] It thus harbors within itself deep pessimism, disavowed, however, through a mobilization of affect—specifically, empathy toward a distant other that creates a sense of imagined community, even communion, with the suffering world. Humanitarian reason's central paradox is that while conjuring vectors of identification across lines of difference, it serves to sustain the regimes of what I call humanitarian containment—keeping the suffering other at bay, and more generally, keeping both the victim and the sympathetic observer in their proper places.

This book argues that while circa 2001 writers and filmmakers understood and depicted Afghanistan almost exclusively through a humanitarian mode, the allure of human rights rhetoric began to wane considerably in the second decade of the 9/11 wars, when the horrific failures of the two US-led wars (in Afghanistan and in Iraq) that were framed as humanitarian interventions became widely understood. The implosion of Iraq and the stalemate in Afghanistan following these interventions has shaken the liberal belief in human rights and humanitarianism as a vehicle for alleviating suffering, bringing into view the many tensions and paradoxes of humanitarianism as a moral framework.[22] The Afghanistan corpus of cultural texts thus serves as one of the prime examples of the humanitarian imaginary while also indexing this imaginary's progressive fracturing and destabilization. The three texts discussed below emerge in the cultural context of the human rights era and exemplify its paradoxes as they seek to portray the country that they all assert, in various ways, has been forgotten by the world: Taliban-era Afghanistan. In these texts, humanitarianism figures as the dominant framework for global action, and empathy serves as the moral response par excellence to distant suffering. The discussion of these texts will serve as a starting point for tracing the specific limitations of the humanitarian imaginary, and for bringing into view its deep embeddedness in the post-Cold War melancholia and its many impasses. This discussion is also key if we are to understand the ways in which writers, critics, filmmakers, and other cultural producers try to navigate these impasses and double-binds as they begin to write their way out of the humanitarian imaginary during the second decade of the 9/11 wars.

Humanitarian Sublime

Kandahar opens with an image of a solar eclipse that fills the screen ominously, the black disk indexing the unnatural quality of what will be represented in the film. It is followed by an image of a woman facing the camera in a burqa—the protagonist—who then lifts the burqa to reveal her face and state her name. The conjoining of the eclipse and the burqa-clad figure conjures a metaphoric equivalence of the solar eclipse lifting to reveal the sun and the lifting of the burqa to reveal the identity of the woman hidden beneath. The voiceover explains that the protagonist—an Afghan-born journalist living in Canada—is traveling to Afghanistan to save her sister who tragically was left behind when the family was escaping the country years prior. Set on committing suicide on the day of the last solar eclipse of the twentieth century, the protagonist's sister in her letter blames the horrific conditions endured by Afghan women under the Taliban for her resolve to end her life, urging her more fortunate sibling to enjoy her life in the West, cherishing the freedoms she is allotted. A narrative of an attempted rescue, *Kandahar* thus equates the Taliban's oppression of women to a solar eclipse—positioning it as a temporary yet horrific humanitarian crisis to be relieved by outside intervention, suggesting that women's liberation will follow the Taliban's fall just as the sunlight is restored when the eclipse ends. Via this sequence, the viewer is conscripted into desiring to grant visibility to the burqa-clad characters—the desire that is articulated by the aphorism issued by the American doctor who the protagonist meets later in the film: "For a woman living under full cover hope is the day she'll be seen."[23]

Immediately after the opening, a new sequence features a Red Cross helicopter flying low above what appears to be a small refugee camp at a desert site. On the ground, miniature figures recognizable

Figure 1.1. *Kandahar*'s opening images.

as people missing limbs are seen running on crutches toward the helicopter as it passes over them, making it seem as if the helicopter missed its aim. The next shot, however, reveals the purpose of the flight: prosthetic legs of various shapes and sizes have been dropped on parachutes in singles and pairs. The camera lingers on the image of the parachuted prosthetics descending—a peaceful image against a clear blue sky—before showing again the people on the ground in a race toward them. The scene thus congeals into a humanitarian image: a glimpse of suffering on the ground to be relieved, via distance, by an aid package; a distant lack corrected through foreign assistance. This scene metonymically constructs Afghanistan as a body with missing parts, as a site of dismemberment and privation, while inserting into the frame a humanitarian apparatus designed to provide a remedy, a way of filling this lack. The film unfolds in this idiom, offering the figure of helper (a humanitarian) as a proxy for the viewer, thus mediating the viewer's access to the site of suffering.

The film offers a number of these helper figures. In the opening scenes at a refugee camp, humanitarian workers educate the children about the dangers of landmines, distribute dollar bills, take photographs of the refugee families, and instruct them on the value of keeping hope alive. Other helpers include the Red Cross nurses who distribute the prosthetic limbs delivered by the helicopter to those waiting, and an American "doctor"[24]—a former jihad fighter who stayed in Afghanistan to help the needy after the jihadists' victory over the communists. All of these characters are one-dimensional figures defined entirely by their function as donors. They distribute money, dispense medication, offer food to the starving—without wanting or needing anything back. Most importantly, the protagonist (called Nafas) herself is a humanitarian proxy; the film follows her journey from an Afghan refugee camp in Iran into Afghanistan in a desperate attempt to reach Kandahar before the solar eclipse to prevent her sister, Diana, from committing suicide.

The role of spectacle in conjuring humanitarian response to distant suffering is key.[25] To paraphrase Laura Mulvey who wrote, famously, that sadism requires a story, one can argue that humanitarianism requires a scene to render distant (and thus abstract) suffering proximate and concrete through putting a suffering body to work, telling the story of its misfortune and displaying its wounds. Luc Boltanski observes: "Pity is not inspired by generalities . . . a picture of absolute poverty defined by means of quantitative indicators" will not inspire this sentiment (11). He continues, "To arouse pity, suffering and wretched bodies must be conveyed in such a way as to affect the sensibility of those more fortunate" (11). Suffering, in other words, must be exhibited, made scenic; distant atrocity viewed from above has to become a tragedy unfolding in a close-up take on the ground. Makhmalbaf's film offers the viewer precisely this close view. First, disguised as one of the wives of a returning refugee family and later accompanied by various other guides, Nafas journeys through the devastated terrain, proffering a cornucopia of humanitarian scenes to the audience, along with dispensing dollar bills to the locals. Although she fails to reach her destination, she is reintroduced to the land she left behind many years prior, getting a firsthand view of the unimaginable poverty, devastation, hunger, and despair of Taliban-era Afghanistan. The film conjures a "humanitarian triangulation" (Slaughter's term)—a structure common in a humanitarian narrative, where the protagonist serves as an *aucteur*, a proxy figure who mediates between the suffering characters and the spectator who observes them.[26] Positioned as capable of both observing and acting (relieving some of the suffering observed), the aucteur's function is to compensate for the viewer's necessary passivity; in addition, the aucteur's selflessness serves to assure the reader of the moral nature of partaking in the spectacle. In *Kandahar*, Nafas is presented as utterly selfless and willing to sacrifice everything to save her sister. As the opening scenes document her flying into the Afghan refugee camp on the Iranian frontier, we hear the voiceover: "I'd always escaped from the jails that enslave an Afghan woman. But now I am a captive in every one of those prisons, and only for you, my sister."

The plot of *Kandahar* is thin and seems to be an excuse for staging a spectacle of extreme suffering in a place that is entirely unfit for living. The film delivers a cascade of scenes of ruination and human misery. After the refugee family Nafas travels with is robbed of all their meager possessions and decides to return to Iran, she is left to fend for herself, having to rely on incompetent or reluctant guides: a young illiterate boy she hires, the "doctor," and a poor disabled man who suggests they both join the procession of burqa-clad women on their way to a wedding in Kandahar—a suggestion that results in them being discovered by the Taliban, bringing their journey to an inconclusive end. Most of the scenes featuring Afghan characters seem sloppily choreographed and convey a sense of artificiality as they employ a slew of figures who move around each site in a somewhat circular fashion, creating an impression of purposeless frenzy. While the protagonist supposedly advances in the direction of Kandahar, the scenery—desert—remains unchanged and the same background of distant mud houses is presented several times over. While this visual paucity and monotony most probably results from the crew shooting the entire film in the same location on the deserted stretch along the Iran-Afghanistan border, it creates an aesthetic in which the frenzied movement of bodies has to compensate for the landscape's and the plot's monotony. This seemingly circular motion also serves to further solidify an atmosphere of entrapment evoked by the storyline.

It is not coincidental that the film presents Afghanistan as culturally and geographically isolated, rather than as the geopolitical hotspot that it has been since the days of the Cold War. Surveying the piles of rubble and debris that make up the setting of the film, its dust and visual dreariness, it is hard to imagine this country as the site of the epic battle between socialism and capitalism—the battle in which the state-of-the-art Soviet helicopter met with the slick and compact US-developed and sponsored anti-aircraft Stinger missile, wielded by the jihad fighters who often came from lands far from Afghanistan. As Edward Girardet and Jonathan Walter observe, "no country in the modern era has been the victim of such outright foreign interference by superpowers and its regional neighbors as Afghanistan" (16). Afghanistan's landscape still contains ample evidence of this global conflict, with new layers superimposed. *Kandahar* steers clear of this global history almost entirely, as addressing it would take the viewer's attention away from the realm of affect (compassion toward the suffering Afghans) to stir up uncomfortable questions of culpability and global interconnectedness, which would implicate the Western viewer into the scene of crisis. By refusing to do so, the film is unable to enter into an ethical milieu, remaining instead in the rigidly defined moral universe of humanitarianism.[27]

Yet the film's reluctance to engage with the history of the crisis presented on the screen means that a certain perspective is sold to the viewer implicitly. Specifically, the viewer's perspective is most closely aligned with the two westerners who mediate our access to the site of suffering: Nafas herself and the African American "doctor," Tabib Sahib. This humanitarian "doctor" is a former mujahid—a mercenary who came to Afghanistan from the United States to kill communists (or "to find God," as he proclaims in the film). The actor who plays the doctor is a profoundly controversial figure. David Theodore Belfield (a.k.a. Dawud Salahuddin, a.k.a. Hassan Tantai)—a North Carolina native who converted to Islam at age eighteen—assassinated an Iranian politician in 1980 in his Maryland home, on behalf of the Islamic Republic of Iran, subsequently fleeing to Iran to escape arrest.[28] In the 1980s, Belfield went to Afghanistan to join the jihad against the "godless" socialist state. Nelofer Pazira, who plays Nafas in the film and on whose family story the plot of the film is based, was herself an active participant in the anti-communist jihad movement in the 1980s, as she describes in her memoir, *A Bed of Red Flowers*, written after the film was made. Thus, although the socialist era is not discussed at all in the film, anti-communism subtends the film in subtle but powerful ways, by aligning the perspective of the viewer with these two westerners—an African American-turned-Islamist-fighter and a jihad enthusiast who later immigrated to Canada. The victory of the radical Islamist movement over the "godless" socialist state in 1992, however, brought forth precisely the crisis the film exposes: the collapse of the state infrastructure and the patriarchal restoration of women's subjugation embodied in the burqa—four years prior to the arrival of the Taliban in 1996. The particular melancholy exhibited in the film is the one of victors—with the Afghan socialist state defeated, humanitarianism seems to be the only way of ameliorating the resulting crisis, and the global West figures as the only imaginable site of progress and liberation.

Both Makhmalbaf's and Pazira's accounts of filming *Kandahar* shed light on the paradoxical position of what one could call a "humanitarian filmmaker." In his essay "Buddha Was Not Demolished in Afghanistan, It Collapsed out of Shame," Makhmalbaf describes the process of filming *Kandahar*, as well as the difficulties associated with accessing Afghanistan during the Taliban rule. Makhmalbaf's initial approach was to enlist the help of the United Nations. The film director contacted Bangladesh native Dr. Kamal Hossain, at the time the UN special rapporteur (adviser) on Afghanistan, for help with obtaining permissions from the Taliban government, as well as with getting access to the areas not under Taliban's control—ideas to which Dr. Hossein was receptive. However, Taliban officials repeatedly refused to grant Makhmalbaf permission to film in Afghanistan, in spite of the director's insistence that his "subject is humanitarian, not political" and that his subjects would be the victims of starvation and drought, not of the regime (Makhmalbaf, "Buddha"). Perhaps these Taliban officials wisely ruled that humanitarianism is always political. To Makhmalbaf's plea that he needed to make visible the victims of hunger, the officials replied that there were "2.5 million Afghans in Iran. Why not film them?" (Makhmalbaf, "Buddha"). The crew then resigned to shooting the film in Niatak, a refugee camp in Iran, where, indeed, many Afghans were starving.

However, this too was fraught with difficulties. Pazira's account of filming *Kandahar* in *A Bed of Red Flowers* provides further details on the humanitarian filmmaker's paradoxical positioning. A passing presence, the crew cannot change the lives of the refugee families they encounter—

and try to employ—as they are shooting the film. Pazira recounts considerable difficulties associated with finding actors for the movie, as the refugees were resistant to the crew's requests and promises. She describes the problem with actors showing up for a few days of shooting but then defecting and expresses her frustration in having to track them down and plead with them to return:

> Sado [a young boy] is upset and doesn't want to work with us anymore. Mullah Qader manages to convince him to finish the sequence. Sado is making more money by working with us than by crossing the border [selling dates], but he is unhappy, he says. "You'll leave," he contemplates, "and I'll have to deal with the insults." The pressure from people in the community—who are at best ignorant and at worst jealous—is very strong. (309)

Makhmalbaf similarly describes difficulties the crew experiences when trying to convince the refugee community to participate in their project. He writes:

> Once when we had asked an Afghan woman to be in the film, her husband said: "Are we unchaste to expose our wives?" I told him that we would film his wife with her burqa on but he said that the audience knew that it was a woman under the burqa and that would be unchastity. (Makhmalbaf, "Buddha")

The humanitarian filmmakers thus have to contend with the fact that their cameras are as invasive as they are ephemeral. The tension between the crew and the refugee community highlights the disconnect between the reality of daily suffering in the refugee camp brought forth through a historical process, on the one hand, and the spectacle of suffering manifested in the film, on the other. It also posits the uncomfortable question of the crew's exploitation of the suffering bodies—the question neither Pazira nor Makhmalbaf are able to fully articulate in their accounts on the production of the film. Pazira's memoir makes evident, however, that it is clear to the prospective film actors that the filmmakers will shoot their scenes, pack up their equipment, and leave their subjects behind, on their way to Cannes, to Canada, and to the world, taking the spectacle of suffering with them, while the world of the refugees will remain unchanged.

Pazira describes several attempts made by the crew to intervene, which are as futile as they are random. On one occasion, the filmmakers buy food for the starving families they find in the ruins of an abandoned building. The sight of them will haunt the crew for a while, but ultimately, they are unable to help as they are a temporary fixture in this landscape, and because they have to keep on filming. "Please leave us in peace," pleads the father of a girl selected to play a role in the film. "Please let us be" (303). Actors join in for a day or two, but fail to return to the set, leaving the crew to have to contend with wasted footage. Pazira can't help but blame the community for being jealous and the actors who fail to return to the set for being unreasonable—after all, they are making money on the set—a spectacle for dollar bills, a story for sympathy. Pazira's account, unwittingly, betrays a crucial bit of information: The community is resistant to the filming project and payment is not a sufficient incentive for engagement, which is in tension with the plot of the film, where, when the protagonist proffers her dollar bills, the characters cooperate.

The film culminates in a scene of humanitarian sublime—a vivid display of choreographed suffering that dramatizes the central contradiction of humanitarianism—the conflict between the immensity of need and the insufficiency of assistance. The scene takes place at a Red Cross station—a few tents in the desert—staffed by two Eastern-European nurses who appear exhausted and desperate, besieged by a crowd of people needing medical help. The camera offers close-ups of the injuries displayed to nurses by the exasperated patients—Afghan men who lost their limbs to landmines—accompanied by the soundscape of overlapping voices narrating the experience of suffering: "I haven't slept in months," one man complains. "There are no legs, no medication," complains another. "It hurts all the time," echoes a third man. The nurses examine the wounds, ask how bad the pain is, and explain that the men will have to wait for up to a year for an available prosthesis.

This scene then erupts into comedic relief as the patients spot a Red Cross helicopter flying above them, which prompts them to move toward it. In a sequence that mirrors the scene at the beginning of the film, the viewer is treated to a choreography of mutilated bodies that appear to be moving synchronously, as if dancing, in their race for succor. Unable to run, the disabled men hop awkwardly up and down, looking up to the sky from which prosthetic legs are descending, their dance accompanied by a quickening musical tune. The image of parachuted legs that captivates and mobilizes the men on the ground is as obscene as it is sublime. Allegorizing Afghanistan's post-Cold War relation to the global North, the ruined bodies on the ground dance for the viewer as they are waiting to receive aid, while the prosthetics—a figure for humanitarian assistance—descend slowly—too slowly—against the backdrop of the beautiful, peaceful sky. The concrete image of the parachuted prosthetics—captivating yet insufficient and always too late—also can be said to represent, as in the Kantian version of the dynamic sublime, the failure of imagination to grasp the magnitude of suffering, thus bringing its immensity into the foreground. By viewing the choreography of need and aid, and their incommensurability, the spectator indulges in a sense of humanitarian sublime—a negative pleasure in which the spectator has to come to terms with her ineptitude while recognizing herself a part of the moral community of viewers who feel eager to help yet equally powerless in the face of enormous suffering.

The Aesthetics of Enclosure

Akin to *Kandahar*, *The Swallows of Kabul* is a novel steeped in the humanitarian imaginary: while staging the conditions that enable an affective resonance between the victim and the reader, the author erects boundaries that limit such identification. Published in 2002 in French under the female pen name Yasmina Khadra, the novel was written by Mohammed Moulessehoul, an Algerian army officer who claims to have taken his wife's name as a pen name to avoid censorship. As Moulessehoul explains, *The Swallows* was the first novel in a trilogy in which he sought to explore the key issues that plague the contemporary world. Set, respectively, in Kabul, Tel Aviv, and Baghdad, this trio of novels portrays the landscape of religious extremism and repression, examines East and West tensions, and investigates the causes of terrorism and violence. The trilogy, according to the author, is set to correct "the tremendous ignorance in the West about Arab and Islamic culture."[29] An English translation of *The Swallows* was published in the United States in 2004, following the dizzying success of Khaled Hosseini's *The Kite Runner* in 2003. As in *Kandahar*, the plot of *The Swallows* is set in the Taliban era, exploring the near complete breakdown of social relations and the plight of women under their rule.

In the early post-9/11 context, the novel was well positioned to become a didactic text through which Western readers would learn about Afghanistan. Upon its publication in France, the novel, no doubt, benefited from the public believing it to have been written by a woman, which

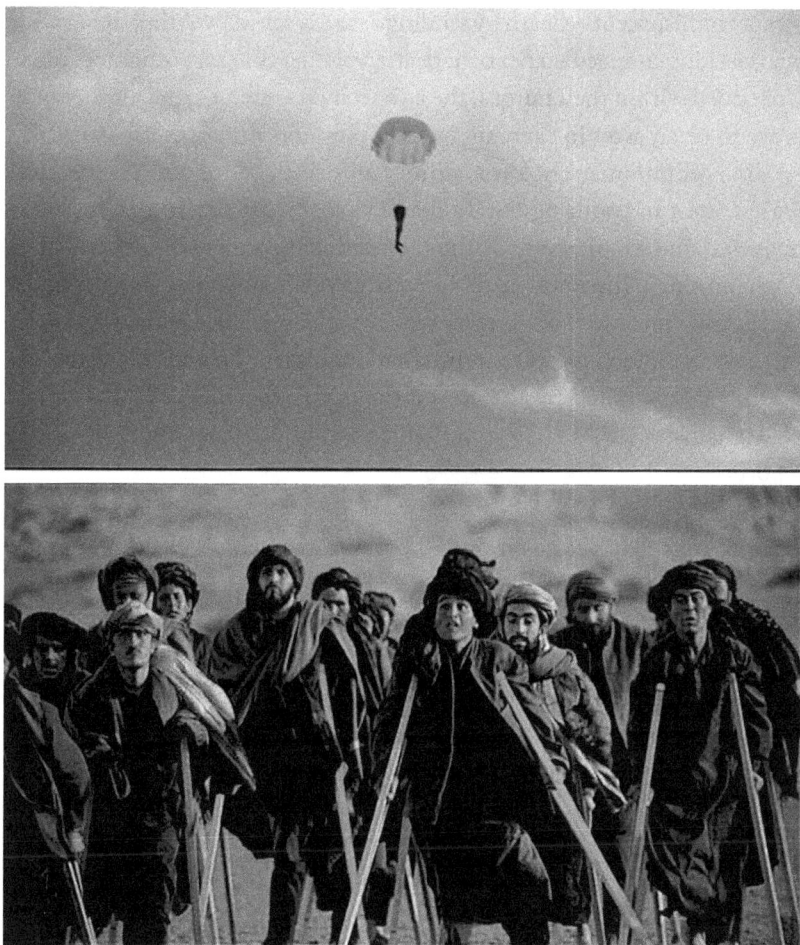

Figure 1.2. Humanitarian sublime in *Kandahar*.

may have positioned it as a feminist critique of the Taliban coming from the Arab world. The novel's plot follows two couples—a barely literate Taliban jailor, Atiq, and his terminally ill wife, Musarrat, and Mohsen and Zunaira, educated, former middle-class residents of Kabul who suffer the loss of status, the daily humiliation of poverty, and a sense of hopelessness under the Taliban regime. Zunaira, a champion of women's rights who aspired to be a magistrate in the past, suffers bitterly from the removal of rights and what she sees as the utter denigration of women as a group under the Taliban. When she is accused of her husband's murder (his death is an accident but occurs while the two have a fight) and is about to suffer the utmost punishment—death by stoning—she is saved by Atiq's dying wife, who, seeking to speed up her own death, volunteers to take Zunaira's place. Concealed within their burqas, the two women's interchangeable identities prove to be an asset in carrying out this ploy and Zunaira's life is saved.

The central image of a woman's stoning in the novel reflects the post-9/11 interest in featuring the Taliban's violence against women both as a *casus belli* and *raison d'être* of the international community's presence in Afghanistan.[30] There was little interest in Afghan women's plight under the Taliban prior to 9/11. Fowler observes that, in the aftermath of 9/11, there was a sudden increase in international attention and interest in the documents compiled by the Revolutionary Association of the Women of Afghanistan (RAWA)—an organization in existence since 1977. She reports:

> a RAWA film, posted on the association's website, of a woman being executed in Kabul Stadium was offered to media outlets two years previously, including the BBC and CNN, but it was turned down on the grounds that it was too shocking to show to news audiences. After September the 11, however, the Pentagon took the film from the website without permission, and brought it into the public domain to justify military action against Afghanistan. (191)

This was the same footage, shot secretly by Freshta, a RAWA member, that feminist playwright Eve Ensler brought back to the United States from Afghanistan in 2000. "No one could understand [back then] what the terrible plight of Afghan women had to do with their own interest, their own comfort and security," Ensler writes (36). As Carol A. Stabile and Deepa Kumar remark, "until Afghan women proved rhetorically useful, their tragic circumstances merited little coverage in the mainstream media" (771). They also report that only fifteen newspaper articles on Afghan women appeared in media in the period between January 1, 2000, and September 11, 2001 (eighteen months). By contrast, ninety-three such articles appeared between September 11, 2001, and January 1, 2002 (six times more in three months than in the eighteen months). The contrast in broadcast programs is even more telling: thirty-three programs in the period between January 1, 2000, and September 11, 2001 (eighteen months), as compared with a staggering 628 broadcasts in the three months after September 11 (771–772).

On the cusp of the US-led Operation Enduring Freedom, high-profile feminist organizations, such as the Feminist Majority Foundation and *Ms.* magazine made public their support of the US-sponsored "liberation" of Afghan women[31] and were in turn criticized by RAWA spokeswomen. The suffering of Afghan women, as well as the mystery of Afghan society as a whole, became embodied in the burqa—a tomb-like symbol of a captive, circumscribed, and ultimately ruined life. Exemplifying westerners' fascination with and wholesale reprobation of the burqa are columnist Rob Norland's *New York Times* essay that described Kabul as "a misogynistic desert," or *The Scotsman*'s similarly toned indictment: "The Afghan female is one of the most maltreated beasts of burden in the world."[32] Jasbir Puar observed that in the post-9/11 climate, "[t]he head scarf . . . (along with the burka and the hijab, often decried as masks), has become a perverse fetish object—a point of fixation—a kind of centripetal force, a strange attractor through which the density of anxiety accrues and accumulates" ("Queer Times" 133). Positioned as battlefields for human rights and dignity, women's bodies became synecdoches of the global West's victory or defeat in the months following Operation Enduring Freedom. In 2002, *The Swallows* added to the repertoire of images rehearsing Muslim women's victimhood and proffering victims in need of saving.

As in *Kandahar*, Afghanistan in *The Swallows* appears as a cultural wasteland—ruined by decades of incomprehensible war that it appears to have brought upon itself. Free of outsiders or outside influence, Khadra's Kabul is quarantined from the rest of the world and suffers the agony of decay, which is presented as a result of a self-imposed enclosure: "Kabul, the old sorceress, lying there at his feet in the grip of her torments, twisted, disheveled, flat on her stomach, her jawbones cracked from eating dirt" (105). Khadra's corpse-like Kabul is a dangerous city seeming to have mystical powers that make its residents succumb to depravity and barbarism, unleashing violence upon each other. While the Taliban are singled out as the culprit, the causes of the rise of the Taliban are mysterious and are described only vaguely. Zunaira, for instance, says: "We've had some privileges that we didn't know how to defend, and so we forfeited them to the apprentice mullahs" (76), implying that the liberal Afghans who now suffer under the repressive regime have only themselves to blame for the loss of rights to religious extremists. Similarly, her husband, Mohsen, contrasts the oppression of the regime with the good old days when he studied political science at the university and "when children sang in public squares now besmirched by dirt and disfigured by gallows" (72), without explaining the causes of this change. While the former middle class yearn for the unspecified past era ("the good old days" [75]), Atiq, a former mujahid and now a Taliban jailor (thus belonging to the group in power), cannot make sense of history at all. The following passage is telling:

> He can't figure out why he has survived two consecutive decades of ambushes, air raids, and explosive devices that turned the bodies of dozens of people around him into pulp . . . to wind up like this, vegetating in the dark, inhospitable world, in a completely disoriented city studded with scaffolds and haunted by doddering human wreckage—a city that mistreats him, damages him, day after day, night after night, whether he's in the company of some wretch condemned to die and awaiting her fate in his stinking jail or watching over his tormented wife, doomed to an even crueler death. (50)

In Atiq's inner monologue, the city of Kabul is personified as an active force oppressing him. As in *Kandahar*, Khadra's removal of history from the narrative naturalizes the disaster borne by a historical process by turning it into a feature of landscape. It makes the nature of the crisis illegible, explained only through repetition and tautology: "Things in Kabul are going from bad to worse, sliding into ruin . . . a chaos within chaos, a disaster enclosed in a disaster" (71). Such poetic refrains cycling through Khadra's prose create a sense of entrapment, stagnation, and claustrophobia, as well as induce a psychic stupor that prevents the reader from asking questions about the cause of the disaster.[33] Images of endless circulation of trapped matter (dirt and dust) conjure a vision of violence as a jammed repetition. The very first sentence in the novel invokes the whirlwind as a figure of enchantment and petrification that locks the terrain into a timeless figure of despair: "In the middle of nowhere, a whirlwind spins like a sorceress flinging out her skirt in a macabre dance; yet not even this hysteria serves to blow the dust off the calcified palm trees thrust against the sky like beseeching arms. [. . .] A deathly silence pervades the dereliction as far as the eye can see" (1). As in *Kandahar*, the aesthetic of circularity is poignant; a figure of meaningless rotation and entrapment, the whirlwind is a useless frenzy that fails to advance or enact even a small change, as a regular wind gust might, such as clearing the dust from the palm trees.

The elision of history by Khadra and his resulting reliance on hyperbole and repetition creates an image of suffering so immense that the reader feels immune to it. The novel unfolds in the atmosphere of humanitarian containment. The reader is invited to witness the loss of humanity experienced by the characters while shielded from seeing the interconnected global histories that contributed to Afghanistan's demise. Once again, the decades of global rivalry and intrigue reaching their nadir during the Soviet-Afghan war; the US's, Saudi Arabia's, Iran's, and Pakistan's meddling; as well as the presence of internationally sponsored terrorist networks in Afghanistan are erased in gestures through which the desolate terrain is supposed to stand in for an explanation: "It seems that the whole world is beginning to decay, and that its putrefaction has chosen to spread outward from *here*, from the land of the Pashtuns, where desertification proceeds at a steady, implacable crawl even in the consciences and intellects of men" (2). Instead of the world coming to fight in Afghanistan, in Khadra's text we have the image of Afghanistan contaminating the world—its decaying matter breeding death that spreads from its core.[34]

While *Kandahar* offers several humanitarian proxy figures that mediate the viewer's access to the site of suffering, *The Swallows* removes such mediation from the scene, portraying Afghanistan as a zone of total abandonment and desertion. Even humanitarian workers, it seems, cannot pierce Afghanistan's self-enclosure. The aesthetic of containment is used strategically by Khadra, seeking to create a sense of catharsis when the novel ends. In his interview to *The Guardian* (2005), the author says: "I gave a talk in Amsterdam recently, and a woman said to me, 'Monsieur Khadra, when I finished the novel and left that world I felt I was re-entering the light. Could you tell me why I felt that?' I said the light is the luck you have in not being an Afghan."[35] The humanitarian narrative model employed by Khadra offers his readers characters who are victims—the four suffering Afghans who no longer know themselves abiding in the zone of mass sacrifice brought forth by mysterious forces. It also seeks to provide therapeutic effects to the reader, who is invited into that world of suffering not only to emerge unscathed, but to feel relieved, feeling the luck of "not being an Afghan." The therapeutic effect depends both on the strong hierarchies between the suffering Afghans and the reader, and on the invitation to feel empathy. It is further noteworthy that the breakdown of empathy in the novel (the characters' succumbing to barbarism and violence) is compensated for by surplus empathy expected from the global community of readers. As the novel describes the diminishing compassion of characters toward each other—Atiq's resentment toward his dying wife, Mohsen's moral fall as he participates in the stoning of a woman, Zunaira's resulting contempt toward Mohsen, and so on—the reader's empathy is bound to grow stronger. The characters are meant to be forgiven for their loss of compassion for each other because of the magnitude of their suffering.

This empathy indexes the reader's moral positon, her or his belonging to the global community of moral subjects who condemn violence and express moral outrage toward the perpetrations of suffering. Indeed, while the novel's explanatory arsenal is inadequate, its affective reach is impressive. This is evidenced most vividly by reader responses posted online. As of May 2019, Goodreads features 6,516 ratings and 751 narrative responses to *The Swallows of Kabul* by readers from around the globe, and most responses convey a sense of being affected by the suffering described. Reader-reviewers call it "a heart-piercing book" (Kim Allen-Niesen) that is important to read because of the truth expressed in it ("Reading *Swallows* is like reading science fiction without the fiction part," writes William), valued because of its capacity to "make you think" (Alisson). It is praised for its imagined ability to raise the consciousness of the reader: "I think it's important for the rest of us to realize how priviliged [*sic*] and pampered we have become living here in our safe and secure little corner of the world where we are free to live the way we choose," writes Trisha. Along the same lines, another reader (Kay) writes, emphatically: "It is about men, by a man, and I wanted to weep for all of them,"[36] while Fantasy4Eva confesses: "Despite the fact that I sat among others in the library, my urge was so strong to shout that I had to put the book down for a minute."

These reader testimonies are important. According to Boltanski, what distinguishes a (moral) humanitarian reader from self-serving readers who consume scenes of violence for their own pleasure (akin to consumers of pornography) is a membership in the moral community of like-minded readers constituted through an actual or imagined public expression of moral outrage. He writes:

> The criterion of public speech or conversation is precisely what enables us to distinguish a way of looking that can be characterized as disinterested or altruistic, one that is oriented outwards and wants to see suffering

ended, from a selfish way of looking which is wholly taken up with the
internal states aroused by the spectacle of suffering: fascination, horror,
interest, excitement, pleasure, etc. (21)

In other words, an altruistic way of looking is differentiated from a quasi-
pornographic gaze through public testimony ("This is unacceptable!"), as
if, through testimony, a hailed reader can confess and be absolved from the
guilt caused by her morbid fascination, and then feel as if meaningful action
has been taken through the act of publicly condemning the perpetrators
of violence.

In sum, *The Swallows* succeeds as a therapeutic text while falling short
of the didactic mission envisioned by its author. By relying on hyperbole in its descriptions of suffering, by evading history and geopolitics as
frameworks for explaining the Afghan tragedy, and by offering, instead,
phantasms of landscape-induced violence, *The Swallows* fails at making
such suffering apprehensible. In fact, the deployment of humanitarian
imagery serves to create a form of affective governance in which the hierarchies of humanity, such as the hierarchy between the reader and the
suffering other, are preserved and strengthened ("the joy you feel of not
being an Afghan"), which in turn create a context and justification for the
unfolding "humanitarian" invasion.

Humanitarian Unconscious

Kushner's celebrated play premiered in New York in the early winter of
2001, shortly after the start of US-led Operation Enduring Freedom in
Afghanistan, with its print version released in 2002. The play, however, was
not a response to the 9/11 attacks; Kushner began writing it in the late 1990s
when Afghanistan and the strife of its people seemed largely irrelevant
to the majority of Western actors. Composed over the course of several
years, with the events of the play set in 1998 (the height of the Taliban
era), the play seemed prescient in that it sought to position Afghanistan,
improbably, as central to global affairs, attempting to bring the forgotten
country into mainstream visibility. The play's uncanny positioning as a work
that in some ways predicts and foreshadows the attacks on the Twin Towers
has come to define its post-9/11 reception. Among other things that seem
clairvoyant in retrospect, the play contains a line: "You love the Taliban
so much, bring them to New York! Well, don't worry, they are coming to
New York!" (85).[37] Notably, the play offers a critique of the humanitarian

mode of representation that relies on empathy as a vector of relating to the suffering other; it also opposes the practice of turning distant suffering into spectacle. While exposing the guilt and melancholy as the psychic malaise that subtends the liberal empathy project, the play proposes, instead, a quasi-religious action plan of seeking repentance through sacrifice. An alternative to empathy's impotence and an antidote to melancholic withdrawal from action, such sacrifice is imagined to have curative powers. And yet, as I will demonstrate, the play suffers from the same set of ailments as the previous two works—the omission of history and the resulting mythologization of Afghanistan—that prevent it from bringing its critique to a meaningful end.

The play centers on an English woman referred to as "homebody" who is stifled by her domestic existence—a life of perpetual, self-inflicted confinement in her apartment in London. A voracious reader, she develops an obsession with Afghanistan, especially as it was represented in discarded travel guides (obsolete and useless today) as they depict the country as it once was: a beautiful, serene place framed by the snowy peaks of the Hindu Kush mountains—a tourist hot spot and a site of successfully implemented modernization.[38] This image of a peaceful past, as contrasted with homebody's knowledge that Kabul since then has become a site of violence, bloodshed, and modernity's failure, is deeply troubling for her, and it makes her decry the present as "an awful place to be" (11).[39] Rejecting the actual present as a site of "wreckage rack and ruination" (25) and, more enigmatically, as "the scene of our crime" (11), homebody suffers in her confinement, presented to the audience through her fragmented, semi-coherent monologue that comprises the entire first act of the play.[40] Homebody's protracted oration is an example of neurotic speech, pulled in different directions by profound yet unknown psychological forces. Homebody's psychic suffering exemplifies what Enzo Traverso calls "Left melancholia"—a background feeling that arises in the world that has lost an expectation for a better future and is haunted, simultaneously, by the past imagined as wreckage. As if echoing homebody's lamentations over the canceled future of Afghanistan as she peers over mid-twentieth-century guides, Traverso writes: "Utopia seems a category of the past—the future imagined in a bygone time—because it no longer belongs to the present of our societies. History itself appears as a landscape of ruins, a living legacy of pain" (7). Homebody's melancholy turns into a neurotic obsession over unidentifiable losses and into the hunt for a shimmering image of the ruined past that might contain something akin to a cure.

Homebody allegorizes excessive empathy—being an obsessive yet distant witness to the "wickedness perpetuated now, in August 1998, now now now, even as I speak and speak and speak" (Kushner 17) leaves her exhausted and succumbed to compassion fatigue. That homebody's state indexes a generalizable condition is supported by the fact that all other Western characters in the play are represented as psychologically ill, requiring psychotropic medication. Both homebody and her husband, Milton, abuse antidepressants, their daughter, Priscilla, attempts to commit suicide by overdosing, and the only westerner to be found in Kabul (in act two)—a shifty embassy worker, Quango—is depicted as an opium addict. Self-medication figures as a necessary numbing—a price that these westerners have to pay for their "luxury" and safety (10)—more generally, for their privileged position in the hierarchy of humanity (the hierarchy of grievable lives).[41] Homebody is vaguely aware of the causes of her malaise, saying, here "stands homebody, safe in the kitchen, on her culpable shore, suffering uselessly watching others perishing in the sea, wringing her plump little maternal hand, oh, oh. Never *joining* the drowning" (28, emphasis in original).[42]

Homebody's psychic suffering is interrupted by her encounter with an Afghan salesman while buying exotic hats for her party, which marks the end of act one. Preparing to pay for the purchase, she suddenly notices the merchant's hand—a piece of mutilated flesh. She observes: "three fingers on his right hand had been hacked off, following the line of a perfect clean diagonal from middle, to ring, to little finger" (21). The transaction exposes homebody's placement within global consumer capitalism, bringing into focus her privilege (she is shopping for postcolonial exotic), as well as potentially implicating her in the violence unleashed on the merchant's body.[43] Conventional treatments of suffering as spectacle, typical of the humanitarian narrative, are disrupted by Kushner describing the injury in a way that pays attention to its specificity, akin to a forensic report. Additionally, the play brings attention to the mutilated hand turning up where it is not supposed to: While exotic commodities (the hats) are seen as belonging in England, the hand that proffers them must remain hidden from view. Homebody's exclamation—"Here, in London, that poor ruined hand" (21)—implies that the mutilated body's proper place is in Afghanistan—a cordoned-off zone of suffering. The ruined hand's manifestation in London turns it into a grievable injury, one that is subject to an investigation: How did this happen? The hand then "speaks." In a trance-like state at the shop, homebody imagines hearing: "Look, look at my country, look at my Kabul, my city, what is left of my city? The streets are as bare as the mountains now, the buildings are as ragged as mountains and as bare and empty of life, there is no life here only fear . . . *you will never understand*" (23–24, emphasis in original). An Afghan body—usually an abstract signifier of *distant* suffering—here appears in central London, challenging homebody's ability to comprehend or relate to its suffering.

The encounter with the merchant is visceral and is described as a touch ("being touched by the mutilated hand" [24]). As such, it closes the gap between spectator and scene, and propels homebody from empathetic passivity to action, resulting, in act two, in her decision to travel to Kabul, where, according to one account, she is murdered and, according to another account, finds redemption and healing. By turning up at the heart of London, the ruined hand globalizes Afghanistan's tragedy, which in turn causes homebody to "provincialize" her European body by leaving her "culpable shores" and going to Kabul, thus traveling to the epicenter of suffering. Homebody's excessive, melancholic empathy prior to the encounter with the merchant is exposed as detached from the scene of suffering and thus lacking—"a touch that doesn't understand" and thus "corrupts" (28). In this encounter, however, the touch of the ruined hand opens up new paths for affinity, action, and understanding. In act two, homebody's response becomes illiberal and exits the domain of feeling (empathetic or melancholic); it is taken into the public sphere—the dangerous streets of Kabul. Homebody's physical presence in the Afghan capital as a body is an act of solidarity and sacrifice. Her silence in act two implies a psychic cure—the melancholic monologue seizes and we never hear her speak again.

While humanitarian narrative conventions frequently portray or call for a rescue mission in which the suffering is relieved by the victim being transported to the West, *Homebody/Kabul*, at least in acts one and two, insists on the Western body's relocation to mayhem's headquarters. By staging this transfer, Kushner seems to suggest that, instead of melancholic witnessing from afar, the Western body has to partake in the violence in which it is implicated. Homebody's unpublicized yet baffling relocation proclaims, much more loudly than her neurotic orations, the radical equality of all lives—an idea that subtends the humanitarian project while being erased in it—and exposes the hierarchy of grievability. Homebody's subsequent alleged death in Kabul—reported by Reuters and documented in a (questionable) forensic report—brings to the fore the invisibility of the suffering of the Afghans whose deaths are not reported or documented. The forensic, profoundly anti-sentimental mode of documentation here, once again, features as an alternative to spectacularized portrayal of suffering designed to induce compassion. Homebody's corporeal sacrifice, the play suggests, conjures a politics of solidarity as an antidote to the politics of pity; the insistence on the radical equality of bodies capable of suffering paves a path out of the empathy-induced melancholy that requires medication.

While in *Kandahar* and in *The Swallows*, Afghanistan figures as just another zone of suffering, Kushner tries to present Afghanistan as a point of intersection for multiple global forces, thus inviting a conversation about its role in global rivalries. At the end of act one, homebody says, "There is a country so at the heart of the world the world has forgotten it, where one may seek in submission the unanswered need" (28). Homebody's statement signals a connection between her location (London) and Afghanistan—a dotted line between the two sites that the play promises to explore. Gesturing toward historical complicity or guilt, Kushner's invocation of culpability in act one has the potential to disrupt a simplistic narrative of West-instigated liberation, in which the forces of democracy bring freedom to the Afghan people suffering the barbarism and cruelty of an archaic and incomprehensible Taliban. Similarly, the insistence of Afghanistan's centrality, the idea of needing to seek answers in Afghanistan, positions Afghanistan as key to the West's questions, a way of cure for the melancholic psyche, and a place of atonement where the Western subject must travel to be absolved of its historical sins. By tracing homebody's trajectory as she seeks such atonement via a trip to Kabul, the play issues a moral imperative for engagement, remembrance, and reparation, reminding the world of its unfinished business in Afghanistan. Such need for repair and remorse also comes through in the following dialogue between homebody's daughter, Priscilla (who traveled to Kabul along with her father, Milton, to collect her mother's remains) and Khwaja, an Afghan poet:

Priscilla: We've brought our misery to your city, my family, I'm sorry.

Khwaja: *(Angry)* What have you ever brought us besides misery? Gharbi? Ferengi? The West? And many among us would like to give your misery back to you. *(He stands to leave)* You have to take home with you nothing but the spectacle of our suffering. Make of it what you will. (115, emphasis in original)[44]

This dialogue, as many others in the play, is both evocative and enigmatic. While Priscilla is apologizing to Khwaja about bringing their family drama to Kabul, the poet himself speaks of a broader historical connection. It is not clear from Kushner's text alone how the West and the world more generally are implicated in the Afghan suffering or why repentance is needed. Kushner's references to history and historical events in the play are plentiful, but they are always vague. The play mentions, for instance, the coalition strikes of 1998 authorized by the Clinton administration—the strikes that, according to the play's Taliban official, made the people "very angry against Western aggression-disrespect-disregard" (33); on several occasions Kushner gestures nebulously toward the Cold War hostilities. These equivocal invocations are not sufficient, however, to ascertain historical culpability or prescribe reparations.

When it comes to history, the play leaves much to be desired, which is especially surprising given the sheer plentitude of historical material that Kushner brings in, both from the travel guides, and presumably, from history books. In fact, it is precisely such excessive quotation and enumeration of historical data that renders history meaningless. Here is an example of such enumeration:

> In the middle of the second century bc, during the Greco-Bactrian Confusion, a Chinese tribe, the Hsuing-Nu, attacked a rival tribe, the Yueh-Chih, and drove them from their homes to what is now southern Afghanistan. Then the Hsuing-Nu, displaced from their new homes by another Chinese tribe, also migrated to Afghanistan and once again displaced the Yueh-Chih, who emigrated to the Kabul Valley. (16)

Paradoxically, these historical facts and stories do not add up to a narrative that has meaning; they do not cohere and fail to make an impression. Instead, we are left with a repository of facts that explain nothing. An agglomeration of data reveals a succession of catastrophes; stories pile up, negate each other, while contradictory accounts coexist and clog up the avenues of meaning-making. Kushner is Benjaminian (and melancholic) in his view of Afghanistan's history as "pile of wreckage upon wreckage" brought forth by an unknown force—akin to Benjamin's storm blowing from paradise (Benjamin, "On the Concept of History"). This clogged up history lends itself to circularity and jammed repetition, which is the domain not of history, but of myth. When Priscilla, guided through the city of Kabul by Khwaja, is shown a pillar indicating the spot where hundreds of British soldiers were slaughtered, she wonders whether they were going in circles, since they have already passed such a pillar. To this, Khwaja replies, cryptically: "There are many pillars, many slaughtered British soldiers" (55). Where Priscilla is looking for a linear chronology and a conventional map, she is presented with a circular, disorienting geometry, designed to obfuscate, rather than explain. This circularity is reminiscent of Khadra's whirlwind as a figure for entrapment, as well as of the frenzied choreography in *Kandahar*. Just as in Khadra's novel and in Makhmalbaf's film, the play's landscape appears petrified. While supposedly using history to grant Afghan suffering greater visibility, Kushner's actual use of it produces a condition of illegibility, where meaning collapses, faced with the sheer magnitude of wreckage. "But in Kabul now there is no history. There is only God," as the Mullah in the play solemnly declares (36).[45]

And this indeed is true. As Kushner's history is flattened into wreckage, Kabul, in turn, becomes the very figure of history as catastrophe. It is described simply as mountains of rubble (111), as a city of death (107), wreckage rack and ruination (25), holocaustal effacement (25), "great heaps of rubble" (21), and unlucky city (114). Its landscapes are nothing but "rubble-strewn streets," "piles of bomb debris" (31), beautiful to the extent to which Hiroshima after a nuclear explosion could be beautiful (as Priscilla declares [56]). Afghanistan is offered as the very figure of disaster: "the fifth worst country on earth . . . not a country, really, a . . . populated disaster" (53). Here, again, we have humanitarian sublime—an overpowering image of destruction that obfuscates a social and political relation.

This neutralization of history and the resulting resort to the humanitarian sublime are disappointing, especially after Kushner's gesture, in act one, toward the rich potential contained by old travel guides that disrupt and problematize conventional chronology. The guide that homebody extensively quotes from was published in 1965. As such, it harkens back to the era when Afghanistan was a rapidly modernizing monarchy that espoused education, women's freedom, and global connectivity. In fact, women were granted the right to vote in 1964—a year before the guide was published—which spurred the era of women's active participation in governance and social movements. Because of the country's proximity to the USSR, modernization of mores often had a distinct socialist tint as many elite members studied in the Soviet Union. The year 1965 was a landmark year for the consolidation of Afghanistan's social justice movements: Afghanistan's socialist party (the People's Democratic Party of Afghanistan or PDPA) was formed that year. The first women's group, the Democratic Organization of Afghan Women (DOAW) was created that year as well with the objectives to improve women's educational levels and ban forced marriages.[46] A closer look at the old travel guides thus has the potential to deconstruct both the idea of linear progress and the idea of Western "liberation" as a long-awaited delivery from the grip of Oriental darkness. An in-depth look at the historical moment captured by a 1965 guide could problematize a vague but neat, diphasic history timeline that both *Kandahar* or *The Swallows* offer—a timeline in which the Afghan people (and especially Afghan women) oppressed by a seemingly timeless fundamentalist regime are then liberated (or expected to be liberated) by the global West. Instead, and disappointingly so, the play leaves us with an image of spectral pasts (what once were) and spectral futures (what could have become but did not) as additional images of ruination that remain abstracted from the actual historical process.

This removal or neutralization of history is present in many scenes, and the scene in which homebody examines the mutilated hand of the merchant provides, possibly, one of the most vivid examples of such neutralization. As homebody imagines the merchant speaking in response to her silent question, his answer renders all historical explanations insufficient and ultimately meaningless. This effect is achieved though an agglomeration of mutually exclusive possibilities:

> I was with the Mujahideen, and the Russians did this. I was with the Mujahideen, and an enemy faction of the Mujahideen did this. I was with the Russians, I was known to have assisted the Russians, I did informer's work for Babrak Karmal, my name is in the files if they haven't been destroyed, the names I gave are in the files, there are no more files, I stole bread for my starving family, I stole bread *from* a starving family, I profaned, betrayed, according to some stricture I erred and they chopped off the fingers of my hand. (23, emphasis in original)

It becomes clear that while embedding historical actors into the storyline (such as the mujahideen or communist party leader Babrak Karmal), Kushner simultaneously divests them of significance through a piling up of incompossible scenarios that amount to nothing in the end. The injury is thus beyond historical explanation; for Kushner, to assign a causation is to take away from its significance. This is a strategic choice. Through this gesture, Kushner positions Afghanistan as a site of an ontological rather than an ontic (historical) trauma.[47] This ontological valence crystallizes most vividly in Kushner's mythologization of Kabul as a place where Cain—Adam's son—was buried.

As historical injury (ontic trauma), is transposed into ontological injury, homebody's travel to Kabul acquires mythological significance. What initially seemed to be a political statement (asserting the radical equality of all bodies) instead turns out to be a pilgrimage—a trip to a site that may contain answers to an ontological question: the origin of violence itself. To designate a site as a pilgrimage destination is to insist on the place's worth as a heritage site. To imagine Afghanistan as a site of global pilgrimage is a difficult task, since Afghanistan, at least in the 1990s, when the play was written, was seen as a place of no significance (and hence a zone of abandonment). After all, what can one expect to find in a place almost completely destroyed by war? To assign such significance, Kushner amplifies and strengthens the legend that he claims to have found in one of the guidebooks, about Kabul being the gravesite of Cain, Adam's first son—a biblical character who brings murder into the world by killing his brother, Abel, when God rejects his sacrifice. Tracing the journey of her mother, Priscilla discovers homebody's fascination with Cain's grave, along with evidence that she had prayed at the site. Presumably, while Cain sowed the seeds of murder, homebody travels to his gravesite to repent, seeking atonement and forgiveness for humanity as such. Early on, in London, homebody remarks: "Murder's grave. Would you eat a potato plucked from *that* soil?" (22, emphasis in original). Her dismemberment (her body was allegedly torn into pieces by a street gang in Kabul) could be then seen as ritualistic act—a sacrificial reseeding of the land that breaks the cycle of violence Cain started.[48]

This plot twist further solidifies Kushner's interest in Afghanistan as a mythological, rather than historical, location. In proximity to Cain's gravesite, Kushner's prose becomes denser, offering an agglomeration of images that connote danger and destruction, becoming hyperbolic, almost *Heart of Darkness*-like at times, suggesting that the site contains the key to the central questions asked in the play. It is described as "[a]n open place, mountains of rubble. Terrible fighting took place here. There are signs posted warning of the danger of undetonated mines" (111). Once there, Priscilla exclaims: "Look up there! Look at that sky! Black! Black! Those stars! Crikey. We could be on the moon! Oh sweet Christ it's. . . . Unearthly!" (112). Kushner then explains the religious and political significance of the site:

> [Cain] was many years older than a thousand years old when he arrived. His heart was worn out with regretting, after so many centuries of remorse, it must have been. And Kabul has always been welcoming of strangers, weary travelers. Even so, it was a great mistake, burying him here. Unlucky man. Unlucky city. (114)

The biblical reference turns the rubble of Kabul ("terrible fighting took place here," 111) into a ruin of a globally significant past, into a heritage site ("the genesis of evil," 148). Cain's grave, therefore, holds the key not only to the tragedy of Afghanistan, but to the larger metaphysical questions of the origin of violence, the possibility of repentance, and the means of atonement. The sheer negativity of the rubble, the minefield, and a depression in the earth that is Cain's grave thus acquire positive value as a ruin of world heritage. Reimagined as Cain's gravesite, Afghanistan's piles of rubble turn into a portal, a gateway into a shared past—a global ruin to be revered and preserved, even though it is the darkest heritage one can imagine ("Would you eat a potato plucked from *that* soil?" 22).

There is an important difference between ruins and rubble. The ruin is an affectively invested site of belonging, while rubble is a place of dispersal and shattering—a no one's place. Cultural anthropologist Gastón R. Godrillo points out that one's desire to see rubble as ruins is never politically innocent. He writes: "Rubble is matter that belongs to everyone and to no one" (265), while, in turn, "ruins are rubble that has been fetishized. . . . [B]eyond the fenced perimeter [of the ruin] lie constellations of rubble created by ongoing forms of disruption" (9). Ruins are rubble that has been singled out as significant while the remaining debris lies unclaimed. There is a long history of European colonial fascination with ruins that foregrounds the fact that ruins are profoundly constructed objects, being situated as high up on what Godrillo calls "the hierarchy of debris" (9): they are superior to rubble, trash, fragments, or useless matter insofar as they are perceived to be remnants of significance (26). Ruins are affect-inducing objects, fecund in their incompleteness. In *The Aesthetics of Ruins*, Robert Ginsberg eulogizes the ruin as a freeing, creative force:

> The ruin liberates matter from its subservience to form. As the chains of form are smashed, matter emerges in our presence, reformulating itself for our refreshed experience. [. . .] The destruction of the structure is rewarded with the resurgence of the substance. (1)

Forces of destruction, unleashed by the ruin, are thus seen as creative in their essence. Destruction here is sutured to resurgence, rejuvenation, and reformulation. The materiality of ruins is thus profoundly spiritual, and a source of insight into the deepest regions of our psychic being: "the ruin bares what is hidden in ourselves. [. . .] The durable and creative stuff shines forth through the transitory and broken patterns applied by human beings" (Ginsberg 2). This history of valorization of ruins explains why Kushner uses the ruin as a way of writing Afghanistan's rubble into the global (and ultimately, Western) imaginary. Restored from its rubble and imagined as a ruin, Kabul can then become a node of collective identification, indexing the dormant forces of resurgence, rejuvenation, and spiritual rebirth. As such, the Afghan past can be recast as significant to world history and spirituality—a site of pilgrimage important for three world religions—Judaism, Christianity, and Islam.

The adherence to the logic of the ruin exposes the limitation of Kushner's project, however. Ultimately, Kushner's Afghanistan as a myth and a site of ontological trauma remains in tension with Afghanistan as a site of a complex historical processes (the ontic trauma) throughout the entire play. What remains foreclosed in this approach is Afghanistan's specificity as a site of historical breakdown and shattering in which the West is implicated in very specific ways, and which I will discuss in subsequent chapters. Here, the reader remains uninformed about the extent of this implication, although Kushner refers to it in vague, indirect ways throughout the play. The last section of the play features Mahala, an Afghan woman, whom Priscilla and Milton smuggle out of Afghanistan and bring to England, thus rescuing her, presumably, from death or at least from impending madness. As if having seamlessly exchanged lives with homebody, Mahala is depicted in homebody's yard gardening. The play concludes, enigmatically, with her words: "In the garden outside, I have planted all my dead" (140). This last line evokes T. S. Eliot's *The Waste Land*, a work concerned with the question of concealment and resurfacing of the past:[49]

> That corpse you planted last year in your garden,
> Has it begun to sprout? Will it bloom this year?
> Or has the sudden frost disturbed its bed?

Why does Mahala plant her Afghan dead in the English garden? Why
do they belong there? What do we do when the past resurfaces? What are
we called to address, who is culpable, and why? The reader is left uncertain as what to make of Afghanistan's tragic history, its ontic trauma.
The play's focus on the corpse of Cain, supposedly buried (planted) in
Kabul, takes our attention away from the landmines that powerful global
players have planted in Afghan land. It remains unclear, at the end of
the play, whether we are to ponder and redeem the primordial "Act of
Violence" (Cain's) or the violence we find ourselves implicated in, by virtue
of historical processes. While attempting an excavation (and as I show in
subsequent chapters, an excavation of Afghanistan's history is required
if we are to understand our contemporary post-9/11 moment), Kushner's
play digs in the wrong place, excavating the sentimentally charged ruins
of Biblical history. As such, it ends up using Afghanistan as a mere setting for the Western subject's search for forgiveness—and for the abstract
original sin—rather than for historical wrongdoings. The radical potential
for transnational solidarity glimpsed in homebody's relocation is replaced
in the end by a weak version of solidarity through cross-cultural fertiliza-
tion (planting the Afghan dead in the English garden) and a recourse to
a shared mythical past.[50]

  In *Human Rights Inc.*, Slaughter observes: "In the contemporary context of the 'War of Terror' in Afghanistan and Iraq . . . the trigger finger
of military invasion is justified by the projective human rights ink of the
'purple finger' of popular democratic elections" and other humanitarian concerns, primarily literacy and women's rights (121). *Kandahar* and
The Swallows of Kabul enter the post-9/11 Operation Enduring Freedom
moral universe by crafting images of extreme victimhood that require
an intervention from the West. The Afghanistan they imagine figures as
flat Earth—a land of no history, inhabited by people trapped in a cycle of
medieval oppression that have been caused, these works suggest, by the
landscape itself. In chapter five, we shall see how this flat view is disrupted
and redefined by Nadeem Aslam who excavates not only Cold War legacies
(the short *durée* of recent history), but insists on seeing Afghanistan from
the perspective of deep time. In the absence of such historically grounded
framework, *Kandahar* and *The Swallows* function as weaponized narratives[51] (inscribing the US invasion as liberation and thus legitimizing it).
The universe they construct is morally unambiguous as they fail to examine
the ethical quandaries posed by humanitarianism as a representational

mode that relies on turning distant suffering into a spectacle, as well as failing to loosen the hierarchies of humanity entrenched in the humanitarian imaginary.

By comparison, Kushner's play is much more nuanced insofar as it offers an examination of the humanitarian imaginary, issuing a critique of melancholic empathy and resisting representing Afghanistan as an object of empathetic humanitarian intervention. As such, *Homebody/Kabul* can be seen as diagnosing our "humanitarian present"[52]—defined by compassion fatigue, melancholy, self-medication, postcolonial exotic, preservation of inequality in humanitarian sentiments, and hierarchies of grievable/ ungrievable lives. The play contains a strong imperative for engagement and remembrance that is not based on the idea of humanitarian intervention, but is framed as sacrifice and repentance. In addition, Kushner's Afghanistan is no longer an insular, cordoned-off zone of suffering. The play inscribes Western culpability and global interconnection, as well as (vaguely) reminds the world of its unfinished business—the corpse buried in its backyard (Afghanistan is often referred to as the graveyard of empires). However, there are significant limitations to Kushner's project as well. By focusing too much on the sublime global ruin, a site cursed by the presence of Cain (an ontological trauma), it turns away from the rubble that is a product of a concrete historical process. This, paradoxically, results, once again, in a historical flattening and illegibility of suffering similar to *Kandahar* and *The Swallows*. While offering a critique of the humanitarian mode of relating to distant suffering, the play can be said to suffer from a humanitarian unconscious, at the end resorting to the domain of myth. Proffering the ancient biblical ruin as an antidote to the unease triggered by the rubble and other residues of failed Afghan modernity, *Homebody/Kabul* also dehistoricizes, aestheticizes and mythologizes the Afghan crisis. Symptomatic as well is the desire in all three works to inscribe the Afghan woman as an object of rescue—even Kushner's play ultimately cannot resist the temptation to save a Muslim woman, Mahala, by having his characters bring her to London—contributing to the 2001-era obsession over rescuing Afghan women critiqued most famously in Lila Abu-Lughod's piece, "Do Muslim Women Really Need Saving?"

Ultimately, the underlying tone in all these works is melancholic insofar as the suffering they portray seems beyond redemption—a jammed repetition from which there is no escape. No amount of mourning, it seems, will ever be adequate to sufficiently grieve the victims of the atrocities committed. Salvation will be available, but to a select few—Mohsen's wife, perhaps Diana (Nafas's sister in *Kandahar*), or Mahala. Even in Kushner, the liberal West figures, at the end, as the only imaginable site of progress and liberation. Without historical depth, without indigenous social justice movements, with no valid claim to modernity, Afghanistan as presented in all three works has to appeal to the West—not only for physical rescue but for everything else, too, including ideas and dreams. It is noteworthy that the three cultural texts discussed in this chapter are silent about Afghanistan's socialist past—when they gesture in its direction, they provide no context or framework for making it legible.[53] These glaring omissions are fascinating as they reveal the absence of a language in which to talk about the defeated socialist projects in the aftermath of the Cold War's end. Ultimately, it is this very erasure of Afghan revolutionary history that results in a humanitarian capture of Afghanistan's present. The next two chapters extend the critique of the humanitarian mode of representing Afghanistan by bringing into focus the relation between the humanitarian imaginary and post-Cold War impasses. These impasses, in contemporary NATO-centric cultural texts, present as aphasias—gaps in representation that signal the work of erasure. An inability to speak about histories of real existing socialism outside of the discourse of failure, we shall see, makes it impossible to represent the Afghan revolutionary subject, and Afghan socialist modernity, in a positive light (or at all).

2

Imagining the Soviets: The Faustian Bargain of Khaled Hosseini's Kabul "Trilogy"

Bad Soviets

Circa 1980, Joseph Brodsky—dissident poet and Soviet exile—wrote a poem entitled "Lines on the Winter Campaign, 1980." In this poem, Brodsky condemned the Soviet intervention in Afghanistan that began on December 27, 1979, painting a dramatic picture of a ruthless Northern Empire that used the heavy machinery of war to subsume—and ruin—the stark and delicate beauty of an Oriental landscape. From this encounter, the poet recoils in horror and shame. Shame is something that the Soviets are supposed to feel, according to the Nobel Prize-winning poet, but are no longer able to—"the color of shame has all gone to the banners." The poem then warns its reader of the coming of the new Ice Age, the cold wave of totalitarianism whose "moraines" are spreading from the North to the South, bringing with them nothing less than enslavement of peoples and destruction of cultural memory: "The Ice Age is coming—slavery's ice age is coming / oozing over the atlas. Its moraines force under / nations, fond memories, muslin blouses."[1] In his passionate condemnation of the Soviets, who intervened on behalf of the unsteady communist regime that came to power in Kabul in April 1978, Brodsky was not alone; by 1980, politicians, ideologues of all persuasions and castes, humanitarians, reporters, writers, poets, and activists joined each other in a thick chorus of voices urging the Soviets to withdraw from Afghanistan. Many of these voices belonged to members of the global Left who saw in the Soviet intervention an occasion for their final disenchantment with real existing socialism and its world-making project. Characteristically of that period, a group of left-wing intellectuals in France devoted an entire issue of 1980 *Les Temps Modernes* to the situation in Afghanistan, denouncing Soviet actions.[2]

Of all the socialist superpower's twentieth-century misadventures, nothing, arguably, received as wide a condemnation as the intervention in Afghanistan in 1979. By 1989, pressured from within and from without, the Soviet government of the USSR—the last Soviet government as it turned out—decided to end the almost-ten-year-long affair and pulled its armed forces out of its southern neighbor's territory. The Cold War was over. The Soviet Union itself disintegrated two years after the end of its Afghanistan mission, outlived by the Afghan socialist state by one year. In 1992, Kabul and its last socialist government fell to Islamist fighters—the mujahideen—and the Democratic Republic of Afghanistan, the world's youngest socialist state, became the Islamic State of Afghanistan.

In post-9/11 NATO-centric cultural texts set in Afghanistan, the Soviet invasion occupies a key role. It figures even more prominently than the recent US-led invasion, being an object of scrutiny, denunciation, contention, blame, and ongoing reassessment. The US-led war in Afghanistan following the 9/11 attacks led to a reissue and republication of Cold War-era anti-communist narratives that depict and condemn the Soviet intervention, such as Atiq Rahimi's *Earth and Ashes*—a Cold War-era story that saw its first publication in French in 2002 (also turned into a film in 2004 and published in English in 2010), along with his *A Thousand Rooms of Dreams and Fear* (2007). M. E. Hirsh's little-known Cold War-era *Kabul*—a novel I discuss later in this chapter—was first published in 1986 and then republished in 2002. Edward Girardet's memoir *Killing the Cranes* (2011) and Didier Lefèvre's (with Emmanuel Guibert and Frédéric Lemercier) graphic memoir *The Photographer* (2009)—the texts I discuss in detail in chapter three—are stories based on their authors' experiences in the 1980s as war reporters "embedded" with the anti-Soviet Islamist fighters. While laden with post-9/11 ruminations on global terror and revamped for post-9/11 consumption, these memoirs furnish a typical Cold War-era anti-Soviet perspective, indexing the sentiments of bewilderment and condemnation as their authors face real, existing socialism from the jihad fighters' mountain

bases. Svetlana Alexievich's Cold War-era account *Zinky Boys*, first published in English in 1992 and bringing "the truth of the Soviet-Afghan
war" to the Anglophone audience, was propelled into renewed visibility by
the author winning the Nobel Prize in literature in 2015.[3]

Moreover, aside from recycled material from the Cold War era, there
also are numerous new texts that tackle the matter of communism's legacy
in Afghanistan. While it is easy to understand the polarizing moralisms
of the 1980s Cold War rivalry—the war in which writers, scholars, and
humanitarians often had to take a side—representations of the Soviet
intervention in post-9/11 texts often betray a more complex, paradoxical
set of investments in seemingly contradictory ideas. What is at stake in
post-9/11, post-Cold War stories of the Soviet invasion? Most immediately, for fiction writers as well as politicians, the Soviet invasion provides
an explanatory matrix that renders the more recent, US-led invasion legible
and legitimized. For instance, Donald Rumsfeld, in his memoir *Known
and Unknown* (2011), invokes the Soviet invasion when describing his
first impressions of Afghanistan in the first weeks of Operation Enduring
Freedom. He contrasts the USSR's "failed conquest" and the US-led "successful liberation" of the country:

> On December 16, 2001, I made my first visit of many to a liberated
> Afghanistan. . . . We landed at Baghram Airfield, a decaying facility
> built by the Soviet Union. . . . MiG fighter jets, battered and unus-
> able, lay scattered along the tarmac, vestiges of the Soviet occupation.
> Parked alongside them were American C-130 transport planes, AC-130
> gunships, Black Hawk and Chinook helicopters, and rows and rows
> of supplies. I was struck at seeing symbols of these two different eras
> side-by-side—*one of failed conquest, the other of successful liberation.* (404,
> emphasis my own)

The triumphalist juxtaposition of the two interventions—Soviet *occupation* and US-led *liberation*—in Rumsfeld's unapologetically US-centric
account provides both justification for the American mission and comfort
in remembering a prior victory—the victory over socialism that now is only
visible in socialism's rubble and wreckage, vestiges of its once powerful
past. In the background of such triumphalist accounts, nevertheless, there
lurks the persistent lingering question—are we in as much trouble as the
Soviets yet?—which fuels some of these comparisons. Girardet, reflecting

on the decade of the post-9/11 coalition mission in Afghanistan, remarks
on the similarities between the two invasions by noting that, "[n]ot unlike
their Red Army counterparts during the 1980s, the Americans and their
military allies are increasingly perceived by ordinary Afghans as an unwelcome foreign occupation force" (3). To this, he adds:

> Often, while examining how the Americans, British, and other NATO
> forces are fighting this latest Afghan conflict, *I am reminded of the
> uncanny resemblance* to the anti-Soviet jihad. Coalition efforts to hunt
> down the guerillas by "clearing" areas only to find out that the insurgents
> slip back in again once they have left hark back to similar efforts by the
> Red Army. (8, emphasis my own)

Here, the stark difference between a failed conquest and a successful liberation gives way to the "uncanny resemblance" between the two. After all,
the vestiges of the Soviet era mentioned by Rumsfeld look a lot like the
artifacts brought to Afghanistan by the Americans, suggesting the possibility that the new empire will meet a similar fate (consider the frequency
with which the heavily mythologized idea of Afghanistan as "a graveyard
of empires" is invoked in post-9/11 Anglophone texts).[4]

Yet perhaps the most important stake in representing the Soviets in
Afghanistan and, even more importantly, portraying socialist Afghanistan
of 1978–1992 lies in the controversial issue of representing socialism in the
aftermath of its historical failure, or rather, its historical defeat. That the
past of formerly socialist countries cannot be effectively articulated in the
contemporary NATO-centric context has been noted by many researchers.[5] After the end of the Cold War, the second world disappeared, and
the postsocialist space became a silent non-region.[6] These difficulties are
further compounded when it comes to minor socialisms, such as Central
Asian socialism, as compared to the more prominent Eastern European,
Cuban, Chinese, or Soviet socialisms. While the best studies of nostalgia
emerged out of considerations of how people in Eastern Europe and the
former USSR dealt with their loss, addressing the possibility of communist
nostalgia in Afghanistan has been a topic hard to breach. The post-9/11
attempts to tell the story of socialist Afghanistan exemplify, perhaps, what
Ananya Jahanara Kabir calls "post-amnesias"—the collective work of erasure of the Afghan socialist dream, a dream that solidified around 1965
and by 1992 was ruined. Socialist Afghanistan is only conceivable as a

ruin—its inception, its existence, its troubled attempt at survival, its end, and finally, its complete erasure readable only through jumbled fragments and gaps in discourse, through its spectral remnants and toxic residue. And yet, these fragments and residue power up many narratives I examine in this book. Traces of such are detectable in many accounts, although mentioned only in passing: "While some [residents of Kabul] formerly supported [mujahid commander] Massoud, I detected a distinct nostalgia for the Soviet occupation days," writes Girardet, known for his sympathies for the anti-Soviet mujahideen with whom he traveled throughout the Soviet-Afghan War era (*Killing the Cranes* 296).

Furthermore, in the 1980s and beyond, the failures of state-sponsored socialism in Afghanistan, resulting in the Soviet-Afghan War, have become "a global symbol for the failure of Moscow's Third World policies" (Westad 378)—a figure for Soviet political, economic, and moral bankruptcy, as well as the insolvency of its world-making project. The violent end of socialist Afghanistan is thus not only a historical event in its own right, but a potent symbol of socialist ideology's absolute and final defeat—a symbol that, when invoked, must remain so unambiguous that it settles all disputes about the future, and socialism's potential role in that future. More than the end of Eastern European socialisms, the failure of the Soviets in Afghanistan continues to function as a global symbol of Soviet insolvency, even in the post-9/11 climate. International relations scholar Anthony James Joes, in his 2010 book aptly titled *Victorious Insurgences*, writes, characteristically:

the Afghan struggle was more than an embarrassing colonial defeat for the world's last multinational empire. By successfully refusing to be bullied into a Central Asian imitation of Ceausescu's Romania, the Afghan freedom fighters inflicted the first (but not the last) *indisputable reverse* on the "historical inevitability of Marxism-Leninism" in which Brezhnev had so devoutly believed. This double defeat helped stimulate the profound pressures for change that were already building inside the Soviet empire, hastening its process of decomposition. (228, emphasis my own)

The Soviet failure in Afghanistan here is proffered as an indisputable argument against socialism as such; it is presented as something that any freedom-loving people would have to be "bullied" into. In Joes's text, we have what Alain Badiou calls "the propagandist use of the notion of

failure"—one invoked to foreclose a horizon of possibility, not only for
the past, but for the present and future (6). Here is another characteristic
quote from Joes:

> *indisputably*, by their resistance to the Soviet invasion, the brave, sorrow-
> ful, martyred people of Afghanistan helped to alter the course of world
> politics. Thus Trotsky's aphorism about the connection between Central
> Asia and Europe was vindicated with supreme irony: the cries of battle
> in the Afghan mountains found an echo in the shouts of freedom at the
> Berlin Wall. (229, emphasis my own)

A psychoanalyst might argue that the almost compulsive rhetorical emphasis on indisputability in both paragraphs quoted from Joes's book reveals
a deep-seated anxiety precisely about such a dispute: What would happen if we started questioning the rhetorical uses of socialism's failure in
Afghanistan? How would it change our view of post-Cold War world
politics, our view of ourselves and the values to which we subscribe? As
Badiou argues:

> What really remains of the great ideological machinery of freedom,
> human rights, the West and its values? It all comes down to a simple
> negative statement that is as bald as it is flat and as naked as the day it
> was born: socialisms, which were the communist Idea's only concrete
> forms, failed completely in the twentieth century. (3–4)

Here I seek to call into question this indisputability by suggesting that,
when it comes to writing about Afghanistan in NATO-centric contexts,
we succumb to what writer Chimamanda Ngozi Adichie in her TED
talk calls "the danger of a single story." This chapter (and the next one)
seeks to open a space for a different story, recovering the image of Afghan
socialism from its ruins and restoring Afghan revolutionary history
and the Afghan revolutionary subject to visibility. This effort is needed
to correct a set of deeply entrenched Cold War-era biases that exist on
both ends of the political spectrum and lead one to equate "the brave,
sorrowful, martyred people of Afghanistan" (Joes 228) only with those
who fought against socialism, condemning to historical invisibility those
other Afghans who shared in the dream of universal emancipation and
social justice. In truth, the people of Afghanistan, like any other people,

were divided among many lines of difference—traditionalist, monarchist, nationalist, anti-imperialist, fundamentalist, communist, and so forth. Afghanistan's revolutionary era is a testament to how these differences, and the corresponding political projects, played out on Afghanistan's soil.

Given the symbolic value of Afghanistan as a ruin of communism, it is not surprising that the first properly didactic narrative on Afghanistan to emerge in the NATO-centric world after 9/11—Khaled Hosseini's *The Kite Runner* (2003)—proffered the ruins of Kabul as resulting from "the communist *coup d'état*" and the subsequent Soviet invasion, pointing at the Soviets as the sole culprit and cause of destruction (36). In *The Kite Runner*, the Soviet invasion heralds the "official end" when "Russian tanks would roll into the very streets where Hassan and I played, bringing the death of the Afghanistan I knew" (36). In this immensely successful global best seller, the invasion by the Soviets is described as a grisly, macabre, overnight takeover by a savage force from the North (Brodsky-style), comprised of bulldog-faced, shameless soldier-rapists led by corrupt officers. In the wake of the invasion, the novel's protagonist promptly flees the country with his father to resettle and start a new life in Freemont, California, only to return to Kabul in 2000. The scene of the return is situated perfectly just a few months prior to the NATO-led invasion. Overwhelmed with the landscape of ruination that welcomes him, and noticing that Kabul's formerly lush, tree-lined streets are now stripped, Amir, the main character, asks his local guide what happened to the trees. "The *Shorawi* [communists] cut a lot of them down," the guide explains—leaving out the entire era of civil war that followed the Soviet *withdrawal*, the era during which entire orchards were destroyed by the four years of rocket shelling by the warring militants who took Kabul in 1992 (246).[7] This grisly story of Kabul's protracted siege by the mujahideen is told by another Afghan writer, Qais Akbar Omar, whose work I discuss in chapter four. In the 2007 cinematic version of *The Kite Runner*, the phrase morphs into an even more stark charge: "The Russians chopped them down" (Figure 2.1).

Why does Hosseini—a debut novelist seeking to break into the post-9/11 NATO-centric literary market—as well as the film director who further condenses the message for greater effect—resort to such gaudy anti-Sovietisms? Is it because one might expect that, in NATO-centric contexts, the audiences are well primed to see the Soviets as evil—ones who would chop down the trees in Kabul out of sheer hatred for nature, perhaps? In her aptly titled article, "'The Russians Acted Like the Russians,'"

Figure 2.1. Amir returning to Kabul in the 2007 film by Marc Forster.

Joanne P. Sharp suggests that the othering of the Soviet Union in mainstream US media in 1980–1990s was extreme. Her analysis of *Reader's Digest* during this time period, reveals homogenizing, unsympathetic representations, reinforcing "the picture of a homogenous population" (62), timelessness ("unchanging Soviet character," 63), the trope of degeneration (64), irrationality (64), "a moral void" (69), and an insistence of the radical difference between Americans and the Russians. Capitalizing on the legacy of the Cold War-era anti-Soviet bias is thus an easy shortcut for a writer seeking to make Afghanistan legible for the American public.

What happens if we accept, for a minute, that the Soviets portrayed in global Anglophone contexts, during the Cold War and beyond, are just an image born out of fear, a figure of the global West's own anxiety that persists, improbably, beyond the Cold War and into the 9/11 wars? While literary theorists today are deeply conscious of the dangers of Orientalism, and are resistant to both the generalization and the abstractions that may result from it, they are much less aware of the entrenched power of the deeply rooted Cold War tropes associated with the portrayal of socialism—abstractions of "red terror" that today, no doubt, serve to stave off any possibility of socialism's revival. The cultural imaginary that proffers the image of what Jodi Dean calls "our Soviets" marks the Soviets as an abstract force of destruction, as the very figure of "authoritarianism, prison camps, and the inadmissibility of criticism"—a constellation that, according to Dean, has little explanatory or historical valence but has tremendous consequences as it attempts, again and again, "to repress the communist alternative" as a vehicle of futurity and hope (29–32). This demarcation of socialism as a figure of total oppression circumscribes NATO-centric cultural imaginary in such a way that it is hard, if not impossible, to imagine socialism as an object of desire. And yet, in 1970s Afghanistan, socialism was precisely such an object. In his 1978 *New Left Review* article, historian Fred Halliday wrote that the 1978 communist revolution "at least temporarily embodied the hopes of a wide section of the population. . . . The novel character of the new regime soon became even more apparent. It committed itself to land reform, to equality of nationalities, to emancipating women, to a solution to the nomadic question" (4).[8]

In this chapter, via my analysis of Khaled Hosseini's literary works on Afghanistan, I seek to bring into view Afghan socialism as an object of Afghan people's desire, restoring to visibility the Afghan revolutionary subject doubly erased: first, by erasing the difference between Afghan socialism and the Soviet invasion, and second, by reducing the Afghan people to those who fought against communism. I also seek to inscribe the much-needed ambiguity into the heart of the narrative of the demonic Soviets, as well as into the corresponding narrative of the helpless Afghan victim conjured in Cold War–era texts (such as Brodsky's poem) and perpetuated in post-9/11 writing.[9] I argue that, by summoning anti-Soviet cultural capital, and thus taking advantage of the accumulated bad press that the Soviets and the invasion received in the NATO-allied world during the Cold War and beyond, Hosseini, in *The Kite Runner*, strikes a Faustian bargain that both makes the text easy to consume (in NATO-allied contexts), and simultaneously, forces him into a representational stalemate from which his subsequent two novels struggle to find a way out. To capitalize on the Soviet defeat and the Evil Empire as a literary commodity that would help the novel in the global literary market, *The Kite Runner* has to foreclose the possibility of Afghan agency, casting the Afghans as passive sufferers rather than revolutionary dreamers engaged in their own project of world-making. To bring the Faustian bargain of *The Kite Runner* into further relief, I juxtapose it with M. E. Hirsh's *Kabul* (1986)—a long-forgotten, Cold War–era novel that focuses on the same period of Afghanistan's history—the socialist revolution and the subsequent Soviet invasion—but results in a very different portrayal of

these events with very different consequences in terms of representing
Afghan political agency. I also demonstrate that Hosseini's choices in *The
Kite Runner* result in a highly distorted, flawed narrative of Afghanistan's
recent history, thus betraying the novel's didactic-realist premise. One
of the main distortions was the author's choice to not describe the forces
(the US- and Saudi Arabia-sponsored Islamist fighter groups) that actually caused the destruction of Kabul in 1992, three years after the Soviet
withdrawal and one year after the collapse of the USSR. I demonstrate
how his following two novels—*A Thousand Splendid Suns* (2007) and *And
the Mountains Echoed* (2013)—struggle to correct and amend the earlier
narrative by including parts of history omitted in *The Kite Runner* and
reframing the legacy of the Soviet period. These subsequent two novels at
times exemplify, and at other times break through, post-Cold War aphasias, mapping the writer's quandaries as he tries to articulate the project of
Afghan socialist modernity and its place in the country's history.

From the perspective afforded by the second decade of the 9/11 wars
(which led to the proliferation of failed states in the aftermath of US-led
"humanitarian" invasions) and the widespread economic crisis, Hosseini's
novels' ideological vacillations look particularly intriguing as they might
index the changing zeitgeist. The market crash of 2008 and the Occupy
Wall Street movement of 2011 exposed the crises of capitalism, forcing
many to wonder whether the idea of communism as an alternative to market capitalism that privileges the one percent is not without merit. More
notably, the void left by the defeated Left becomes palpable as the specters
of fascism rush to fill that space. While I was writing this book, even in
NATO-centric contexts the question of the future was no longer bound
by the promise of liberal capitalist democracy only. If in 1989, Fukuyama
wrote about "the total exhaustion of viable alternatives to Western liberal-
ism" (1) and contended that "the class issue has actually been successfully
resolved in the West" (8), by the onset of the second decade of the 9/11
wars, a wave of massive economic and political crises enveloped the global
North and the phrase "we are the 99%" indexed the return of class politics.
To add, residents of the post-socialist world continue to suffer from what
has been discussed by many as "communist nostalgia"—a nostalgia for the
past but also a nostalgia for a particular vision of the future enabled by
socialist dreaming. As Svetlana Boym puts it, "[c]ommunist teleology was
extremely powerful and intoxicating; and its loss is greatly missed in the
post-Communist world" (59).

As I trace Hosseini's initial staging, and subsequent revisions, of his narrative of Afghanistan's recent history, as thrown against the background of Hirsh's work, I deploy the concept of time as a shortcut to signal each text's investment in a particular mode of inscribing Afghanistan's revolutionary era. The first temporal mode (exemplified by Hosseini's *The Kite Runner*) is an ahistorical (frozen) time of trauma; the second—a messianic, revolutionary time, as depicted in M. E. Hirsh's *Kabul;* the third is the nostalgic mode of *A Thousand Splendid Suns* in which the revolutionary era is seen, retrospectively, as women's time. Finally, in *And the Mountains Echoed,* the revolutionary era disappears from view completely, as if time itself vanished inexplicably. By suturing the notion of socialism to the imagery of sexual violence (ahistorical trauma), as I will demonstrate, *The Kite Runner* attempts to write the socialist leftist project out of history, disallows an articulation of Afghanistan's political diversity and subsequently, its agency, and justifies US interventionism and neocolonial ambitions. By contrast, Hirsh's *Kabul* situates the invasion as a moment (one among many) within rich, revolutionary (messianic) time during which the people of Afghanistan are propelled into major political changes. By describing the diverse revolutionary forces that flourished in pre- and post-1979 Kabul, Hirsh's novel resists issuing a call for rescue, suggesting that Afghans have a unique political history and culture that will allow them to find their own way to liberation and peace. Hosseini's *A Thousand Splendid Suns* inscribes the Soviet period in Afghanistan's history as women's time, revising the simplistic narrative of ruination-via-the-Soviets of *The Kite Runner* and offering, paradoxically, a version of communist nostalgia—a nostalgia for the interrupted project of Afghan modernity. Yet this nostalgia dissipates in the last novel, as Afghanistan's revolutionary history vanishes from view, leaving us with a vision of a bleak, corrupt, violence-ridden world without any hope for a better future.

Before proceeding with the analysis of the novels, a brief note on the history of the events that unraveled in Afghanistan in 1978–1979 is in order. The Soviet invasion of Afghanistan occurred in December 1979, eighteen months after the Saur (April) Revolution of 1978, through which the Nur Muhammad Taraki-led faction of the socialist party (the People's Democratic Party of Afghanistan or PDPA) came to power. Afghan socialists overthrew the regime of Mohammed Daoud Khan, a member of the royal family, who had himself deposed his cousin's kingdom and abolished the monarchy in 1973, coming to power with the help of multiple revolutionary groups, including the PDPA. Contrary to a commonly held belief, declassified historical documents now clearly show that the revolution was not orchestrated by the USSR, and in fact, it caught the Soviet political elite off guard. Furthermore, the Soviets were extremely loath to send their troops to assist the revolution unfolding in Kabul.[10] The USSR's reluctance is well documented. In response to Taraki's repeated requests for military backing in the months following the revolution, Leonid Brezhnev—"by temperament a cautious and circumspect man on international issues," was not taking the idea of a military intervention lightly (Crews 319). He is known to have warned the newly minted leader that full Soviet intervention "would only play into the hands of our enemies."[11] Brezhnev also advised Taraki to slow down, seek support for his regime in the villages, and reconsider the timeline for his ambitious social reforms that were becoming increasingly unpopular, especially in the countryside. Alexei Kosygin, USSR chairman of the Council of Ministers, also criticized Taraki for his methods and warned him that Soviet "troops would have to fight not only with foreign aggressors but also with a certain number of your people. And people don't forget such things."[12]

The Politburo's attitude started to shift, however, after a protracted time of anxiously watching Taraki's brutal means of enforcing reform compliance in the countryside, which caused major uprisings, as well as the purges that resulted in hundreds of party members being imprisoned. The Soviets urged Taraki to broaden the regime base by setting up a coalition government, which would include not only members of the rival factions of the PDPA, but also members of the old regime (Westad 311). They also urged the new government to stop purges of the party and to release political prisoners. The final decision to send troops was made as the result of the assassination of Taraki by Hafizullah Amin—an even more radical member of the PDPA.[13] Paradoxically, the Soviets intervened in December 1979 not on behalf of but *against* the radical left-wing regime, deposing Amin and installing a much more moderate leader of the other wing of the socialist party (*Pagram*, "banner") Babrak Karmal, who they believed could work successfully with the countryside and with the opposition. The Soviet invasion quickly led to even more resistance in the rural areas and the rise of jihad fighters (mujahideen), who were subsequently armed and supported financially by the United States and trained by the CIA.[14] The resulting civil war between the Soviet-supported Afghan state and the (increasingly transnational) jihad groups resulted in loss of life and displacement for millions of Afghan people.

The Time of Trauma

Arguably, no one has done as much as Khaled Hosseini to popularize the image of Afghanistan within the global Anglophone context. *The Kite Runner* was published just eighteen months after the US invasion of Afghanistan, and propelled Hosseini into fame by explaining to the US-based and subsequently global audience curious about Afghanistan's history and culture why the country was in such sorry shape. As Timothy Aubry points out, readers "seem to approach *The Kite Runner* either as an accurate record of Afghanistan's recent history or as a preferable substitute for such record" (34). The most successful novel ever written about Afghanistan and written entirely in the humanitarian mode, *The Kite Runner* seeks to make Afghanistan relatable, that is, empathetically consumable by global, primarily Western audiences. As of the year 2018, it has been published in 46 languages. Teachers around the globe use the novel to introduce their students to the culture and history of Afghanistan. The film version of the story was screened in the White House upon its release in 2007. Laura Bush recommended *The Kite Runner* as one of her and her husband's favorite books.[15] Criticized by some scholars,[16] it is lauded by others as a didactic narrative useful for teaching.[17] My reading here brings into view something that existing literary criticism does not address, but that, in my view, constitutes the crux of the novel—the set of distortions and omissions that I refer to as Hosseini's Faustian bargain.

The Kite Runner constructs pre-1979 Kabul as a simplistic geography of imagined social cohesion, free of political dissent—a beautiful city spoiled only by the racism of the few. By contrasting the images of beautiful pre-war Kabul with the images of bone-chilling destruction and violence that the Soviets initially bring and the Taliban complete, the novel issues, post-2001, a powerful call for a humanitarian (presumably US-sponsored) intervention that would restore the city to its former glory: "I dream that *lawla* flowers will bloom in the streets of Kabul again and *rubab* music will play in the samovar houses and kites will fly in the skies" (218). The narrative arc of the first part of the novel unfolds in one of Kabul's wealthy neighborhoods—the artfully chiseled site of Amir's (the protagonist's) childhood sold to the reader with a pinch of Orientalist spice. The exoticism of the bazaars, along with descriptions of mysterious desert nomads caravanning with their camels through the streets of Kabul are pleasantly contrapuntal to the scenes depicting Amir's protected, rather modern life in his father's mansion. In the narrator's memory, pre-war Kabul emerges as a peaceful, provincial, yet strikingly beautiful place— "a perfectly encapsulated morsel of good past" (123):

> Friday afternoon in Paghman. An open field of grass speckled with mulberry trees in blossom. Hassan and I stand ankle-deep in untamed grass, I am tugging on the line, the spool spinning in Hassan's calloused hands, our eyes turned up to the kite in the sky. [. . .] From somewhere over the low brick wall at the other end of the field, we hear chatter and laughter and the chirping of a water fountain. And music, something old and familiar. I think it's *Ya Mowlah* on *rubab* strings. Someone calls our names over the wall, says it's time for tea and cake. (122–123)

In this sentimental sketch, Kabul is presented as a tranquil paradise of an Oriental variety through a rather extreme agglomeration of positively coded imagery that appeals to all of our senses: an open field, blue skies, trees in blossom, the chirping of a fountain, chatter and laughter, music, a friend's calloused hands, tea and cake. Such descriptions work well to conjure the image of pre-war Kabul as a city of social cohesion almost completely free of social antagonisms and conflict.

Racism is foregrounded as the main, perhaps the only, issue that troubles pre-socialist Kabul. It is presented as an exception to the general rule of social harmony, and becomes central to the novel's plot. Racism is examined through Amir's relationship with his best friend and servant, Hassan. The issue of race is a clever device employed to solidify the connection between the Afghan protagonist and an American reader.[18] I use the term *racism* instead of the term *ethnic difference* because *The Kite Runner* strategically reduces Afghanistan's ethnic diversity to a binary vision of race that an American reader will find easy to grasp: Amir, the master's heir, is a Caucasian-looking Pashtun, and Hassan, a servant, is an Asian-looking Hazara. What is being erased by the binary depiction of race is Afghan specificity; the ethnic structure of Afghanistan is in no way binary but consists of four major ethnic groups: Pashtuns, Tajiks, Uzbeks, and Hazaras. The complex web of ethnic differences (including linguistic and religious, such as Sunni and Shia differences) would be harder to explain to a Western audience and would interrupt a seamless process of identification with the characters. The racist binary the novel constructs serves to exemplify all that is "bad" in pre-socialist Afghanistan.[19] In the novel's central scene, the narrator watches Hassan get raped by a sociopathic racist named Assef and becomes implicated in the crime when he does nothing to rescue his friend. Hassan's racialized body ("He is just a Hazara," says Assef [76]) is also a feminized, penetrable body that connotes passivity, powerlessness, and a silent acceptance of its fate. The logic and the vocabulary deployed in the description of Hassan's rape are then redeployed in the descriptions of the Soviet invasion and later in Amir's encounter with the Taliban.

It is hard to overstate the centrality of the image of rape in Hosseini's book. Its efficacy lies in its visceral nature; Hosseini's messages about Afghanistan's history are organized and maintained around the imagery of sexual violence. The act of rape Amir witnesses scrambles the narrative flow, causing it to become fragmented; the scene is recounted through a mix of flashbacks and disjointed associations that take the narrator in and out of the event, back into the past and forward into the future. Perception becomes fragmentary, erratic, and the senses themselves unreliable:

> I stopped watching, turned away from the alley. Something warm was running down my wrist. I blinked, saw I was still biting down on my fist, hard enough to draw blood from the knuckles. I realized something else. I was weeping. From just around the corner, I could hear Assef's quick, rhythmic grunts. (77)

The image that Amir's memory blasts out of the sensory shock of having witnessed an act of sexual violence is the image of Hassan's face. Hassan's face resembles the face of a sacrificial lamb—an image of resignation, ritual sacrifice, and above all, purity (76). Profoundly good-natured, loyal, and chaste, yet lacking the power to resist the thugs, Hassan metonymically stands for the country itself—also "good," yet passive, feminized, and unable to resist its invaders. Hassan's fate is linked to the fate of Afghanistan, and his rape serves as an allegorical representation of the fate suffered by the nation at large.

The underlying image of Kabul as a "good" (even if tragically flawed) place frames the novel's representation of the Soviet invasion of 1979—a pivotal event of Amir's childhood that propels him and his father away from the country into exile in California. Visceral images of sexual violence are used to frame and explain the event to the reader. *The Kite Runner* mobilizes a Western reader's preexisting set of beliefs pertaining

to socialism as an illogical and an unnatural system, depicting the arrival
of the Soviets as a "rape" of the pristine terrain by foreign forces seeking to
impose an incomprehensible political system upon an internally coherent
culture. Reminiscent of Brodsky's poem, the novel dramatizes and explains
the invasion as the rape of Kabul—tanks are ripping through the streets
of a sleeping city at night, Kalashnikov-wielding (phallic) soldiers march-
ing up and down the boulevards, "their turrets swiveling like accusing
fingers" (113). In his representation of the invasion, Hosseini employs a
variety of Cold War-era "othering" strategies best captured, for lack of a
better word, as Cold War Orientalisms.[20] In Hosseini's text, the Soviets
are presented as both the *destroyers* of the Oriental landscape but also
as themselves Oriental. This depiction reveals the novel's NATO-centric
position, a cultural location from which both Afghanistan and the Soviet
Union appear to be Oriental "other"—the first constructed strategically
as benign orient, a passive feminized victim in need of saving; the second
depicted as aggressive, malevolent orient, a ruthless sexual predator. Sharp,
in her review of late Cold War-era representations of the USSR, asserts
that while there are many similarities between Orientalism as described
by Edward Said and the set of tropes that serve to frame representations
of the Soviet Union, they diverge when it comes to the issue of gendering. Specifically, "the gendering of the USSR seems to be the opposite to
that of the Orient. *RD* [*Reader's Digest*] articles [about the USSR] do not
evoke the West's penetration or subjugation of its Other. Instead the Soviet
Union is pictured as the aggressor or the forceful masculine courter" (67).
One can trace the residue of this framing in the more recent obsession in
the US culture with Vladimir Putin's masculinity, leading, at times, to
rather absurd anxieties about feminized America.[21]

The Soviet invasion in Hosseini's book is depicted quite literally as
an instance of an inexplicable, sudden violence inflicted on virgin land
by a stranger, with no connection to the history of Afghanistan. It occurs
in the "frozen" time of trauma—time outside of a historical process, as a
singular event without a cause that creates a rift in the continuity of the
protagonist's psychic life and in the coherent narrative of national history.
Amir's memories of that time are fragmented, inconsistent, and do not
cohere into a continuous narrative. They form a constellation of jumbled,
gut-wrenching sensations, all of which are unwelcome intrusions into the
psyche, and importantly, into the body of the narrator. They are convul-
sions caused by sonic waves, acrid fumes, and nausea:

scattered bits and pieces of memory that come and go, most of it sounds and smells: MiGs roaring past overhead; staccatos of gunfire; a donkey braying nearby; the jingling of bells and mewing of sheep; gravel crushed under the truck's tires; a baby wailing in the dark; the stench of gasoline, vomit, and shit. (123)

The implicit link between socialism and rape becomes explicit in the scene where Amir and his father are being smuggled out of Afghanistan. The Soviet soldier who searches the truck wants to rape an Afghan woman (a nursing mother with a baby on her lap and a terrified husband by her side), and Amir's father heroically saves her. In this powerful, viscerally gripping scene, the Afghan family assumes the status of the Holy Family while the Soviet soldier is cast as a pervert who interrupts the heteronormative family structure seen as indigenous, proper, and sacred:

The soldier wanted a half hour with the lady in the back of the truck.

The young woman pulled the shawl down over her face. Burst into tears. The toddler sitting in her husband's lap started crying too. The husband's face had become as pale as the moon hovering above. He told Karim to ask "Mister Soldier Sahib" to show a little mercy, maybe he had a sister or a mother, maybe he had a wife too. The Russian listened to Karim and barked a series of words. [. . .] "Agha Sahib," Karim said, "These *Roussi* are not like us. They understand nothing about respect, honor." (115)

The description of the soldier is packed with images of sexual predation: he is "bulldog-faced," "grinning," with a "cigarette dangling from the side of his mouth," has a barking voice, and is humming a wedding song as he expresses his wish to rape the young mother (114). "There is no shame in war," he says (115)—a phrase evocative of Brodsky's "the color of shame has all gone into banners." The narrator finds himself hypnotized by this terrifying scenario, experiencing a sense of disassociation and shock reminiscent of the moment he witnessed the rape of Hassan (Figure 2.2).

Hosseini deploys sexual imagery consistently and to a great effect to outline the contours of the enemies of the land—the Soviets and later the Taliban, who are, not surprisingly, also the enemies of the Anglo-American geopolitical axis. If communism is explained through the image of a soldier-rapist, the Taliban are later explained through Assef, who has grown

He says,
there is no shame in war.

Figure 2.2. A scene from the 2007 film. The truck is pulled over during Amir and his father's escape from Afghanistan and the refugees are confronted by a Soviet soldier.

up to become a child molester and a Talib commander. Thus, the fanatical Taliban is, paradoxically, positioned as a successor to the atheist Soviet rule. In turn, Afghanistan's continuous victimization is explained through the continuity of suffering endured by Hassan, and during the Taliban era, by his son, Sohrab: both innocent children, they are likened to sacrificial lambs in the hands of their assailants. The body of a communist is thus sutured to the Talib body through the idea of perverse sexual violence that disrupts heteronormative family structures by preying on children and nursing mothers.

In doing so, the narrative also sutures the notion of heteronormativity to the vision of the nation, and the idea of the child's purity to the image of Afghanistan, trafficking in what Elizabeth Anker calls "patronizing fictions of Third World purity" (*Fictions of Dignity* 41). This is not entirely surprising. As Jasbir Puar explains, "queerness is always already installed in the project of naming the terrorist; the terrorist does not appear as such without the concurrent entrance of perversion, deviance, deformity."[22] To this one can add that queerness is also installed in the project of naming a communist, who cannot be articulated outside of the discourse of failure: moral failure, the failure of heteronormative family structure, and ultimately, historical failure.

The imagery of sexual violence punctuates the narrative strategically; it decontextualizes the key developments in Afghanistan's history, rendering them ahistorical and illogical. For instance, upon Amir's brief return to the land of his childhood, Kabul is a spectral city, a mere skeleton of what it used to be:

> The cratered streets were flanked by little more than ruins of shelled buildings and abandoned homes. We passed the rusted skeleton of an overturned car, a TV set with no screen half-buried in rubble, a wall with the words ZENDA BAD TALIBAN! (Long live the Taliban!) sprayed in black. (251)

This spectacular destruction is blamed on the Soviets (246) and the Taliban where both are presented as mythical forces of violence, leaving the narrator, along with the reader, bewildered at the sheer scale of Kabul's ruination.

The way in which the Soviet invasion is represented in *The Kite Runner* is troublesome for three distinct reasons. First and foremost, it betrays the impossibility of narrating socialism other than as failure, aberration, and perversion, foreclosing the prospect of any discussion of any transformative potential it might have contained. In doing so, it forecloses the possibility of discourse of and about socialism as a political project that has any kind of validity in the future. Second, by presenting the Soviet invasion as the prime cause of the destruction of the country, Hosseini conveniently avoids all mention of the CIA-trained mujahideen (the jihad fighters),[23] and therefore absolves the US of its key role in arming, financially supporting, and coaching the jihad fighters, a legacy that continues to create instability worldwide today and that came to bear on 9/11. Hosseini's

omission of the mujahideen and their chief role in the complete destruction
of Kabul in 1992 is so glaring that the author had to address and correct
this misrepresentation of the country's recent history in his second and
third novels. Finally, *The Kite Runner* perpetuates the Orientalist idea of
a third-world nation's purity and passivity, which has long-reaching consequences. Afghanistan appears as having no political history or political
culture of its own, and thus no agency and no role in its own history other
than that of a victim or a pawn. The novel thus renders invisible the Afghan
revolutionary subject—a gesture that is brought into relief through a comparison with a late Cold War-era novel by M. E. Hirsh: *Kabul*.

Revolutionary Time

Hirsh's text describes the same time period and serves as an important
counterpoint to Hosseini's international best seller. It was originally published in 1986 by St. Martin's Griffin and seems to have received very
little attention that year.[24] It was reissued in the aftermath of 9/11 (June
2002) when the reading public developed an interest in Afghanistan due
to the events of 9/11 and subsequent US-led invasion. A survey of reader
responses on *Amazon* and *Goodreads* reveals two facts: *Kabul* boasts a much
smaller readership as compared to *The Kite Runner*, and the readers of
Kabul are self-selecting as they disclose that they had a preexisting interest
in regard to the history and culture of Afghanistan as a result of their prior
exposure to other texts, often *The Kite Runner*.[25]

The novel *Kabul* is similar to *The Kite Runner* in many ways. Written
in English and for the Anglophone, NATO-centric audience, it offers
descriptions of the Afghan capital by focusing on the very same period:
1973–1980. However, it avoids many of the pitfalls of Hosseini's text. For
instance, it carefully contextualizes the Soviet invasion by describing a
series of internal sociopolitical transitions that occurred in Afghanistan in
the years preceding the invasion (1973–1979), from monarchy to republic
and then from republic to Afghan socialist rule. Specifically, it describes
the protagonists' discontent with monarchy and later the republic and
follows them in their fascination with the promises of nationalism and
socialism. It also examines the reasons why students in Kabul favored and
put their hopes in the socialist party of Afghanistan (PDPA).

Critically revisiting a novel from 1986 (that in many ways serves as
a ghost image to the more popular *The Kite Runner*) allows for an articulation of the Afghan socialist project from a historical "elsewhere"—the

moment before its historical failure, when it was still a real possibility
for the future. The novel is Afghan nationalist in its political orientation
(postcolonial nationalist) and speaks powerfully against the invasion
by the Soviets. It is also a Cold War-era text published in the United
States—all of which contribute to its anticommunist pathos. At the
same time, however, the novel manages to accommodate a multiplicity
of voices and political perspectives. The characters' identities are complex and paradoxical: the main character, Mangal, is a "nationalist who
couldn't tie his own turban" (12)—a royal minister's son and a journalist
for *Kabul Times* (an official newspaper), who now conspires against the
monarchy by coordinating the production of a revolutionary newspaper
called *The New Homeland*. Roshana, Mangal's fiancée, is a feminist whose
face features a scar from an acid attack, but who puts on a burqa to conceal her identity when she goes to the underground political meetings
held at a bazaar shop. Mangal's father is a royalist and works for the king.
He says, "If the monarchy falls, that's the end" (53). Mangal's brother,
Tor, a perpetual troublemaker and a college dropout, will eventually join
the mujahideen in the mountains.

The socialist perspective is represented by Mangal's younger sister,
Saira, who has legitimate reasons to be skeptical of Afghan nationalism,
since she is driven into exile because of the culture's double standard
regarding women's and men's premarital sexual behavior. The author is
thorough in describing this double standard: both siblings—Mangal and
his sister—attend college in the West (Europe and the United States),
and each have a lover during their college years. While Mangal remains
unscathed by his premarital sexual escapades, his sister's marriage is
called off when her personal diary containing evidence of her premarital affair in the United States is discovered. Later, while in exile in
the United States, Saira dates a communist, Andrew, a Soviet official
working for the embassy of the Soviet Union. The novel thus brings into
view the various characters' emancipatory desires; specifically, socialist
ideology with its emphasis on women's rights, represents, for Saira, an
alternative to the patriarchally inflected Afghan nationalism her brother
subscribes to.

In stark contrast to the works discussed in chapter one, Hirsh's Kabul
is featured as a global city and an active participant in global conversations.
Tensions between the Kabul-Moscow and the Kabul-New York axes are
foregrounded, but the agency of the Afghan people is never diminished.

The novel unfolds in a messianic, revolutionary time—a point in time when various futures seem equally possible. If in *The Kite Runner* Afghanistan's capital city is presented as peaceful and provincial, Hirsh's novel depicts Kabul as a global place that is mercurial, unstable, and ripe with possibilities, with various underground political movements trying to capitalize on the unsteadiness of the king's regime. While *The Kite Runner* inscribes the Soviet invasion as an ahistorical trauma, *Kabul* positions it as a moment in the revolutionary period in Afghanistan. The novel's beginning chapters capture the moment in time when various futures hang suspended in potentiality (1973), giving way to a quickly unraveling era of revolutionary changes (from 1973 on).

In his "On the Concept of History," Benjamin introduces the notion of a messianic time that he views as true historical time.[26] Messianic time is contrasted with empty, homogenous time that is inseparable from the idea of repetition. The "new" is forever destined to reproduce the "old," that is, until the advent of a "zero hour"—a messianic moment that is nonlinear and open-ended, "blasting open" the continuum of repetition and fate. In a similar gesture, Fanny Söderbäck positions revolutionary time as "a movement of return that, through displacement and alteration, generates renewal while acknowledging the unpredictable status of the future (that we are 'still to come')."[27] Messianic time has an affective quality to it. It is pregnant with the promise of redemption, the aptitude for making things right. In such a time, the past exerts pressure upon the present, while the present becomes molten, plasma-like, and the future unpredictable.

Hirsh's portrayal of this remarkable period in Afghanistan's history is consistent with contemporary historical research that emphasizes the extent to which Afghan revolutionary movements were both self-conscious of their role in shaping the country's history and bound with global political movements. In *Afghan Modern*, Robert D. Crews writes of Afghan political actors'

> conviction that something truly momentous and universal was underway in Afghanistan from the late 1970s. "Revolution" was the key word that seemed to capture the political moment. From left to right, these [revolutionary] thinkers resembled so many others in the twentieth century who saw themselves as participants . . . in an entangled drama of war and revolution that was "of cosmic significance." (231)

Fred Halliday, in his analysis of the events that predated the Saur Revolution of 1978, talks about "a highly charged atmosphere in Kabul" in 1970s (24); he notes that "by the early seventies, an air of suppressed but intense militancy existed at least among the intelligentsia" (25). The revolutionary time described in *Kabul* is characterized by a sense of a crisis of the old royalist regime and a sense of potential for change. Reminiscent of Lenin's description of a revolutionary situation, the ruling elite is depicted as weak and corrupt while powerful forces gain prominence and influence from below, such as nationalist groups, right-wing Islamist, and left-wing socialist and feminist groups.[28] In Hirsh's *Kabul*, traditional structures of society are set into motion, and even family loyalty—so central in traditional Pashtun life—is not exempt from this sense of rupture and crisis. Mangal, a king's minister's son and an aspiring bureaucrat himself, is depicted in his fascination with the idea of the regime change. On the eve of the coup of 1973 that ends the monarchy in Afghanistan, he agrees to join Prince Daoud in his takeover and becomes a member of his government, effectively betraying his royalist father who loses his post as a result of the coup.

Kabul explores the city's internal geography to expose sites of difference and political diversity, revealing a complex geography of dissensus. This geography forces the reader to suspend judgment and interrupt the deployment of stereotypes about what Kabul, or Afghanistan, ought to be:

> The bazaar edged the old quarter—a labyrinth of mud-brick houses climbing the rock face in ragged tiers. Stooping as if to adjust a sandal, [Mangal] glanced behind him, then slipped down the alley in back of Khalid's tea shop.
>
> Six tense faces looked up from the table as he came into the room. Tonight only a fraction of the group would participate, to minimize the risk, and except for Ahmed they had all arrived before him. Since tea shops were still a male preserve, Roshana always carried a basket, like a delivery, and it stood filled with peaches in the center of the table. A pleated gray silk chadri was folded over the back of her chair. (20)

Here the bazaar—an Orientalist stock image—is just a façade, a prop for underground political life, a complex geography of conspiratorial activity and political agitation. And so is the burqa (*chadri*) that Roshana wears—it is also just a front that conceals her revolutionary identity. The market and the identities of the characters are not what they seem to be; impenetrable for an outsider, they reveal their meaning to those who know how to read their secret code. The bazaar, perhaps the most unmodern of all places, here figures as a space where different projects for the Afghan modernity are discussed, disputed, dismantled, and put together again; a place where political alliances are forged, transnational connections are made, and various possibilities for the political future of the country are rehearsed. By describing the city's microgeography of political dissent, the novel manages to demonstrate how the global political conversations and struggles traverse Kabul, turning it into a global city in the epicenter of a transnational ideological battle for the hearts and minds of both the workers and the intellectual elite.

Because the city's internal geography of political diversity and dissent is so thoroughly described, the ways in which certain pivotal events are interpreted changes as well. For instance, the Soviet invasion is depicted as a consequence of a series of political upheavals, one of many, rather than the main cause of everything that has gone wrong. This, again, is in line with historical research; Westad, among other contemporary historians of the Cold War, explains that by the late 1970s, US elites were "seeing revolutions [in the Third World] as the *result* of Soviet involvement rather than a cause of it" (332, emphasis in original). Contrary to this notion, as Westad, Crews, and Maley demonstrate, the April revolution was unexpected by the Soviets and caught them off guard. Crews writes:

> The successful 27 April 1978 Khalq coup in Kabul was . . . as much a surprise to Alexandr Puzanov, Soviet ambassador since 1972, as to other diplomats in the Afghan capital. In his first comprehensive report to Moscow after the coup, Puzanov gave a sober assessment of the new regime and its coming to power. The coup had been badly prepared, Puzanov explained, and its main figures—Taraki and Amin—were both given to ultra-left initiatives. (302)

While in Hosseini's novel, the Soviet invasion of 1979 (an event he does not distinguish from the Afghan homegrown socialist revolution of 1978) figures as the ultimate trauma; in Hirsh's text, the events that are traumatic differ for each character because of their political affiliations. For the father—a royalist—the overthrow of the monarchy in 1973 signals catastrophe. For the older son, Mangal, who joins the king's overthrower, Prince Daoud, the downfall of the monarchy is a good thing, but the coup by the socialist party of Afghanistan (1978) signals ruination. As Daoud's government is deposed, Mangal loses his post and eventually his life. The "tanks in Kabul" image, although chilling, is contextualized as well. The reader learns that the arrival of the tanks marks an internal revolution in which the left-wing Afghan socialists come to power—the Saur Revolution of 1978. The Russian tanks that surround the palace, although built in Russia, are piloted by the Afghan military that allied itself with the socialist revolutionary forces, and so are the Russian-built MiGs that traverse the sky.

The novel is didactic: It explains why the reluctant Soviets eventually do send their troops in December 1979, not to install communism, but to depose Hafizullah Amin, an Afghan communist who seizes power in September 1979 and who is seen by the Soviets as too radical for a traditional society such as Afghanistan. The Soviets install a much more moderate leader, Babrak Karmal. The Soviet invasion (although the author condemns it passionately) is thus presented not as an exceptional event, but one among many political transformations, coups, and upheavals that take place in Afghanistan in the 1970s—during its "messianic," revolutionary era. By uncoupling homegrown Afghan revolutionary identities from the Soviet troops,[29] and by allowing various visions for Afghanistan's modernity to be articulated, the novel resists the ideological closure present in *The Kite Runner* and complicates the dominant modes of consuming Afghanistan's history, ultimately bringing into visibility the Afghan revolutionary subject. As such, this text from a historical "elsewhere" provides an alternative model for imagining Afghanistan in twenty-first-century Anglophone literature.

Communist Nostalgia

Given the intensity of Hosseini's anti-communist sentiment in *The Kite Runner*, it is remarkable that, in his second novel, he undertakes a revision of his narrative of Afghan socialism and conjures a cautious vision of communist nostalgia. This revision not only dislodges the symbolic value of Afghanistan as a ruin of communism, but also inscribes the Afghan socialist era as the high watermark for women's rights in Afghanistan. This positive image of socialism is unstable, as Hosseini, in this novel as well, is anxious to distance himself from communism *in general,* and various complaints about communist repression are found throughout the novel. And yet, Hosseini must be credited for breaking through the

post-Cold War aphasias that result in Afghan socialism's complete erasure (or its reduction to a Soviet imposition). The inscription of socialist
modernity as the era of women's emancipation also dislodges the status
of the pre-socialist past as the golden age. Where *The Kite Runner* finds
an idyllic landscape of social cohesion, *A Thousand Splendid Suns* reveals
geographies of pervasive gender and class inequality, which the socialist
project is meant to interrupt. Additionally, Hosseini's sophomore novel
revises the prior narrative of Afghanistan's history by describing in detail
the atrocities committed by mujahideen forces in Kabul and contextualizing the mujahideen rule, more generally, as an era in which the advances
of women's rights were halted, and then dramatically reversed. These
revisions indicate that Hosseini is serious about his didactic-realist project
of educating Western publics about Afghanistan's history and culture.
However, even these efforts contain elements of the Faustian bargain:
Afghanistan is still represented primarily in the humanitarian mode, and
questions of historical complicity—ones that implicate Western audiences
in the very scenes of Afghan women's crisis—are still largely bracketed
out. The mujahideen are presented as a violent, but an autochthonous
force, and questions of Western involvement in this patriarchal restoration
are left unaddressed.

Published in 2007, *A Thousand Splendid Suns,* although failing to
achieve the success of its predecessor, nevertheless boasts significant readership and the status of a top *New York Times* best seller. By centering on
the lives and fates of two female characters—Mariam and Laila—the novel
capitalizes on the success of the specific genre that gained ascendance in
the era of the 9/11 wars: stories written about the plight of third-world
Muslim women—"women of cover," as George W. Bush referred to them.[30]
The novel begins in the same time period as its predecessor—the golden
age of Afghanistan (prior to revolutionary changes), which is now presented less favorably, due to the differences in the class and the gender of
the protagonists. Whereas Amir (*The Kite Runner*) is a privileged son of a
prominent businessman in Kabul, Mariam—the older of the novel's two
central characters—is a *harami*: an illegitimate child fathered outside of
wedlock, a daughter of an unmarried, poor, mentally unstable mother who
commits suicide when Mariam is still a youth. Such unfavorable circumstances result in Mariam's early marriage to a man in his forties who takes
her from her native and provincial Herat to metropolitan Kabul. Socially
and religiously conservative, Mariam's husband insists on her wearing a

he rapidly modernizing city where many women choose not to
head coverings, adopting a modern look during the last years
ionarchy—a trend that becomes the new state-sponsored norm
during the socialist era that follows. Mariam's world is one of confinement
and submission; lacking education or practical skills that would enable
her independence, Mariam is resigned to her fate as a captive housewife.
When multiple miscarriages prove her useless to her older husband, she
finds herself trapped in a relationship that is physically and emotionally
abusive. The issue of class is addressed not only via Mariam's lack of opportunities for personal development, but also through her husband's response
to the news of the socialist revolution. When Afghan communists come
to power in Kabul, Mariam asks her husband whether this is good or bad.
"Bad for the rich, by the sound of it," her husband responds. "Maybe not
so bad for us" (102). Her husband, who is a shoemaker earning a modest
income through his craft, neither fears the communists nor expects his life
to change with the advent of the new regime.

The changes brought forth by the revolutionary government are
exemplified by the novel's second main character, Laila (Mariam's
neighbor), who belongs to a new generation of Afghan women—those
who grew up during the socialist era. Laila embodies the Revolution
most literally. She is known at school as *Inqilabi* Girl (Revolutionary
Girl) because she was born on the day of the socialist revolution in April
1978 (112). Raised to believe in her limitless potential realized through
education and hard work, Laila comes of age in a world that not only
tolerates but actively promotes gender equality. Laila's timid and loving
father, a university-educated man and a vocal advocate of women's rights,
says: "This is a good time to be a woman in Afghanistan." He insists
that she put all her energy into learning: "Marriage can wait, education
cannot... a society has no chance of success if its women are uneducated,
Laila. No chance" (114). A generation apart, Laila and Mariam have
dramatically different experiences as Afghan women. Laila is born into
a world where women see a radical expansion of their rights and enjoy
full access to public life. Laila's world is also one in which strong Afghan
women who can serve as role models for independence and success are
abundant. While in *The Kite Runner*, sexual assault and phallic, harassing
Soviet soldiers served as figures for socialism, in *A Thousand Splendid Suns*,
the socialist era is captured via a completely different figure, one of an
empowered Afghan woman:

[Laila's teacher] was a sharp-faced young woman with heavy eyebrows. On the first day of school, she had proudly told the class that she was the daughter of a poor peasant from Khost. She stood straight, and wore her jet-black hair pulled tightly back and tied in a bun so that, when Khala Rangmaal turned around, Laila could see the dark bristles on her neck. Khala Rangmaal did not wear makeup or jewelry. She did not cover and forbade the female students from doing it. She said women and men were equal in every way and there was no reason women should cover if men didn't. (111)

This passage serves as a counterpoint to claims—found in many overviews of the Afghan socialist era—about the unbridgeable divide between Afghan city and Afghan countryside that resulted in the defeat of socialism. Such difference, no doubt, existed and proved to be a considerable obstacle to both the literacy program and the land reform initiated by Taraki's and Karmal's governments; however, it is also true that many Afghans who supported the socialist project were first-generation students whose parents had been peasants. Additionally, the social mobility created by the socialist state's endorsement of the universal literacy program and its investment in higher education country-wide cannot be overstated. The key role of the state in promoting gender equality and thus empowering women's flight from patriarchy are exemplified by scenes from Laila's school; her teacher's rhetoric of personal emancipation reflects the official position of the Afghan socialist party that in its first declaration proclaimed that one of its chief aims was "ensuring the equality of the rights of women and men in all social, economic, political, cultural, and civil aspects" (Westad 399).

While Hosseini supplements his portrayal of the positive aspects of socialist educational reforms with critical remarks that seek to expose other aspects of the regime that he sees much less favorably (for example, Laila's progressive father was fired from his position as a schoolteacher by Afghan communists), this revision of the narrative of Afghanistan's history is significant. The Afghans in this sophomore book are presented as active adopters rather than passive sufferers of the new ideology. This is consistent with historical accounts of that era. Describing the changes in gender relations during the socialist period, Timothy Nunan, a historian of Cold War-era Afghanistan, argues, that "Soviet ideas about 'the woman question' found fertile soil in Kabul. The more women attended Kabul University and Soviet-sponsored Kabul Polytechnic University, the wider their worlds grew" (186). Indicative of the changes occurring during this time period is the following anecdote that serves well to illustrate the cultural climate in the Afghan capital, in which women's growing participation in public life grated against some of the commonly held assumptions:

> One alumna saw a team of five Soviet engineers—four men, one woman—moving into an apartment in the Mikrorayon neighborhood. Reared on stories about the evils of Communism, she assumed that the woman was the men's shared property. Only later did she discover that the woman was their *supervisor.* (Nunan 186, emphasis in original)

In her *Narrating Post/Communism*, Nataša Kovačević reminds us of the historical significance of Marxist ideology and communism as "a line of flight" from colonial dependence upon Western Europe, from "the stigma of economic and cultural inferiority, escape from the logic of capital and the logic of being the 'other'" (17). Similarly, Marxist ideology served as a "line of flight" from patriarchal oppression endemic in many traditional societies. Women's advancement during the socialist decade in Afghanistan was unprecedented. Shahnaz Khan writes that, by the end of the 1980s, Afghan women occupied

> prominent positions in urban areas and in the PDPA government as members of the National Assembly, members of the Revolutionary Defense Group militias, chief surgeons in military hospitals, and construction workers and electrical engineers who often supervised male staff. Ariana Airlines employed female as well as male flight attendants. And the female announcers who read the news were neither veiled nor wore a headscarf. Women were members of trade unions and worked as printers, soldiers, parachutists, and veterinarians. (par. 29)

Signaling a notable departure from the earlier narrative of Afghanistan's history, the pre-socialist "golden age" idealized in *The Kite Runner* is superseded in Hosseini's second novel by the socialist era that represents "the golden age" for women's rights. As Laila's father puts it:

> *Women have always had it hard in this country, Laila, but they're probably more free now, under the communists, and have more rights than they've ever*

had before . . . it's a good time to be a woman in Afghanistan. And you can take
advantage of that, Laila. Of course, women's freedom—here, he shook his
head ruefully—is also one of the reasons people out there [in the countryside]
took up arms in the first place. (135, emphasis in original)

The prior "golden age" no longer seems idyllic but filled with social antagonisms along the axes of gender and class. The insurgents—hailed by
Washington as freedom fighters—here, according to Laila's father, take up
arms to fight *against* women's freedom and seek a patriarchal restoration.
The novel brings into relief the oppressive customs that limit Mariam's
(the older character) participation in public life—her lack of access to
education (she received basic literacy classes from a village mullah), her
lack of options for professionalization and employment (her husband does
not think that women should work), and the resulting lack of confidence
that leads to her compliance with her husband's demands, including the
demand to wear a burqa, even during the time when most women in Kabul
opt to roam the streets uncovered. All of these factors compound to seal her
fate leading to her tragic death during the Taliban era. By contrast, Laila,
the "Revolutionary Girl," has the confidence to dream of a future unhin-
dered by the constraints of her gender, even during the times that turn
"bad for women"—the mujahideen era (1992–1996), and later, during the
Taliban's rule (1996–2001). Laila's nomination as the *Inqilabi* Girl established a historical continuity. The spirit of Saur Revolution, it is suggested,
survives in young women whose fate will be to live through the unbearable
oppression of the subsequent fundamentalist regimes. In a curious parallel, Taraki (the leader of the Saur Revolution and the first head of state
in socialist Afghanistan) liked to tell those around him that he had been
born in October 1917, during the days of the Russian Revolution.[31] The
emancipatory lineage—from 1917 to 1978, and into the future—marks
an alternative history that survives in spite of many defeats, in Afghan
women's hearts.

In this new narrative of Afghanistan's history, the destruction of
Kabul—one of Hosseini's persistent themes in all three novels—is no
longer blamed on the Soviets but placed in a more historically grounded
context and explained in great detail. The novel's title—*A Thousand Splendid
Suns*—refers to a seventeenth-century Iranian poem "Kabul" in which the
sun reflected in the myriad of Kabul's rooftops connotes the beauty and
cultural richness of the Afghan capital city. In Hosseini's novel, the image

also connotes a shattering—a shattering of an image in a multitude of its reflections—thus foreshadowing the destruction of Kabul in 1992 by the warring militants—the mujahideen—who pillage the city after they defeat the last socialist government.

"Ask Afghans when the worst period of time was in Kabul," writes journalist Kim Barker, "and they'll never mention the Soviets or the Taliban. They'll talk about this time, the civil war, when chaos and crazy ruled. They'll talk about the warlords" (*The Taliban Shuffle* 57). The Revolutionary Association of the Women of Afghanistan (RAWA) members are especially outspoken in condemning the fundamentalist takeover that followed the Soviet withdrawal: "the darkest period in our history began when fundamentalists took power in 1992. . . . They turned Kabul into a graveyard, where you could only see tears, fear, destruction, and blood."[32] Mujahideen were the jihad fighters, and to use the language of the revolutionary Left, counterrevolutionaries. They were comprised of various groups of insurgents who formed an armed resistance to the socialist government as early as 1978, sabotaging the state through ambushes and bombing of both military and civilian targets. Cold War-era historians Ralph H. Magnus and Eden Naby point out that during the Reagan era, the mujahid (a jihad fighter) in the US context was a positively charged term that held appeal for the US Christian Right and that served as a "legitimizing concept" across the political spectrum (259). The phrase "legitimizing" is surely an understatement; the mujahideen were widely celebrated in the West by both right-wing and liberal observers. Tony Kushner's case is symptomatic: A liberal, queer, left-leaning Jewish American playwright, he admits that, during the Soviet-Afghan War, he found himself, improbably, supporting Ronald Reagan because of his heavy-handed approach to the Soviet problem in Afghanistan and his backing of the fundamentalist Afghan jihad fighters.[33] In *Homebody/Kabul*, Kushner states, via Mahala, that the ultraright mujahideen are preferable to other forces who have been in power in Afghanistan since the 1970s. In the eyes of the West, the mujahideen stood for the people of Afghanistan in general, as in Joes's quote, where he speaks of them as "the brave, sorrowful, martyred people of Afghanistan" (229). I will discuss this mythologizing of the mujahideen as "the real Afghans" in detail in the next chapter. The mujahideen were divided along ethnic lines (consider, for instance, the intense rivalry between Ahmad Shah Massoud and Burhanuddin Rabbani, both Tajiks, and Gulbuddin Hekmatyar, a Pashtun) and competed with each other for funding that came from the West and the Arab world. Magnus and Naby, overall sympathetic to the mujahideen cause, nevertheless note that "wholesale destruction of villages, irrigation works, and agriculture" by the mujahideen were hallmarks of that period (147). Contemporary historians offer a more somber assessment of mujahideen methods of warfare, pointing out that mujahidin "had butchered pro-PDPA tribal elders" and massacred entire villages along the Soviet border, bombed symbols of Afghanistan's modernization, such as Kabul University and the Polytechnic Institute, and conducted attacks on women's schools.[34] Nunan quotes a Soviet adviser who recalls the following:

> *Mujahidin* bombed stalls in Jalalabad's bazaars, and once, when Wahidov [a Soviet advisor] visited Jalalabad's main market, he had to dive for shelter as a fully loaded camel with a bomb surgically implanted into its stomach exploded, leaving gore and mayhem behind. (159)

Mujahideen also boasted an extensive agenda designed to halt and dramatically reverse the progress of women's rights in Afghanistan. Shahnaz Khan observes that, in contrast to the position of women in the socialist state, in the mujahideen resistance movement, there was "no public space for women as ideologues or as spokespersons nor in any other form. . . . [Women were meant] to serve the needs of the community through giving birth to future warriors" (par. 30).

In its second half, *A Thousand Splendid Suns* dramatizes the loss of rights and freedoms suffered by women in the aftermath of the socialist government's fall in 1992, and describes the incredible violence unleashed upon Kabul and its residents as the mujahideen enter the city. The tragedy of that period is captured by the novel's most unforgettable image of the body of a child ripped apart by an explosion of a missile blasted by one group of the mujahedeen fighting another in the streets of the city. In an expository passage, Hosseini explains how the word *mujahid* during this era becomes an insult, used as a synonym to "warlord":

> [Laila learns that] this road, up to the second acacia tree on the left, belonged to one warlord; that the next four blocks, ending with the bakery shop next to the demolished pharmacy, was another warlord's sector; and if she crossed the street and walked half a mile west, she would find herself in the territory of yet another warlord and, therefore, fair game

for sniper fire. . . . Riflemen. Others still called them Mujahideen, but, when they did, they made a face—a sneering, distasteful face—the word reeking of deep aversion and deep scorn. Like an insult. (176)

The Soviet modernity described in the first half of the novel is thus short-lived and followed by a period of unraveling and violence, along with the redefinition of Afghanistan's identity and a transition from a secular to a theocratic rule, from women's empowerment to a patriarchal restoration. The fall of the socialist government—the secular ("godless") Democratic Republic of Afghanistan—heralds the advent of the Islamic State of Afghanistan that reverses women's gains achieved during the socialist era:

> The freedoms and opportunities that women had enjoyed between 1978 and 1992 were a thing of the past now—Laila could still remember Babi saying of those years of communist rule, *It's a good time to be a woman in Afghanistan, Laila.* . . . The Supreme Court under Rabbani [the mujahideen head of state] was filled now with hardliner mullahs who did away with the communist-era decrees that empowered women and instead passed rulings based on Shari'a, strict Islamic laws that ordered women to cover, forbade their travel without a male relative, punished adultery with stoning. (260, emphasis in original)

During this era of mujahideen-induced violence, and to her father's great sorrow, Laila stops attending school as it becomes too dangerous. Laila's life course is then even more dramatically changed when she loses her parents to a rocket fired by the mujahideen and has no other option but to seek shelter in Mariam's house, which means becoming Mariam's husband's second wife. The era of opportunity for women has closed. After four years of incessant violence, Kabul is "liberated" from the mujahideen by the Taliban forces, and women's oppression becomes enshrined as law. As the husband's behavior turns progressively violent toward both women, and the misogynist laws offer the women no protection or escape, Mariam takes matters into her own hands by murdering their husband to protect her and Laila's life, and is subsequently executed by the Taliban. Laila remarries, and with her new husband, flees to Pakistan, only to return to Afghanistan following NATO's arrival. At the onset of the American era, Laila "hears of schools built in Kabul, roads repaved, women returning to work," which brings back to life the memory of her father's voice that says: *"You can be anything you want, Laila"* (389, emphasis in original). Seen from the perspective of women, the socialist period—the golden age of women's rights—is thus sutured to the NATO-led era as the two periods in the country's history during which women were encouraged to be free. In the new Afghanistan, Laila can get back to her childhood dream nurtured by the socialist teachers—the dream of being somebody, being successful, and working for the greater good.

The suturing of the Soviets to the Taliban as the two evils in *The Kite Runner* thus gives way to the symmetry of the Soviet and the American-sponsored visions of gender equality and personal liberation. The promise of Soviet modernity is hereby rescued—and restored from its ruins, paradoxically, by the American intervention that revives women's emancipatory longings halted by a theocratic intermission. This is an important revision of Hosseini's prior narrative as well as a notable intervention into the post-9/11 discussions of Afghan women's plight. The legacy of the Soviet period in relation to women's rights was poorly understood by westerners who came into Afghanistan during the reconstruction era. Overwhelmingly, they saw the burqa as a timeless symbol of Afghan women's oppression rather than an unstable marker of the recent political change from secular to religious government form. Historian Robert D. Crews writes: "Most of these foreigners subscribed to the conventional wisdom that they were pioneers entering 'a forbidden land,' whose landscapes and people were reminiscent of biblical times" (282).

There were indeed many similarities between the ways in which the socialist and the American-sponsored regimes sought to promote gender equality. The focus on literacy was central to both the socialist and the US-led program. Additionally, both regimes measured the success of their policies in Afghanistan more generally by monitoring women's presence in the public domain. "Unwittingly," Crews continues, "[Americans] revived many of the promises that Afghan socialists, the People's Democratic Party of Afghanistan, had made in 1978. . . . Schools for girls became the measure of Afghan reconstruction" (282). Crews explains that during the socialist period, "[t]o many Afghans and foreigners alike, the most striking change in the revolutionary capital was the mobilization of women. The first thing a European anthropologist noticed upon arrival in Kabul in 1979 was 'the large number of unveiled women in the streets'" (244). Quite similarly, as Jason Burke points out, the number of unveiled women in the streets of Afghanistan's cities became a measure of progress during the American occupation era. Burke calls it the "*burqa* ratio":

> One key element that became rapidly woven into the post-war project for Afghanistan was the issue of women and women's rights . . . to the point of becoming a *casus belli* in itself. . . . [T]he concentration on the rights of women had the effect of establishing the "*burqa* ratio," as one senior European diplomat in Kabul cynically put it, as a key metric for success in Afghanistan with domestic opinion in the West. (82–83, emphasis in original)

When seen from Afghan women's perspectives, the socialist era no longer appears demonic; on the contrary, it comes into view as a unique period in Afghanistan's history during which women were propelled into the public sphere and gained relief from traditional customs and gender roles that relegated their lives to the private domain. Laila's embrace of the American people's arrival signals a nostalgia for socialist modernity. Revived and redeemed by NATO's resolve to "save" Afghan women, the socialist prelude is rescued from the ruins of history. Women's time, alive in Laila's and other revolutionary women's hearts, promises to return to Afghanistan with the American troops, both prompting a nostalgia for a socialist era and a new hope for women's emancipation. Instead of Rumsfeld's socialist "conquest" versus US-led "liberation," we have two emancipatory visions that are separated in time by a fundamentalist interlude. This version of Afghanistan's history is intriguing, and in the NATO-centric context, countercultural. It is certainly problematic, as the dream of US-borne restoration pins any idea of an acceptable future for Afghanistan on foreigners' intervention. It also fails to acknowledge the Western sponsorship of the very fundamentalist regimes that the United States then intervenes to topple.

The Time of Disappearance

In his third novel, Hosseini revisits Afghanistan's recent history once again, covering a time span of sixty years, beginning in 1952, during the age of the monarchy, and ending somewhere around 2010–2012, during the NATO era. Published in 2013, *And the Mountains Echoed* is much more skeptical in its assessment of NATO's ability, or willingness, to "rescue" the Afghans. It no longer believes that the United States will resuscitate the halted modernization project in Afghanistan. This revisitation of Afghanistan's history is, once again (for the third time), a revision. In this iteration, the devastation of Kabul is blamed entirely on the mujahideen; they are presented as "vandals" and mobsters who come back, after the Taliban's ouster, to rule the Afghanistan they had looted in the 1990s, with the support of NATO forces. More importantly, as far as this chapter is concerned, both Afghan revolutionary history and the Soviet invasion vanish from view—the socialist period is neither condemned nor figures as an object of hope, but simply disappears from Afghanistan's timeline, as if it were nothing of significance. The vanished Soviets in this third novel are mystifying, given the emphasis on their brutality and the intensity of condemnation of socialism in *The Kite Runner*. Gone, also, is a quest for a better social order or any hope for a future that is more just. The American era, in this novel, signals a return not of socialist modernity, but of mujahideen-borne corruption and violence, which in the end cancels all hope for a better future.

This reassessment of the NATO period—which by 2013 was a notable twelve years—is a significant divergence from the previous novels. As others have pointed out,[35] *The Kite Runner* calls for a rescue operation that would liberate the country from the evil Taliban, thus not only implicitly justifying Operation Enduring Freedom, but depicting it as the ultimate moral act. The second novel, through tracing Laila's trajectory, asserts that the new NATO-led Afghanistan, in spite of some difficulties associated with the transition to peace, is a good place to come back to, and that is it once again "a good time to be a woman" in Afghanistan (*A Thousand Splendid Suns* 260). By contrast, *And the Mountains Echoed* offers vignettes from US-led reconstruction-era Afghanistan that is swarming with foreigners—doctors, nurses, volunteers, journalists, and expats who return to claim their properties that have risen in value—to offer a verdict that attests to the era's fatal failures. It tackles the issues of entrenched corruption, security problems, interpersonal violence, the drug economy, and widespread uncertainty about the nation's future, despite the presence of international troops and thousands of NGO workers. The most self-reflective of the three novels, it also explores the issue of ethics inherent in narrating tragic histories, critiquing the Western desire to vicariously experience Afghanistan's suffering via texts, such as Hosseini's own previous two novels, as voyeuristic and self-serving. In this novel,

Hosseini seems to begin to search for alternatives to the humanitarian mode of narrating Afghanistan, its impetus similar to other texts written in the second decade of the 9/11 wars (see chapters four through six).

The novel is written as a collection of overlapping stories told from the varied perspectives of its characters who belong to three different generations of Afghans. It effectively represents the continuity between Afghanistan's violent period after the fall of the last socialist government (1992–1996) and its neoliberal, yet also troubled present. Reconstruction-era Afghanistan is riddled with violence and corruption reminiscent of the civil war. In NATO-era Afghanistan, the most striking acts of cruelty are prompted by property disputes rather than by political divisions. Economic inequalities are extreme. The international community, while there, lacks the willpower to remedy the situation, and even worse, supports the wrong people. Forestalling the narrative of American-sponsored redemption, the novel highlights the injustices and the violence that not only persist in the aftermath of the NATO invasion, but are a direct result of NATO's alliance with the warlords. It dramatizes the fact that the former mujahideen militants (a.k.a. the Northern Alliance) whom the Taliban forces kept at bay in the northern provinces of the country until 2001, were brought back by NATO troops as allies and were allowed to take over the cities they had ruled in the disastrous 1990s. The novel's criticism of NATO's unsavory dealing amplifies the complaints voiced by many Afghans. As one Afghan feminist Sonali Kolhatkar writes in "Saving Afghan Women": "Afghan women are perfectly capable of helping themselves if only [your] governments would stop arming and empowering the most violent sections of society" (par. 5).

In this third attempt by Hosseini to dramatize Afghanistan's history, the mujahideen period acquires utmost importance and its dark legacies are foregrounded. While in *The Kite Runner*, Hosseini explains the destruction of Kabul as an act of Soviet brutality, here the mujahedeen are singled out as the cause of the city's destruction:

> The 1980s [the Soviet period], as you know, Mr. Markos, were actually not so terrible in Kabul since most of its fighting took place in the countryside. [. . .] It was in the 1990s that fighting at last broke out within the city limits. Kabul fell prey to men who looked like they had tumbled out of their mothers with Kalashnikov in hand, Mr. Markos, vandals all of them, gun-toting thieves with grandiose, self-given titles. (122)

The mujahideen are presented in this novel as "vandals," "mobsters," and "thieves." Their reinvented selves—Land Rover-cruising, self-aggrandizing narco-barons who now rule the land—are described with great scorn. Exemplifying this continuity is a vignette that centers on a former mujahid commander who is now a powerful political figure and a drug lord. Hosseini views his "heroic" past with great skepticism and links the violence that he perpetuates in the present to his history as an anti-Soviet jihad fighter. His fiefdom—the village of Shahbad—now features a monument to the jihad fighter—"a nine-foot tall black stone mujahid, looking east, turban gracefully atop his head, an RPG launcher on his shoulder" (244). The statue has been commissioned by the narco-baron himself; everyone in town calls him "commander" to recognize his role in the jihad against the Soviets. The narco-baron's son, Adel, goes through a consciousness-raising moment in the aftermath of a traumatic event in which his friend's father, a poor man from the village, is killed by his father's mobsters. Adel realizes that the villagers' "respect" for the "commander" masks their fear of his brutality. By the end of the story, Adel sees "for the first time his father's house for the monstrosity, the affront, the monument to injustice, that it privately was to everyone else" (274–275).

Hosseini's obsessive revision of history in his trio of novels is symptomatic—signaling the hidden tensions and aphasias found not only in his writing, but in other NATO-centric texts that take Afghanistan as its object. The point of view assumed in *The Kite Runner* deploys Cold War-era tropes, which results in a distorted version of Afghanistan's history. Its narrative of rescue legitimizes the US invasion while casting Afghan socialism as foreign-borne barbarism—a trauma inflicted on the country by its powerful northern neighbor. As a result, the Afghan revolutionary subject is reduced to a third-world victim—a helpless "other" in need of a humanitarian intervention. The second novel, while in line with the global West's resolve to "save Afghan women," seeks to break through post-Cold War aphasias and does not demonize the socialist period; it is unambiguous, however, in its celebration of NATO's arrival to Afghanistan in 2001. The socialists, therefore, are viewed as "good" insofar as they subscribe to the same causes as the Reconstruction-era US-led humanitarians: that is, women's liberation. The third revision in *And the Mountains Echoed* offers a critique of the US's role in Afghanistan. More than ten years after the beginning of the War on Terror, in the wake of the Iraq War disaster, it is difficult to see the US operation in

Afghanistan as an unambiguously "good" humanitarian mission and to be blind to the impending dangers that await the country in the aftermath of NATO's withdrawal.

However, even this latest version of Afghanistan's history contains elements of Hosseini's early Faustian bargain. When it comes to "imagining the Soviets," Hosseini's vacillations are symptomatic; indexing the failures and impasses that haunt the NATO-centric political discourse in the twenty-first century, these best-selling texts at times make use of the vast repertoire of anti-Soviet tropes, at other times resist them, before finally rendering socialist-era Afghanistan illegible. In that, this third novel mirrors Mark Fisher's pronouncement that the contemporary capitalist-realist era is "haunted not by the apparition of the specter of communism, but by its disappearance" (*Ghosts* 19). How does one speak about the failed revolutions of the past? What did the Afghan revolutionary era amount to? In the end, Hosseini does not have an answer. As a result, the story of Afghanistan's recent past cannot be told. It does not cohere into a narrative but breaks into fragments that, like jumbled ice, cannot be put back together and jam narration. Communist nostalgia, Nataša Kovačević suggests, is useful insofar as it works to interrupt the process of post-socialist spaces' transformation into "dependent economies, highly stratified societies, and sources of cheap labor" (18)—their relegation to a neocolonial space, one of global capitalism's many resource frontiers. In Hosseini's last novel, even this specter disappears—nothing interrupts Afghanistan's relegation to global capitalism's resource frontier now. The future seems predetermined and bleak; there is no recourse or respite from omnipresent violence.

Moreover, presenting the mujahideen as "vandals" and "thieves" who turned into "mobsters" and narco-barons, once again, fails to tackle the issue of US systematic involvement in funding, arming, and training the mujahideen in the 1980s—the issue I will explore in the next chapter. Hosseini's word choice—"vandals"—invokes recklessness, the lack of care, and cultural illiteracy, presenting Afghanistan's tragedy as a war between those who appreciated culture, stability, and peace and those who lacked such appreciation having benefited, in turn, from instability and conflict. What is subsumed in this word choice is the Cold War context in which this conflict unfolded. Hosseini's "vandals," who had been referred to as "holy warriors" and "freedom fighters" by the Reagan administration, were anything but a disorganized group of pillagers and looters. Cold War historians Magnus and Naby explain that the mujahideen did not exist in isolation, but were embedded in the vast transnational network that supported the anti-Soviet jihad with billions of dollars spent on training, weapons, and favorable coverage by the international press. By 1989, they write, mujahideen

> field commanders communicated via satellite phones, and [state-of-the-art anti-aircraft] Stingers were the elite weapon of the day. The fighter in the field had to be supported by an array of others, he had to be supplied, and materiel had to be donated or purchased, the donor had to be convinced of the justness of the advantage of the mujahideen cause, and an army of journalists, diplomats, spies, and aid workers had to be kept informed and sympathetic. (149)

Hosseini's novel thus still contends with the impossibility of articulating the role of the US, and the West more generally, in cultivating the jihad fighter it now fears. This best-selling author's inability to talk about the role of the West in fueling the Soviet-Afghan War also forecloses the possibility of understanding the dark origins of twenty-first century wars that we are witnessing today. Terrorism today signifies something the West recoils from in utter horror, failing to recognize its own complicity and its own role in creating conditions for war's proliferation. Hosseini's didactic project, while set to explain Afghanistan's tragic history to global audiences, thus fails to bring into view or make legible the "dark histories" of covert operations and ghost wars that played a key role in Afghanistan's unraveling. This is something that the texts discussed in the next chapter attempt to do.

3

Humanitarian Jihad: Unearthing the Contemporary in the Narratives of the Long 1979

The Devil's Kitchen

Destined to provoke humanitarian outrage, the instantly famous 1985 *National Geographic* cover was a high-profile ad for the bustling Afghan jihad against the Soviets. From the outskirts of Peshawar's Afghan refugee camp in northern Pakistan, a preadolescent Afghan girl with piercing green eyes condemned the viewers who failed to do their share to protect her, and others like her, from the atrocities of the brutal socialist regime. In the same high-impact issue, journalist Debra Denker, a member of the crew who traveled to the city of Peshawar to report on the suffering of the Afghan refugees, did not hide the excitement and admiration she felt toward the rugged Afghan jihad fighters—young men who courageously opposed the abuses of the authoritarian state by taking up arms and fighting back. In fact, she believed this excitement was universally shared. "[E]veryone loves the legendary young hero who began fighting when he did not yet have a beard," she exclaims (776). After providing a vague yet gripping overview of the scenery—a deserted valley ("all gray and brown") with a few ruined buildings, allegedly bombed by the Soviets, and "the fly-encrusted remains of a camel," allegedly killed by the Soviets—she concludes with a scene of the jihad fighters' prayer—a tranquil, hypnotic image that connotes harmony and peace, as opposed to Soviet-borne violence. "The holy warriors," she writes, "Ishaq among them, spread their pattu on the ground, their weapons before them, and stand and bow and stand again. In the silence I feel their strong and quiet faith, and wish only for a swift and happy end to the struggle forced upon them" (797).

During the 1980s, journalists from the Western bloc and Afghan jihad fighters enjoyed a torrid love affair that was supported by cash flowing voluminously from various sources—primarily the United States, Saudi Arabia, and Western Europe. The city of Peshawar became a nerve center for the anti-Soviet jihad—a hub for intelligence staff, international jihad recruits, humanitarians, journalists, and random adventurers. Peshawar's economy became bloated with cash. Western reporters, mostly, though not exclusively, male, were drawn to the romance of anti-statist insurgency and traveled with the Islamist fighters into Afghanistan, functioning essentially as embedded reporters with the mujahideen. Edward Girardet, in his 2011 memoir, recalls his encounters with some of the most prominent Afghan and Arab commanders in Peshawar. He eulogizes commander Ahmad Shah Massoud as "the Che Guevara of Afghanistan" (*Killing the Cranes*, 16); of Gulbuddin Hekmatyar, a radical Islamist known for his extreme brutality and indiscriminate violence against Afghan civilians during the civil war, Girardet writes: "One could not help but be impressed. With their turbans, beards, and hawk-nosed faces, these Afghans looked utterly wild, yet dignified" (46). In Western media of the 1980s, use of the word "terrorism" was discouraged and the violence of the mujahideen's attacks on civilians was downplayed. As Salman Rushdie remarks in *Shalimar the Clown*, westerners often referred to these fighters as the "Muj"—which, Rushdie observes, with sarcasm, "sounded mysterious and exciting and concealed the fact that the word *mujahid* meant the same thing as the word *jihadi*, 'holy warrior'" (270–271). As Cold War historian Robert D. Crews notes, "[i]ndiscriminate attacks by the mujahideen on Kabul and the civilian casualties resulting from a campaign of bombings and assassinations had to be given new labels"—"resistance" and "freedom fighters" (261). This language is exemplified by Ronald Reagan himself who stated in 1983 that "the resistance of the Afghan freedom fighters is an example to all the world of the invincibility of the ideals we in this country hold most dear, the ideals of freedom and independence."[1] The Islamic fundamentalists, in short, embodied the American spirit, and Western journalists reported favorably on their operations.

In the previous two chapters, I discussed the difficulties Khaled Hosseini faced when writing about the mujahideen insurgency. Specifically, Hosseini cannot find a way to talk to his Western readers about the US's key role in creating conditions for the rise of transnational terror that haunts the world today, by setting up, in the mountains along the Afghanistan-Pakistan border, what Fred Halliday called "the devil's kitchen in which the ailments and criminal practices that would later be unleashed on the world were first brewed" (*Political Journeys* 52). It is, in fact, impossible to understand the Afghan tragedy, as well as the rise of transnational terror in the 1990s (leading up to the twenty-first-century crisis), without understanding the legacy of the CIA-led covert Operation Cyclone (a.k.a. the "Afghan" jihad). Appropriately titled, Operation Cyclone drew into its whirlpool Pakistani intelligence, Saudi radicals, and European humanitarians, among many other sympathizers, bystanders, and supporters. The covert US support and funding of the radical Islamist forces started in 1978, several months prior to the Soviet intervention (in fact, contributing to the panic in the Soviet camp that might have led to the USSR's decision to intervene).[2] It continued until the fall of the last socialist government of Afghanistan in 1992. In this chapter, I will discuss fiction and nonfiction texts that bring into view and help us imagine, vividly, the West's role in fueling the flames of the Afghan crisis. These texts illuminate dark histories and shed light on ghost wars, drawing attention to the significance of what I call "the long 1979" as the key moment in the genealogy of the post-9/11 contemporary. And so, they make visible the prehistory of the 9/11 wars.

In what follows, I outline my reasons for proposing to designate 1979 as the threshold of the contemporary—a genealogical point of origin for the world we inhabit in the first quarter of the twenty-first century. I then discuss Sorayya Khan's novel *City of Spies* (2015), set in 1978–1979 Islamabad, Pakistan—a book that draws attention to the rapid globalization of Islamabad that became a spy capital of the world (along with Peshawar) and a hub for the CIA during these years. The book centers on eleven-year-old Aliya whose childhood is defined by the epochal events that reverberate across the region: the coup d'état and the resulting military dictatorship in Pakistan, the Iranian Revolution, the socialist revolution in Afghanistan, and the subsequent influx of spies and CIA agents into the Islamabad area. Focusing on the period spanning 1978–1979, the novel examines the interlacing of personal, collective, and global histories as seen through the eyes of an adolescent. I then turn to Nadeem Aslam's haunting, philosophical novel *The Wasted Vigil* (2008); set in post-9/11 Afghanistan, this text excavates hidden histories of terror and dramatizes connections between CIA involvement in the Afghan jihad and the 9/11 attacks. Both Khan and Aslam seek to open the long 1979 to a variety of conflicting interpretations, offering a vision of history as open-ended and of memory as multidirectional, thickly layered, and staged through multiple colliding accounts of the past.[3] These texts' retrospective dimensions are framed by their epistemological commitment to understanding the endless post-9/11 present, illuminating the recent past as key to understanding the 9/11 wars.

Khan and Aslam are critical of the US ghost wars waged in the region in 1980s; however, the other two accounts I discuss in this chapter— memoirs by photographer Didier Lefèvre (with Emmanuel Guibert and Frédéric Lemercier) and by reporter Edward Girardet—are steeped in the romanticization of the anti-statist insurgency, their admiration for the rugged jihad fighters they met in the 1980s mostly unchanged by the crisis of 9/11. It is important to read these texts with a critical eye, and the chapter will provide a framework for contextualizing their accounts. Lefèvre's story is an acclaimed photo-reportage based on his journey through the fringes of socialist Afghanistan with Doctors Without Borders. Girardet's memoir documents his clandestine trips into Afghanistan in the 1980s both with jihad fighters and with European humanitarian teams. These striking accounts are of relevance to scholars and readers interested in the history of embedded reporting as well as in the genealogy of the military-humanitarian alliance we see today. The term "humanitarian jihad" in this chapter's title captures the convergence between late Cold War humanitarian work and humanitarian imaginary, best exemplified by the famous *National Geographic* Afghan girl image, on the one hand, and the radical Islamist insurgency, on the other. Within that context, the jihad fighter figured as a human rights defender while the Afghan state and the Soviet forces were positioned as prime human rights offenders. Lefèvre's graphic memoir in particular sheds light on the role of human rights reportage during the Soviet-Afghan War as well as the part Doctors Without Borders played in the Afghan jihad. The grave contradictions at the core of the humanitarian-military assemblage (which included reporters, fighters, and doctors) become visible, in retrospect, if a reader is willing to suspend, at least temporarily, the deep anti-communist bias that permeates the narrative. Considered together, all these texts make evident that "the long 1979"—marking the Soviet intervention in Afghanistan, the onset of CIA's Operation Cyclone, and the arrival of European humanitarians to the area—is a multidirectional point of origin for many contested histories, and that the meaning of this era remains disputed, the stakes increasing rather than diminishing during the era of the 9/11 wars. These four texts provide a complex, multifaceted view that complicates the meaning of the term "Afghan jihad," contextualizes the humanitarian imaginary of the late Cold War era, and brings into the foreground the dark histories of ghost wars and covert operations.

The Long 1979: Contesting the Primacy of 1989

In *Ghosts of My Life*, the late Mark Fisher writes: "It has become increasingly clear that 1979–80 . . . was a threshold moment—the time when the whole world (social democratic, Fordist, industrial) became obsolete, and the contours of a new world (neoliberal, consumerist, informatics) began to show themselves" (50). His dissenting voice is drowned, however, by the slew of other voices who insist, collectively, on the global significance of 1989 as the imagined point of origin for the world that we inhabit today— a threshold of the contemporary. The concept of a threshold indicates a landmark date that marks a profound transformation, a phase change, an onset of a new condition or a disruption of an existing equilibrium of forces.[4] In assessments of the history of the twentieth century, two such moments are widely accepted: 1945 and 1989. These moments are seen as related to each other. If 1945 marks the year of liberation and postwar reckoning, contending with the reality of concentration camps and nuclear weapons unleashed on civilians, 1989 is seen as a year that marks the end of the Cold War, the coming down of the Berlin Wall, and the triumph of liberal democratic regimes. Some scholars add a third date—1968—to the widely accepted 1945 and 1989.[5] The Eurocentric character of the three accepted thresholds is intriguing, with the epicenter of 1945 and 1989 in Berlin and 1968 in Paris and Prague.

In this tripartite lineage, 1989—the year frequently referred to as an annus mirabilis (a miracle year)—is arguably the most important date. 1989 is an established moment not only in historical studies,[6] but also international relations,[7] political theory,[8] art history,[9] and literary studies,[10] among other disciplines. Political scientist George Lawson observes that "both academics and policy-makers tend to use 1989 and its surrogate frames (such as Cold War/post-Cold War) as the principal normative, analytical, and empirical shorthands for delineating past and present" ("Introduction" 1). Art historians Alexander Dumbadze and Suzanne Hudson theorize contemporary art as emerging after 1989, linking "aesthetic change to the geopolitical changes of 1989" (2). Debjani Ganguly, in her study of the contemporary world novel, argues for the renewed significance of the 1989 threshold in the light of post-9/11 sensibilities (*This Thing Called the World*). In his insightful account of the contemporary novel, which he dubs the "literary anthropology of the contemporary," Amir Eshel argues for the specificity of literature written after 1989 "in the light of the debate about 'the end of history'" (10).

The year 1989, the ultimate spectacle, thus looms large in our collective imagination, and it seems almost pointless to argue against its prominence. Yet a threshold is never universally relevant, but always contested, since it is always *someone's threshold*. A 2010 collection of essays by international relations scholars, titled *The Global 1989*, introduced a much-needed note of discord into the Fukuyama- and Rorty-inspired triumphalist narrative of liberal democracy's victory in the wake of the collapse of the Soviet Union and the fall of the Berlin Wall. While liberal democracy did emerge victorious in several Eastern European countries, this was generally not the case in the global South. Richard Saull, in his contribution to *The Global 1989* volume, states firmly that "1989 is not the historical root of contemporary world politics *tout court*, at least not when viewed from the vantage point of the global South" (181, emphasis in original). It is necessary to provincialize 1989 as a European threshold. Moreover, the era we refer to as the contemporary is never static; it unfolds in the opening between the recent past and the immediate future that constitute its immediate horizons.[11] These horizons are always shifting. We can only know our own recent past through its traces in the present—traces that make manifest that past as exerting pressure upon the present. Given the point of view of the 9/11 wars, after the 2008 global financial crisis, and in the midst of the rise of the right-wing regimes across the world, we might be less eager to accept the triumphalist narrative of the 1989.

It is worth remembering that in 1989, as Europeans celebrated the tearing down of the Berlin Wall and Eastern European countries hoped for their own Marshall Plan (which never materialized), many countries in the global South faced the fallout of the Cold War's end in the form of reactionary governments coming to power, often through violent means.[12]

In 1989, an Islamist government was established in Sudan, Hamas was rising to prominence in Palestine; the Islamic Salvation Front became a party in 1989, and a few months later won elections in Algeria; soon after, the Soviet withdrawal from Afghanistan allowed ultra-conservative Islamist forces to close in on Kabul, putting an end to the secular government form. Assessing the outcomes of the "miracle year" in the global South, Saull writes:

> In two formerly communist countries, Afghanistan and South Yemen, grotesque forms of social regression, violence against women and corruption prevailed, as they did in combat-plagued Iraq, and, even more so, in Somalia. Meanwhile in West Africa, the formerly vanguard socialist state of Guinea-Bissau, the country that produced the outstanding revolutionary leader Amílcar Cabral, fell from 1989 increasingly under the control of corrupt military leaders, with the result that in 2008 it had become the main transit state for Colombian drugs en route to Europe. [. . .] In other words, one of the main legacies of the collapse of communism was the disappearance not only of social provision and a rough commitment to social equality, but of the basic order-providing state. Any balance sheet of the "failure" of communism must, therefore, be matched by acknowledgment of the "failure" of its replacement. (132)

Here, from the view of the global South, a very different narrative of 1989 emerges, connoting not the unequivocal and irreversible triumph of liberal democracy, but the collapse of the state, the loss of rights, the loss of emancipatory expectations and dreams, the end of modernizing efforts, the onset of corruption, narco-trafficking, and infrastructural breakdown. The very insistence on the spectacle of 1989 is an act of erasing these histories of suffering. Upon closer inspection, it becomes obvious that 1989 was the moment of manifestation, not the moment of origin, of multiple developments that took place in the time period around 1979. These developments became manifest in the post-9/11 world. The nomination of 1979 as a point of origin maps a genealogy that signals the rise of transnational terror; the threat to women's rights; the privatization of warfare with the increasingly covert nature of its conduct; and the emergence of the humanitarian-media-military assemblage that manifests today as humanitarian violence—a near complete convergence of the humanitarian and military apparatuses.[13] Yet in our current imaginary,

1979, I contend, figures only as a specter—a figure of our anxiety about the present we find ourselves in—a present defined by increased risk, by progressive militarization of everyday life, and by securitization that does little to calm our fears about the dangers that are erratic and unpredictable. It is also the specter of what Tony Kushner in *Homebody/Kabul* calls our "culpability"—the vague sense that the global West has played a role in destabilizing the very societies it now fears the most, such as Afghanistan, Pakistan, Iran, and Iraq, among others (24). This vague sense of culpability translates into fears of the West's own survival—fears that are reminiscent of nineteenth-century worries of barbarians at the doorstep. As a threshold of the contemporary, 1979 thus connotes the looming disaster—a future moment of reckoning that cannot be averted.

In the spirit of provincializing the Eurocentric 1989, the narratives I examine in this chapter ask us to turn our gaze to Islamabad and Peshawar (in Pakistan), as well as the mountains of Badakhshan (in Afghanistan) as the epicenters of change that occurs around 1979. I call for a recognition of the global significance of these places, all of them sites of profound political and cultural transformation. I also argue for the significance of the long 1979 as an index of these tectonic changes. Seen from the point of view of the Islamic world, there is little doubt that the year 1979 marks a threshold. The axis of change lies in the Iran, Afghanistan, Pakistan (Tehran, Kabul, Peshawar) triangle. "The long 1979" is a period that starts in 1978 and continues through the early 1980s. By the end of 1978, the geopolitical map of Central Asia and the greater Middle East was in flux. The April 1978 socialist revolution in Afghanistan was well underway, and faltering somewhat, with Taraki's government meeting resistance to land reform and the enforcement of women's rights in the countryside. On September 16, 1978, in Pakistan, General Muhammad Zia-ul-Haq became president, having come to power through a military coup, banning all political parties by 1979. Zia's ascent to power presented a unique opportunity for the United States, promising access to the underbelly of the Soviet camp in Afghanistan. On January 16, 1979, the Iranian shah, a longtime ally of the United States, was overthrown by the most popular revolt in known history. At the end of March 1979, Iran became an Islamic Republic led by a spiritual leader, Ayatollah Khomeini, heralding the emergence of a third way—an Islam-based alternative to both socialism and capitalism. On November 4, 1979, the widespread anti-American sentiment bore on the hostage crisis, where 52 Americans were held captive in Iran for 444 days. The unprecedented siege of the Great Mosque of Mecca by a group of radicals on November 20, 1979, led to the burning down of the US embassy in Islamabad the day after (Americans were suspected of having been involved in the siege, which was proven not to be true). A few weeks later, on December 27, 1979, Soviet planes landed on the Bagram Airfield in Kabul in an operation to support the struggling socialist government. Within a few days, Soviet troops crossed the northern border of Afghanistan, thus beginning a full-scale intervention on the ground (Operation Storm-333).

In 1980, Ronald Reagan came to power in the United States and his administration was to become an active supporter of Zia's military regime, declaring it a frontline ally in its war with the Soviet Union. To subvert the Soviet stronghold in Afghanistan, the CIA intensified its covert operations in the region. The CIA's Operation Cyclone (1979–1992), with its nerve centers in Islamabad and Peshawar, was massive in scale and fallout. It was the most extensive and best-funded covert operation in the organization's history, leaving in its wake Al-Qaeda and the Taliban, as well as, arguably, the ruins of socialism. Yet these submerged histories of ghost wars and secret operations have attracted attention only recently, in the wake of 9/11. Books by Mahmood Mamdani (*Good Muslim, Bad Muslim*) and Steve Coll (*Ghost Wars*) made these histories accessible for popular audiences, drawing thick lines between the Soviet-Afghan War and twenty-first-century terror. Khan and Aslam's novels illuminate the significance of the long 1979 as the dark threshold of the post-9/11 contemporary. Both novels—*City of Spies* and *The Wasted Vigil*—are investigations; their plots are arranged around finding out the truth about the past. These novels' epistemological thrust is determined by the desire to understand the conflictual logic of the present, its long wars and humanitarian crises, through mapping its genealogy. And so, they return to 1979.

A Prelude to Unraveling

In a playful inversion of Francis Fukuyama's claim about history having ended in 1989, I propose to accept, provisionally and with Sorayya Khan's eleven-year-old protagonist, that history began in 1979. In her novel that narrates the process of a coming into political consciousness, written for the young adult audience, Khan makes obvious that what I call "the long 1979"—in her case the months preceding the Soviet intervention in Afghanistan in December 1979—are nothing short of what Benjamin would call "messianic time"—not just in Afghanistan, but across the entire region. While in the previous chapter I drew attention to 1978–1979 as a messianic era in Kabul, Khan, similarly, brings into view the epoch of change from her setting in Islamabad. Time itself—pregnant with permutation, saturated with political rivalries, thick with animosities that spill into violent rage—is the subject of Khan's fictionalized account of history as perceived through the adolescent eyes of her narrator. This messianic time is felt locally, spurring a slew of changes in Pakistan, and affects the entire region. With remarkable clarity, the young narrator observes the global significance of the events that unfold in Pakistan's vicinity. The messianism is evident in the events of the Saur (April) Revolution in Afghanistan, in the revolution in Iran, in the rage of Iranian students who take American hostages in Tehran, and in the fury of the students in Islamabad who attempt (and fail) to do the same. Having described the thirty months of rapid, unpredictable change ("phase change" as a physicist might call it), Khan ends her book, dramatically, on December 27, 1979—the day the Soviet troops began their intervention in Afghanistan, acting on behalf of the flailing communist government. Aliya overhears a television news program reporting on the event while in her family home in Islamabad. This framing positions the prior thirty months as a prelude, an introductory chapter to the new epoch that was about to begin. Skillfully, Khan stages a dense interlacing of personal, national, and global histories, demonstrating that the affairs of one's life cannot be separated from the larger epoch-defining events that determine them. "[W]e are all defined by the wars we have lived," Khan writes in the Prologue, "the war of my story . . . is the Cold War" (1).

The novel is marked by a sense of unease and anxiety that is the result of the narrator's progressive realization of the global interconnectedness:

> [T]he world was a small place and what happened in one place affected the other. I was suddenly reminded of Klackers, the game of two balls suspended on a string. When one ball hit the other, the *klick-klack* sent it careering. Countries were connected to each other the same way, which made our world a very scary place. (208)

"Clackers"—the toy the narrator evokes in the passage, was indeed a dangerous toy as the balls, made of heavy hard plastic, would sometimes shatter when hitting each other, producing debris fragments with sharp edges. In the United States, the toy was taken off the market in 1976. In spite of its seeming innocence, the image of clackers thus evokes unexpected violence, cuts to the flesh, and shrapnel resulting from a collision of bodies. The sense of looming danger and the nervous disquiet permeates Khan's novel, resonating with the uncertainties of the post-9/11 universe. The sense of looming danger finds release, for the novel's protagonist, in the event of the US embassy siege in Islamabad. Although she does not experience the burning of the embassy directly, she witnesses the crowd of Islamabad residents flooding the grounds of the American school compound where she is a student, shouting "Amrika Murdabad" ("death to America"). Distant riots, such as the riots in revolutionary Tehran, materialize inexplicably, on the narrator's doorstep, affecting her family, her servant's family, and her American friend's family in an immediate fashion. A *klick-klack* universe is saturated with risk, rendering distant events witnessed through mass media astonishingly close as their reverberations reach Aliya's hometown. And conversely, the events to which Aliya is an eyewitness carry in them a taste of the faraway—a specter of long-distance agencies and faraway rivalries.

City of Spies is, unmistakably, a post-9/11 narrative. Khan notes that she first imagined telling this story in 1989; however, it was September 11 and the wars that followed made her decide that she needed to address, in fictional form, this particular slice of her past:

> The Soviet Union retreated from Afghanistan before my first international journalism assignment. Not long afterwards, the Berlin Wall came down and eventually marked the end of the Cold War. [. . .] But thirteen years ago, under a brilliant blue September sky, airplanes flew into buildings and the world spiraled in a War on Terror that will never end. The United States arrived to Afghanistan and then Iraq . . . and stayed. Today, its drones travel the skies of Pakistan. [. . .] On the ground, Pakistan's cities are bursting with spies, but today they carry guns and do not drive cars with identifying license plates. (223)

By recalling the 9/11 moment, the passage contests the global significance of 1989, positioning it not as the end of history, but as a brief pause, perhaps—a relatively insignificant interlude, overshadowed quickly by the rapid unraveling of a tsunami of new conflicts. The post-9/11 present—defined by the long wars and the renewed sense of global interconnectedness that brings a sense of looming danger, sheds new light, Khan discovers, on her childhood spent in the city of spies. Fittingly, she compares Pakistan to Berlin in the passage above, along with evoking Afghanistan twice: the Afghanistan of the Soviets of 1979 and the Afghanistan of the Americans of 2001. Afghanistan is the reason why, in the 1980s, Pakistan became a global place, competing with Berlin in the number of spies it attracted. General Zia's Pakistan, capitalist-leaning and in need of financial support, was conducive to American efforts to gain access to the Soviet Union's underbelly in Central Asia via North Pakistan. In the wake of the Soviet intervention in Afghanistan, Peshawar and Islamabad become the CIA's most important assets.

Khan's 2015 story captures the atmosphere of suspicion and distrust that pervaded Islamabad in 1979. A daughter of a Dutch mother and a Pakistani father, Aliya describes her discomfort at the US embassy when she is invited there by her American classmates: "I didn't know if their fathers were spies or if they had done anything to conspire against my country, but each time the embassy guard waved me through the gates, my Pakistani half surfaced and made me want to flee from the grounds" (122). Aliya suspects—and later is convinced—that her best friend's father, who claims to be a health project manager and a malaria specialist, is a CIA agent who interferes in "the politics of our country" (127). The school principal, Mr. Hill, is revealed, Aliya believes, to be a spy when he is taken hostage in the US embassy in Tehran:

> Almost as an aside, Mr Mancini offered an explanation for Mr Hill's departure to Teheran. He had taken one week of leave to retrieve some personal effects from his former school in Teheran, including a fountain pen that was a family heirloom. [. . .] The story sounded like a fairy tale to me. [. . .] Mr Hill was a spy, and the fountain pen was his Maxwell Smart or James Bond secret tool. (161)

Becoming attuned to the issues of privilege and power, Aliya notes the superior status of the Americans, who are able to "interfere" in her country's affairs, affecting the course of events far away from their home. A hit-and-run accident in which the family servant's son is killed by an American woman (Aliya's best friend's mother) becomes a figure of such interference. In its wake, Aliya struggles to understand the world of differential grievability—a reality in which American lives are valued much higher than Pakistani lives—and American impunity, which is evidenced by the fact that the killing of the child carries no consequences for the negligent driver. Aliya wonders how much an American life would be worth as compared to the life of a Pakistani child that was valued at 50,000 rupees (about $1,000) in a quick settlement facilitated by the US embassy, which strikes her as an insignificant sum. Aliya's mixed origin marks her point of access to the dynamics of power inherent in American-Pakistani relations. Adjacent to American privilege, she is able to witness it without identifying with it. This double insider view allows Aliya to understand, without condoning, the hatred toward Americans as the locals storm the American school compound—a place where she, as a daughter of a European mother, is allowed to study—as symptomatic of her countrymen's sense of powerlessness. She recalls the game American boys play on the school bus where they spit on Pakistani pedestrians and cyclists. The game—an expression of racism—goes unchallenged because the Pakistani man, the bus driver, has no authority that allows him to restrain the white boys. At the end of the novel, as American personnel are evacuated from Islamabad on school buses in the middle of the night in the aftermath of the embassy siege, Aliya herself becomes the target of schoolboys, being spat on, marking her last encounter with the Americans in Islamabad.

The servant's child, whose death looms large in Aliya's imagination, can be interpreted both as a figure of American interference in other countries' affairs as well as a figure of the costs incurred specifically by Pakistan as a direct result of CIA-orchestrated proxy war against the Soviets in Afghanistan during 1979–1992. Describing the double process through which North Pakistan became not only the hub of transnationally funded Islamic militancy, but also the hub of jihad-financing heroin production and export, Mamdani points out that "[t]he Afghan jihad had a deeper effect on the Pakistani state and society than it did on any other country outside of Afghanistan" (149). As Aliya ponders the cost of the child's death to the American family ($1,000 dollars) and to the child's father (her servant), whose family falls apart as he suffers a mental breakdown, the parallel becomes particularly apt. The child whose life ends abruptly in 1979 connotes the lack of futurity, a historical rupture, the breakdown of intergenerational transmission, and the violent legacies bequeathed by that era. Khan draws a line from the servant whose family disintegrates to Pakistan that is left to endure the costs of the proxy wars:

My home is a barrage of headlines. You see, my country is at war. My cities are burning. My capital is a police checkpoint. My sector borders the Red Zone. My road is a sandbag bunker. My hills, my beautiful Margalla Hills, are an airplane crash site. My Kohsar Market is the site where the Punjab governor was gunned down. Later today, tomorrow, or not until next week (if we're lucky), the list of headlines will have grown. (238)

The agglomeration of possessive pronouns in this passage evidences the narrator's renewed identification with her Pakistani side at the end of the book, which is the direct result of her revisiting the formative events during the thirty fateful months in the city of spies. History, for Khan's protagonist, began in 1979, but this genealogy is framed by the author's knowledge of the post-9/11 state of her home country that has been, once again, drawn into proxy wars. To sum, Khan's staging of memory presents the long 1979 as a period of both regional and global significance—thirty months that changed the world—bringing to the foreground the long legacies of antagonism and violence that eventually came to bear on 9/11 and the crises that followed.

Genealogies of Terror

"History is the third parent," an epigraph to Aslam's 2013 novel (*The Blind Man's Garden*) states. Aslam's previous book, *The Wasted Vigil* (2008), is indeed a novel about history, addressing the ways in which historical forces amplify or circumscribe individual possibilities, inviting us, as with Khan, to examine the issues of culpability, power, and global interconnectedness. Through its choice of characters, who all come to Afghanistan to give proper burial to the traumatic past, the novel examines the ways in which the past acts as a force in the present, impinging, inexplicably, upon the future. Similar to Khan, Aslam returns to the dark era of proxy wars from the post-9/11 point of view, positing Afghanistan as the key to the global present—a key node in global interconnection. He states, "Pull a thread here, and you'll find it connected to the rest of the world" (319). *The Wasted Vigil* is a work of hermeneutics—a hermeneutics of the post-9/11 present through a return to the recent past, which is to say that it is a hermeneutics of the world through the lens of Afghanistan's history.

Much of Aslam's novel takes place between Usha—a town in Nangarhar Province in southwestern Afghanistan—and Peshawar, a frontier city in northwestern Pakistan. The plot switches back and forth between the present (Operation Enduring Freedom era) and the past (the Soviet-Afghan War), most of the events occurring between 1979 and 2001. The reader's access to the past is mediated through the memories of four central characters, all foreigners in Afghanistan: Marcus, an elderly British doctor, who has suffered many losses in Afghanistan, including the loss of his father, his wife, his daughter, and grandson; Lara, a Russian widow in search of her brother, who vanished during the Soviet-Afghan War; David Towne, a retired CIA agent, who had been responsible for coordinating anti-Soviet efforts during the war and who now returns to Afghanistan to try to locate his long-lost stepson; and finally, Casa, a young fundamentalist, an orphan who grew up in an Afghan refugee camp in northern Pakistan. The characters' memories of the recent past are multiply refracted through the point of view afforded by their position in the present. Thus, Lara's view of the Soviet-Afghan War is shaped by her awareness of its aftermath, including the dissolution of the Soviet Union and the fallout in Chechnya that claimed the life of her husband. David's memories are mediated by his knowledge of the attack on the World Trade Center in 1993—an event that was traced to Pakistan-trained Afghan mujahideen— as well as by the fall of the Twin Towers in 2001. Marcus, who has spent most of his life in Afghanistan, is aware of the British colonial legacy along with the role of the Western world in Afghanistan's recent tragedies. The characters contemplate their culpability, albeit in different ways (David and Casa remaining intransigent), and their interconnectedness, as they serendipitously cross paths in Marcus's house outside of Usha.

Memory in Aslam's novel is both palimpsestic and multidirectional. As the four characters converge in Afghanistan, they bear witness to past events through their interactions both with the landscape (loaded with material memory) and with each other. A complex memory ecosystem gradually emerges that allows for a careful articulation of multiple histories of suffering and loss. Taking as a point of departure Michael Rothberg's definition of multidirectional memory as, first, "something that, while concerned with the past, happens in the present; and second, that memory is a form of work, working through, labor, or action" (*Multidirectional Memory* 4), I propose that the novel performs an important kind of memory work, one that brings to light the multifaceted, contested nature of 1979 as the node of conjunction for multiple national and transnational histories. In contrast to Khan, memory work performed by Aslam's text is not tied to identity or group politics, but is profoundly nonidentitarian. Its chief purpose is to hold the past open, resisting its foreclosure into an identity-based narrative, either national (Afghan, Pakistani, Russian, British, American) or political (socialist, nationalist, liberal-capitalist, Islamist). It insists on the coexistence of multiple traumatic histories whose visions collide but do not cancel each other. Taken as a whole, Aslam's text is a novelistic enactment of a nonidentitarian memory ecosystem—a form of memory that cuts across multiple social groups as well as across time periods, rendering simultaneous the present and the recent past.

Echoing Cathy Caruth's famous notion of interconnectedness through trauma,[14] I argue that such memory work, while exposing a rift between self and other through conflicting memories, also binds us to others through shared histories of loss—the "kinship of wounds," as Aslam puts it (318). Multiple resonances and reverberations of memory, distributed along the lines of the four characters, reveal a complex geography of liability and victimhood. We learn that Lara's brother, a Russian soldier killed during the Soviet-Afghan War, sexually assaulted and impregnated Zameen, who happens to be Marcus's daughter and later David's lover. Subsequently, Zameen gives birth to a son who, while biologically related to his Russian father, acquires a stepfather in David, an American. These characters are thus bound together, uncomfortably, in traumatic kinship. This kinship allegorizes the history of Soviet intervention and American support for the anti-Soviet jihad that are interlaced and grafted upon the landscape defined by British colonial history and interimperial rivalry. Aslam's careful articulation of these intertwined pasts contrasts with many ahistorical, mythologizing representations of Afghanistan I have discussed in the previous chapters. More importantly, the novel attempts to introduce uncomfortable complexity into the narrative of the recent US-led invasion of Afghanistan by illuminating the dark legacy of proxy wars that seal the region's fate as a transnational terrorism hub in the period spanning 1979–1992. Addressing the issue of American culpability in Afghanistan's tragedy is a necessary component of the work of truth and reconciliation that awaits us in the future, if we are to grapple, collectively, with the issue of transnational terror. Aslam models a possibility of such transnational memory work ("a kinship of wounds") through the characters' interactions, and points to David and Casa's intransigence. Unlike Russian Lara and British Marcus, they continue to believe in the rightness of their respective causes. David believes in the rightness of the cause of defeating communism at all costs, while

Casa believes in purifying the world via a specific strand of Islamic militancy he has learned in a madrasa. Aslam's attention to CIA-inspired violence in Afghanistan suggests that illumination of dark histories of that war is necessary for any process of transnational reconciliation to begin.

My term "dark history" (as opposed to "bright history") once again deploys the distinction materialist philosopher Levi R. Bryant makes between bright and dark objects. While a bright object is a visible, easily identified node in a specific network, a dark object is an obscure nexus of power. A dark object exudes a force without being seen. A dark history is the opposite of what Guy Dubord calls "spectacle": dark histories are the histories of covert operations exerting influence in the present, without making themselves visible; illuminating such dark histories and legacies of violence is an important task, with literature offering a form of nonjudicial witness to the hidden past. According to Rothberg, the past that remains unseen, that is, "outside the circuits of memory and responsibility" remains "unmastered" and effectively undead, exercising an even more powerful force in the present (*Multidirectional Memory* 285). Aslam's attention to these muted, subterranean histories—"[r]ivers of lava emerging onto the surface after flowing many out-of-sight miles underground" (272)—indexes the novel's truth-seeking impulse while at the same time gesturing toward the limitations of this impulse. Some pieces of the past will remain obscure, some evidence will not be revealed to the characters or to the reader. Not everything in the past can be put to rest, and it will continue to haunt the present.

The history of ghost wars in Afghanistan is dramatized through David and Casa. Their lives are steeped in mystery. While David conceals his identity as a former CIA agent, Casa, an orphan, does not know his origin, and thus is a mystery to himself. Their respective biographies bear the mark of the era, revealing the interlacing of the two recent pasts: of Afghanistan and of the United States. Casa's biography chronicles the emergence of transnational networks of jihad in the Afghan refugee camps around Peshawar, while David is featured as one of the masterminds who helped set up the infrastructure of terror to be unleashed on the Soviets (and later, the world). Casa's character is first presented in the novel through his inner thought process that situates him as a child of the era, bred for the work of "intimidation," "harassment," and "sabotage"[15] of the Afghan state by inflicting violence on (mostly) civilian targets:

Cyanide can be extracted from apricots, Casa knows. He had distilled it at
a jihad training camp, injected it into the bodies of creatures. The memory
comes to him as he walks past a flowering tree at the edge of a street in
Jalalabad city centre, the flowers still not finished emptying themselves of
scent this late in the afternoon. [. . .] Pencils. Lemons. Corn syrup. Die.
As he walks through the street he knows he could fabricate explosives
from many things on the cart and in the shops around him. Sugar. Coffee.
Paint. He even knows how to make a bomb out of his own urine. (89)

Aslam does not sensationalize Casa's mindset but presents him as a type—
characteristic of the generation of Afghans that was drawn into the whirlpool
of proxy wars at a tender age. An orphan, he was raised to become a jihad
fighter with a transnational reach, dreaming, in the early years, of killing
Russians in Afghanistan, then in his adolescent years, of killing Serbs in
Bosnia, ending up in his twenties fighting Americans and rival warlords in
post-2001 Afghanistan. A child of war, he connotes the past's monstrous
legacies, the amputation of memory through forced displacement, and just
as the dead child in Khan's novel, the lack of futurity. He, and others like
him, are the figures of the unburied past, the past that returns to haunt the
present. A member of a transnational militant class, Casa is a foreigner in
his own country that he neither loves nor understands; his point of origin
is not a traditional Afghan village of which he has no memory, but a state-
of-the-art lab, where modern science is fused with the art of killing:

In the laboratories of the camps, stocked with labeled drums of various
acids, acetones, cellulose, wood composite and aluminum powder, he had
learned to mix methyl nitrate, had hit a small drop of it with a hammer
to see it shatter the hammer. He blew up a car with a sack of fertilizer
and ammonium nitrate fuel oil, the burning chassis travelling in an arc
through the air to land a hundred yards away. He crumbled a boulder with twenty pounds of U.S.-made C-4, and, for comparison, others
with C-1, C-2, and C-3. And also with Czech Semtex. He knew the
Americans were trying to get back from the Afghans the Semtex they had
supplied for use in the Soviet jihad, so dangerous was the substance. (90)

Glimpses into Casa's mind offer an insight into David's work as part
of Operation Cyclone. This classified work is never described directly,
but made visible through its consequences—the lives and landscapes it

transforms. Casa's methodical, cataloguing mind exemplifies the modern scientific rationality—the science of terror—that the CIA added as a key ferment to Afghan guerilla uprisings—a ferment that transformed sporadic rural resistance into a highly skilled transnational army of professional fighters. The refugee camps of Peshawar—home of the *National Geographic*'s Afghan girl—became a social laboratory where a new figure of the highly skilled, well-equipped, transnationally capable jihad fighter was selectively bred. By 1982, it became a recruitment zone for radical Muslim youth from around the Islamic world, with Osama bin Laden visiting the grounds. Through David and Casa, Aslam dramatizes Mahmood Mamdani's poignant statement that "[t]he source of privatized and globalized terrorism in today's world, the international jihadis are the true ideological children of Reagan's crusade against the 'evil empire'" (177). Contemporary recollections of 1980s Peshawar are striking, as many Afghans attempt to rethink the past from the view afforded by the 9/11 crisis. In her memoir, written in the aftermath of 9/11, Nelofer Pazira, the star of the film *Kandahar* and a former member of the mujahideen movement who spent a few years in Peshawar, confesses to being surprised, upon arriving to Peshawar, by the transnational character of the "Afghan" jihad. She writes:

> While in Afghanistan, I dismissed any news about Arab fighters as propaganda from the communist government. When I saw the wives of some of these Arab fighters at the school in Pakistan, I realized the extent of their involvement in the Afghan jihad. But their presence seemed more of an anomaly than a cause of alarm. Like most Afghan mujahidin, they too were supported by the West. (320)

In spite of being defined by transnational forces and possessing a transnational vision of his own agency spanning Russia, Bosnia, Pakistan, and the United States, Casa's vision of the world is limited, as he seems to have no sense of personal history or belonging. In fact, Casa seems to be a character without history. His, to use Wai Chee Dimock's phrase, is "the shotgun time frame of military action"—the shallow chronology of war (138). War's operational time—rapid and precise—preoccupies Casa as he plans and executes attacks under the command of Nadi Khan, a local warlord in Usha. Profound, however, also is Casa's immersion into and identification with what Dimock calls deep time—the deep time of

Islam. He was burning, Aslam writes, with "a fury many centuries deep" (184). Lacking personal memory, he is nevertheless an unconscious bearer of collective memory in the *longue durée*. If history, according to Aslam, is a third parent, in Casa's case it is his only parent.

While posing as a gem merchant, David is, like Casa, a professional of war. In his CIA days, he had lived through the siege of the US embassy in Islamabad in 1979 (the one described in Sorayya Khan's novel), waiting to be rescued for hours with 140 others in a secure vault while the building burned to the ground. Several weeks later, in the wake of the Soviet intervention in Afghanistan, he was dispatched to Peshawar:

> David has heard that no other war in human history was fought with the help of so many spies. When the Soviet Army crossed the River Oxus into Afghanistan in December 1979, secret agents from around the world began to congregate in the Pakistani frontier city of Peshawar. It now became the prime staging area against the Soviet invaders, rivaling East Berlin as the spy capital of the world. By then seventeen thousand Soviet soldiers had been killed, and David had been living in the city for two years. [. . .] It has transformed into a city filled with conjecture, with unprovable suspicions and frenzied distrust. Everyone's nerves were raw and everyone had something hidden going on. For most of its history it was one of the main trading centres linked to the Silk Road, and now the United States was sending arms into Afghanistan through here. Wherever David looked he could find evidence of the war in which those weapons were being used. (111)

Aslam's novelistic rendition of Peshawar's transnational character during that era imbues it with gravity, asking the reader to slow down, consider the implication of the events described, and weigh their consequences in the lives of the other characters in the novel: for Lara's brother, who will be tortured and executed by the mujahideen; for Marcus, whose daughter, suspected of socialist sympathies, will be abducted and killed by the CIA; and for Casa, who will be deprived of a childhood as a result of this war.

The characters' personal trajectories as described in the novel make obvious that the massive humanitarian crisis in Afghanistan was cocreated by the Soviet Union's intervention, the United States seizing the opportunity to "bleed" the Soviets by fueling the jihad, and by extremist groups eager to achieve their own aims. There are many parallels between David and Casa: both obstinate, uncompromising characters, fundamentalists, though of different kinds. David does not allow himself to experience doubt; he is referred to as "a believer."[16] His belief—that communism has to be defeated at all costs—is shaken, in spite of his CIA training, after his lover Zameen and his stepson Bihzad disappear, inexplicably, from their apartment in Peshawar. When he starts looking for them, he sees danger everywhere, and the signs of his own culpability— sprawling refugee camps, bombs exploding in residential neighborhoods, poverty, hunger, and despair pervasive in refugee communities. The only moment when David—a believer—feels his faith is shaken happens as he combs through the refugee camps—home to millions of displaced and desperate Afghans—and witnesses a scene where two hungry children make a third child, who has just eaten a meal, vomit, to capture and eat his still-undigested food:

> The little boy stumbled away dazed and fell, his eyes bright with liquid even in the dusk. And David was hurrying through the four-foot-wide "street," trying to find a way out of the maze. He had helped create all of this.
>
> No, this was the Soviet Union's fault because . . . because. . . . He could not complete the thought. He had before and he would later but not just then. (135)

Here, Aslam uses a humanitarian image from the refugee camp—the same camp, perhaps, that was home to *National Geographic*'s Afghan girl—to problematize the trope of Soviet brutality as the sole cause of Afghan suffering. Here, the suffering child indexes the US's interference—a causality disavowed by the very character who exemplifies it. This moment of recognition proves unbearable to David and manifests only as a pause—a break in his habitual thinking—"because . . . because . . ."—as he realizes that his stepson is now lost to the whirlpool of the war he is helping to create.

David never finds Zameen and Bihzad again. "What would become of the child in this place?" he asks himself, wondering about the fate that awaits his stepson (135). The question he needs to ask himself, but cannot, is: "What will become of my child in the world I am creating?" Twenty-two years later and in Afghanistan again, David crosses path with Casa who is "the child of this place," thus having his question answered. He does not find "his" stepson, but encounters many sons of the war he helped create.

Casa, along with other young Afghan militants in the novel, could be—
and symbolically is—David's stepson. When Aslam describes a scene in
which David and Casa work side-by-side at Marcus's house, he emphasizes
their similarity. They resemble each other not only in their ideological
intransigence, in their careers as professional militants, but also in their
interest in technological know-how—a result of direct transmission of
knowledge from one group to the other:

> Casa handles tools expertly and with grace, with perhaps a certain
> delight, and is an efficient mover in any given area. Of course the
> Afghan ingenuity with all things mechanical is a myth, encouraged
> by the United States and the West during the war against the Soviets.
> Most of the rebels were peasants who had little or no military expertise.
> They came from villages in distant pathless mountains and, contrary to
> historical romances, were not natural guerillas or warriors. They needed
> training in weapons and technology, they who were still afraid of eclipses
> and thought communications satellites circling the night skies were in
> fact stars being moved from here to there by Allah. [. . .] They knew
> little about camouflage or maps and would smash a radio in frustration
> when it stopped working because batteries had run out. [. . .] They cut
> a fuel pipeline with an axe and then set it alight, tried to break open
> unexploded bombs with a pistol or a hammer. (258–259)

Casa's technical prowess positions him as a faithful "son" of his Western
"fathers." What would become of a child in this place? Having sought
shelter in Marcus's house for a few days, Casa is then killed in a senseless
attack of one warlord on another. Another young man who shares the name
of David's lost stepson—Bihzad—loses his life in a blast when he drives a
truck full of explosives into a newly built school, taking hundreds of young
lives with his own. The missing children in Aslam's text thus become vehicles of the past, "an uneasy site of memory" (Rothberg, *Multidirectional
Memory* 321), representing the past that haunts and the unresolved issues
that resurface. David recalls a moment in 1993, when, upon hearing the
news of the attempted attack on the World Trade Center, he mutters:
"They are there" (147). David's "children" are indeed everywhere. By
dramatizing the rise of the transnational jihad, by carefully drawing the
portraits of its fighters, as well as by dramatizing the history of its inception
in Peshawar, Aslam's novel calls the reader to witness histories that must

no longer remain "dark." Aslam's novel constructs a legible history of 1979 as a multidirectional point of origin of many traumatic histories that still haunt the world today.

Humanitarian Jihad

As historian Timothy Nunan demonstrates, 1979 marked not only the beginning of the Soviet (and the covert US-led) intervention in Afghanistan, but also the onset of another little-publicized endeavor that he calls the "humanitarian invasion." From 1979 on, he argues, humanitarian agencies, among them Doctors Without Borders (Médecins Sans Frontières or MSF), the Swedish Committee for Afghanistan, and others, engaged in creating in Afghanistan, using the frontier town of Peshawar as a base, a parallel system of humanitarian governance that effectively competed with, and ultimately undermined, the infrastructure of the young socialist state.[17] These humanitarian agencies, aside from providing aid to Afghan refugees in camps around Peshawar (where they had legal standing), also began to send humanitarian aid and medical teams illegally into the Democratic Republic of Afghanistan's (DRA) interior. Operating inside the DRA without visas or permission, they set up a network of clandestine medical clinics in insurgent-controlled areas, such as Badakhshan, the Panjshir Valley, and the Hazarajat. In addition, humanitarian agencies smuggled mining and industrial equipment across the border; paid for by European charities, this equipment was then given to local mujahideen commanders and used to augment the shadow economies that served to finance the war against the state. Other provisions, supplies, medication, and direct financial aid were distributed by European humanitarians in guerilla-controlled areas to ensure their sustainability during unfavorable weather conditions (such as the 1984 drought that caused a shortage of wheat), which further solidified the effective autonomy of these areas from the centralized socialist state while creating dependence upon Western funding. This parallel infrastructure, Nunan argues, served as a force multiplier for the anti-communist jihad, and enabled the fighters to continue and expand their attacks on the state-run infrastructure instead of seeking peace talks with the government.

Nunan's critique of this "humanitarian invasion" allows for a historical contextualization of memoirs by Edward Girardet (a European American reporter) and Didier Lefèvre (a French photographer), who traveled into Afghanistan in the 1980s, illegally, with groups comprised of insurgents and European humanitarians. Lefèvre's and Girardet's memoirs provide ample material that brings into view the routine operations of the "humanitarian jihad"—the daily functioning of the assemblage that included mujahideen fighters, European doctors, and journalists, all of whom were also embedded into the vast transnational infrastructure of the anti-communist jihad. Without the optics provided by Nunan's historical contextualization, these memoirs seem like human rights reportage and are usually presented and interpreted as such. Juliette Fournot, who was featured on Rachel Maddow's show after the memoir's publication in English, speaks of the mission described in *The Photographer* in terms of witnessing and documenting suffering:

> Part of the drama and the tragedy of the Afghan population was this wall of silence and we were some of the very very few witnesses and Westerners to enter that zone. So we basically needed to do the work that normally the journalists and the reporters would do, and the Afghans had a keen understanding of the value of our witnessing and carrying the word out, of their suffering and what they were going through.[18]

Similarly, literary critic Monica Chiu sees Lefèvre's book as human rights reportage. She writes that the graphic memoir "archives the impact of the Soviet invasion on Afghanistan's non-combat citizens—the indiscriminate horrors of war, especially those maiming innocent children" (33). Seen through Nunan's optics, however, these memoirs become windows upon something else. Specifically, they inadvertently reveal how human rights reportage and humanitarian medical work functioned in tandem with the CIA-orchestrated weapons smuggling and Islamist militancy—not only contributing to the tremendous pressure these forces put on the Afghan state, but boosting the economy of violence whose victims they purport to be helping. Both Lefèvre's and Girardet's reportages are, supposedly, a channel through which the suffering of Afghan civilians is made visible in the global domain. Yet this witnessing of suffering is neither politically innocent nor neutral. As Nunan argues: "MSF had brought Afghanistan to the attention of a global public, but what began as a campaign against totalitarianism had enabled a quest to obliterate Afghan statehood" (235). After the collapse of the functioning state system in 1992, Afghanistan becomes, Nunan remarks, a "model of the 'nongovernmentality' about to define much of the former Third World"—and a site that the European humanitarians and reporters then abandon (14). In other words, European humanitarians, in their desire to alleviate suffering brought by the Soviet-Afghan War, contributed to the collapse of the Afghan state, which resulted in a humanitarian crisis on a much larger scale.[19]

In this section, I will move back and forth between the two accounts, focusing on the authors' descriptions of their clandestine trips into Afghanistan's interior during the 1980s. I argue that their points of view are examples of embedded reporting (they are embedded with the mujahideen)—a militarized perspective, which creates a one-sided understanding of the conflict. Furthermore, the authors' complete lack of access to the other side—to ordinary Afghans who studied, worked, and lived in an environment made increasingly unsafe by mujahideen harassment—resulted in a fragmented, deeply skewed understanding of Afghanistan, leading to an anti-statist bias. From the insurgent-controlled mountain bases, socialist Afghanistan—or the Afghan state more generally—cannot be seen; it figures, instead, only as a caricature. As a result, these authors equate the patriarchal jihad fighters and their culture with Afghan people as a whole, condemning to invisibility Afghans who fought on the side of the government against these insurgents. These two memoirs mythologize "real Afghans" as the rugged dwellers of remote mountain villages; they never portray Afghans as urban, educated, professional, and, perhaps, having a stake in preserving a functional Afghan statehood, socialist or otherwise. Since the mujahideen movement, ideologically, was an ultraconservative movement, this gesture erases the Afghan leftist, but also Afghan secular, liberal, and moderate-centrist political subjectivities. Finally, I will address the authors' lack of reflection upon their own complicity in the very war they are trying to document.

Edward Girardet, a European American correspondent, reported on Afghanistan extensively from 1979 into the 1990s, having returned to Afghanistan after 9/11 in the context of the new war. An author of a field guide for humanitarian workers (*The Essential Field Guide to Afghanistan*, 1998, with coauthor Jonathan Walter), a book on the Soviet-Afghan War, and recently a memoir, *Killing the Cranes*, Girardet's writing remains a rich source of information on westerners' roles in the country's unraveling during the 1980s and beyond. Girardet arrived in Peshawar in 1979, a few months prior to the Soviet intervention, and subsequently embarked on many clandestine trips into Afghanistan with various groups of jihad fighters and with MSF medical-humanitarian teams. *Killing the Cranes* is a testimony to that era; it offers a close look into the day-to-day operations of guerilla warfare and provides portraits of people directly and indirectly involved in the war. Most chapters recount the author's encounters with various militants, humanitarians, spies, and other reporters he met in Peshawar and in Afghanistan, among them prominent commanders, such as Osama bin Laden (who, Girardet claims, once threatened to kill him). The memoir is a work informed by the 9/11 crisis, and Girardet is both critical of the US support of the most radical Islamist factions in the 1980s and aware of the destruction the mujahideen brought to Afghanistan after the Soviet withdrawal. Yet even in the light of this awareness, Girardet seems unable to overcome his romanticization of the Afghan jihad and its capital, the city of Peshawar. "For many of us," he writes, "[Peshawar] was the most exciting place on earth—a frontier city that exuded the atmosphere of 1940s Casablanca intrigue combined with twentieth-century Cold War rock, emergency sex, and TV bravado. Everyone felt a part of history in the making. . . . By the early 1990s, with the departure of the Soviets in Afghanistan and the civil war in Kabul, this extraordinary atmosphere had disappeared" (228).

French photographer Didier Lefèvre first traveled to Afghanistan in the summer of 1986, when the anti-Soviet jihad was already at its nadir. Unlike Girardet, Lefèvre was a rather naive, inexperienced traveler, only vaguely aware of the nature of the geopolitical gridlock he was stepping into by agreeing to document, through his photographs, the work of an MSF mission in Afghanistan. Cross-culturally inept yet open-minded, Lefèvre used photography to capture his clandestine journey into Afghanistan's interior with a group of MSF doctors headed by Fournot—a major figure in the Peshawar-based humanitarian community. During this trip, he took four thousand photographs; only six of them were published upon his return in 1986. The rest of the images make up the bulk of the 2006 graphic memoir based on his journey. A product of the collaboration between Lefèvre, illustrator Emmanuel Guibert and Frédéric Lemercier, *The Photographer* is a hybrid text that combines Lefèvre's black-and-white photography with Guibert's hand-drawn frames.[20] The resulting mix is visually and conceptually rich; a sense of immediacy, conveyed via photographs, is augmented by the fictionality of drawings that fill the gaps in the photo reportage and stitch them together into a narrative. The book includes an introduction by Alexis Siegel who briefly explains Afghanistan's role in the Cold War and the factors that led to Osama bin Laden's rise to prominence, thus reframing the story slightly for the post-9/11 era. Siegel suggests that Lefèvre's naivete about the geopolitical quagmire he stumbled into, as well as his "innocence, openness, and eagerness to learn make him an ideal guide for us as readers" (v). And it is so indeed. Lefèvre's images, as well as the stories he recounts, offer a slab of experience and are often open-ended, contradictory, and revelatory, especially if the reader is willing to suspend, at least temporarily, the anti-socialist and anti-statist biases that frame the narrative. At times, these images, as direct glimpses into the past, are directly contrapuntal to the overall narrative, creating an opening through which one may question Lefèvre's assumptions about the conflict he is witnessing.

The Photographer is an early post-9/11 text; it was published in French in three installments between 2003 and 2006; its English version was released in 2009. As mentioned earlier, it invokes the genre of human rights reportage; specifically, the photographs are meant to tell a familiar story of Afghan victimhood and Soviet atrocity. By the time Lefèvre traveled to Afghanistan, the *National Geographic* cover featuring the Afghan girl had become iconic, and many of Lefèvre's images—especially of suffering children—seem to mimic it. As Fournot explained in an interview with Maddow, the MSF wanted to provide an alternative to the official Soviet coverage of the conflict by giving visibility to the suffering of the regular Afghans caught in the mayhem of war. Once in Afghanistan, Lefèvre diligently focuses on this task. He photographs the refugees moving south to the Pakistan border as the MSF team pushes north; he also documents village life and photographs the Afghans who bring their children into makeshift MSF clinics. Most of the suffering he captures is mundane and is not a result of war—the majority of the MSF patients are casualties of accidents and disease. However, the suffering borne by the war—we see the first example halfway through the book—is foregrounded. The photograph of a child fatally injured during an air raid serves as the book's anchor image (133). In this photograph, the boy, who will soon die, looks directly at the viewer with a pained, stunned expression. The image is striking, haunting; it seems to press demands on the viewer, who is expected to feel outrage, perhaps take action through supporting the MSF's humanitarian cause. Operations Chief Fournot (who was known as "Jamila" in Afghanistan) also films the death of the boy using her camcorder. When prompted by Lefèvre, she explains her reason for filming: "The mother said to me, 'Film it, Jamila, people have to know'" (136).[21]

Images of suffering children in the book—the dying child, and on another occasion, a child whose jaw is shattered by an explosion—are striking, unbearable, impossible to forget. And yet, to understand what we are seeing, we need to force ourselves to pause. As Rebecca Scherr reminds us, it is precisely because of the visceral power of the human rights image that we need to be careful. She says, "the ethics of looking at human rights images requires that one adopt a vibrant, critical eye" (123). While Lefèvre's anchor images are meant to tell the story of Afghan victimhood in the hands of the Soviets (which serves to justify the photographer's presence in Afghanistan), many aspects of the memoir suggest that he is embedded in a much more complex media ecology. MSF's focus on witnessing, as Nunan explains, was directly linked to funding: Fournot's documenting the death of a child likely served the purpose of proving that the MSF mission in Afghanistan was warranted; such documents were central to securing funding for subsequent operations, although the book does not mention this.[22] Moreover, as the memoir shows, Lefèvre and the MSF are not the only ones who take pictures or document atrocities. While in the city of Peshawar, Lefèvre recalls meeting a German man (allegedly a reporter for *Der Spiegel*) who talks about his work that involves distributing camcorders to mujahideen commanders in Afghanistan and then collecting footage six months later. He shows Lefèvre filmed recordings of Russian prisoners executed by the mujahideen, which leaves the young photographer both horrified and befuddled. While Lefèvre himself has no explanation for who this man is (he suspects he might be a secret agent) or what role these documented executions serve, this story reveals the complexity of the media landscape. There is clearly a purpose for documenting these atrocities. One might speculate that these documentaries were used by mujahideen commanders to prove their military successes to their Western sponsors in a competitive field of anti-Soviet militancy. Perhaps they also were used to recruit new fighters, similar to how ISIS and other militant groups use execution videos as recruitment tools. These images do not circulate as human right abuses in Western media; they are distributed through the secret channels of CIA-led ghost wars.

Moreover, some of Lefèvre's own frames included in the book unwittingly work against the text's narrative of Afghan victimhood and Soviet atrocity, as well as implicate the doctors, and Lefèvre himself, into the scene of suffering. While summoning the humanitarian gaze in his photography, Lefèvre remains unaware of his own complicity in the very suffering he seeks to document. It is not accidental that the humanitarian gaze that brings evidence of Afghan victimhood into the global public sphere is embedded within the infrastructures of military action (the mujahideen) and is an important party in the landscape of violence. Indeed, the aesthetics of *The Photographer* is a militarized one. Lefèvre's humanitarian team crosses into Afghanistan, concealed under burqas, through a mountain pass near Chitral, Pakistan, as part of a large weapon-smuggling caravan. The caravan is loaded with deadly weapons and is fully a part of the landscape of violence that unfolds in front of the reporter's eyes. The caravan stays in villages along the way, expecting hospitality and shelter, and thus sets the villagers up for aerial bombardment and retaliatory strikes if the caravan is detected. Lefèvre describes the caravan in detail:

> The caravan is assembled, with about a hundred donkeys, some twenty horses, and roughly a hundred men, including some forty armed fighters. I'll explain the system of caravans. They deliver weapons in Afghanistan and return empty to Pakistan to pick up more weapons, continuously, as long as the tracks are usable. [. . .] So we have a pretty substantial escort: forty AK-47s against would-be thieves, and two or three shoulder-fired missiles against the helicopters. (31)

One of the key myths crafted by the West during the Cold War era proffered the Afghan jihad as "a peasant army" fighting a technological superpower with nineteenth-century British rifles or captured weapons.[23] Within the parameters of this myth, the Afghan jihad was seen as a spontaneous, fully autochthonous movement with no support from outside forces, while the enormously complex logistical, political, technological, and military support that the fighters received from their outside sponsors was bracketed out. Even Girardet, in spite of his knowledge of how transnational jihad operations were organized, in his memoir, occasionally perpetuates this myth: "It was a bizarre conflict between a twentieth-century superpower deploying the latest military hardware and a stubborn peasant people whose resistance profile consisted of customs spanning two thousand years" (161). Similarly, Anthony James Joes asserts: "Medical care for the mujahideen inside Afghanistan was poor, but most of the guerillas possessed hardy physiques and stoic attitudes, bequeathed to them by many centuries of Spartan living" (184). In both quotes, the insurgents' success is attributed to their Afghan "character"—stubborn, stoic, and hardy—mythologized as timeless, rather than to the extensive technological, logistical, financial, and medical backing they received. By contrast, Crews reminds of the massive footprint of the Afghan jihad circa 1985:

> The CIA had to import thousands of mules from China to transport the surge of weaponry sent to the Afghan fighters in 1985. This deluge of deadly hardware, manufactured in a dozen countries—the United States, Great Britain, China, Pakistan, Israel, Germany, Switzerland, France, and elsewhere—is but one illustration of the global arms networks that the superpowers unleashed with such lethal effects in Afghanistan. To take just one category of weapon, the landmines deployed by the millions in the country, a source of hundreds of thousands of civilian and animal casualties that persist into the present, were produced in Italy, Great Britain, the USSR, and the United States. To the frustration of the DRA [Democratic Republic of Afghanistan] and Soviet security forces, these weapons moved in large caravans interspersed with commercial goods and people from Pakistan and along inaccessible smuggling routes that only locals knew. (255)

This is precisely the landscape that Lefèvre enters. As his arms-smuggling caravan pushes through numerous mountain passes, his snapshots, often taken in a rush as he is reluctant to stop for more than a few seconds, capture dizzying mountain landscapes, scenes of river crossings, and most often, the backs of the mujahideen fighters walking directly in front of him. Horses, slow and reluctant under their heavy loads, and weapons strapped to the backs of the mujahideen dominate the frames: "In front of me walks a carrier of antitank shells. A man can carry a bundle of those. The heavier missiles are carried by donkeys, but sometimes one of the muj' [mujahideen] will carry one too, in a bag or secured by ropes" (67). Lefèvre's caravan also carries landmines into the DRA—weapons that will be buried in the land and will retain their lethal power for decades, maiming civilians and children. While the group leaders speak with fear of Soviet helicopters, they also are equipped with infrared homing anti-aircraft weapons, provided by the Reagan administration, that can shoot such helicopters down. These details from Lefèvre's account thus grate against the myth of the rugged villagers fighting a twentieth-century superpower with a handful of old British rifles. A frame on page 56 shows Fournot paying the mujahideen at the end of the day. The caption to the photo says: "Juliette handles it like a troop review. The Afghan currency, afghanis, changes hands." The caravan venture is a lucrative enterprise. Most likely the mujahideen pictured here are paid twice for the same journey—by the headquarters of their military organization in Peshawar for the smuggling of weapons and by Fournot for accompanying the MSF team.

Surprisingly, many of the memoir's readers fail to register the presence of an impressive arsenal of weapons (and fighters) in this humanitarian mission story. For instance, Maddow, introducing illustrator Emmanuel Guibert and Fournot to her viewers, says: "Prepare to be impressed, and maybe amazed. This is the story of a walk from Pakistan into Northern Afghanistan at the height of the Soviet-Afghan War. And the walkers were armed primarily with medicine and, in one case, cameras." On the one hand, this statement is startling given the sheer frequency of images picturing guns and other weapons in the book. On the other hand, the memoir's storyline shirks from addressing the issue of the deluge of weaponry brought into the country by the caravan. Lefèvre's narrator never raises questions about his complicity with the very suffering the MSF team seeks to palliate—suffering that the weapons smuggled by the caravan will inevitably bring. Instead, he admires the rugged masculinity of the fighters. The following description is typical of his romanticization of the insurgents: "Najmuddin is in the corner of the room. . . . On his head he's wearing a chapka taken from the Russians. Next to him a vase of plastic flowers adds a poetic touch to his AK-47. He's handsome, this Najmudin. More than handsome, impressive" (44).

Captivated by the romance of both the journey and the insurgency, Lefèvre indulges in photographing the militants as they trek through vertiginously beautiful Himalayan landscapes with their signature AK-47s. Visual repetition here functions as a refrain—frame upon frame of the "muj" and MSF team members walking ahead of Lefèvre, crossing torrents, following narrow trails along mountain passes, ascending, descending, resting, and resuming the walk—underscoring the monotony and the strain of the passage. It takes the caravan close to five weeks to reach its destination, the village of Zaragandara in the province of Badakhshan where the team sets up a clinic. The narrative of this incredibly long, trying journey through the Himalayas thus creates an impression that the village is one of the most remote, inaccessible places on Earth—one that only the most physically able and morally committed individuals can reach.

Lefèvre's commentary supports that impression. "I'd say that Evelyne is the bravest among us," his graphic avatar remarks, "because she's absolutely not cut out for the feats she is accomplishing. She is a normal woman and not a particularly athletic person. Everything she achieves is the result of sheer willpower and determination" (106). Doctors' stories, offered in abundance, attest to their love for the country and its people, which, they claim, allows them to endure the punishing journey to the destination, as well as the daily strain of living and working in unsanitary, Spartan conditions at a makeshift hospital that seems to be perched, quite literally, on top of the world. The caption to the image on page 122 reads: "When I look up from the operating table, this is what I see. This magnificent and unchanging landscape doesn't give a damn about war."

Given this context, the reader is conditioned to believe that MSF doctors bring health care services, at great expense to their own health and wellbeing, to places where none exist, because of the remoteness and inaccessibility of these places. Regis, an anesthesiologist, says: "I know perfectly well why I'm going back. I'm going back because I'll be practicing surgery in a place where people have absolutely no access to healthcare. And I find it deeply fulfilling" (25). Yet, a few frames included later in the story reveal something unexpected, which directly contradicts Regis's statement. A reader not attuned to the subtleties of the Soviet-Afghan War is likely to miss the significance of the photograph on page 150, which shows the skyline of Fayzabad seen from the mujahideen's entrenched position on the mountainside, within walking distance of the MSF clinic. Fayzabad is a city of about 50,000 people and is a regional center and the capital of Badakhshan Province, located about one hour away by plane from Peshawar. A road following the river valley connects it to Kabul—about 270 miles away. It is surprising to learn that the village where the team sets up the clinic is located within walking distance to this regional center that, as we find out from Lefèvre, has a fully functioning hospital equipped with doctors and imaging equipment. One MSF doctor's story recalled by Lefèvre reveals, surprisingly, that the MSF team often sends patients to Fayzabad hospital for x-ray imaging (115). Readers might also miss the significance of a detail from another MSF doctor's account of staying in the village over winter and developing symptoms of appendicitis. He recalls treating himself with antibiotics while monitoring the symptoms, having instructed the locals to bring him "to the Russians" if his symptoms were to worsen (146).

While the term "the Russians" here designates the state-run Afghan hospital in Fayzabad, likely staffed with Afghan rather than Soviet doctors, it again reveals the fact of the availability of medical care in the clinic's vicinity—the care the doctors themselves rely upon for life-threatening emergencies. Going "to the Russians" is, of course, the last resort, but why? The lack of explanation within the memoir itself is intriguing. It leaves the question open, invoking preexisting notions of Soviet barbarity that would prevent a European doctor from seeking help from them, unless his very survival were at stake. However, another, much more plausible explanation is this: Because the MSF team operates in Afghanistan illegally, without visas or permits, and provides assistance to terrorist groups, going to Fayzabad's hospital would create an international scandal and compromise the MSF mission. The strenuous five-week journey undertaken by the MSF team through remote mountain trails, as well as their fear of "the Russians" downhill, therefore, indexes the illegality of the entire operation. The team and the clinic are located in a mujahideen-controlled area and tend to the insurgents who are wounded while fighting the state and thus are unable to use state-run facilities down in the city.

The use of the phrase "the Russians" here is intriguing as well. Cold War mythologies, as I mentioned previously, presented the conflict as one between the Afghan people and the invading "Russians" rather than the conflict between different groups of Afghan people with varied political orientations who were in turn supported by external parties (US/ Saudi Arabia/Pakistan on one side and the Soviet Union on the other). Invocations of "the Russians" (or "the Soviets") in many accounts of that era are misleading as much too often this designation refers, quite simply, to Afghans who lived in cities and/or worked for the state. This slippage further contributes to the erasure of not only Afghan revolutionary leftist identities, but also, more generally, of Afghan secular, urban, moderate, generally pro-government population segments. When Western journalists traveled to Afghanistan in the wake of September 11, this particular use of the term was still common. Jon Lee Anderson's 2001 article "The Warlord" in the *New Yorker* tells a story of a former mujahid recounting how, toward the end of the Soviet-Afghan War, the Russians killed his mother. The article then clarifies that the term "the Russians" referred to Afghan villagers who supported the state and fought against the mujahideen on the side of governmental forces (after the Soviets' withdrawal). One of these pro-government villagers killed the mujahid's mother in retaliation for the mujahideen fighters killing his father. This slippage is important to keep in mind when reading texts about that era.

Lefèvre's embedded perspective (he, too, is in Afghanistan illegally) prevents him from imagining the point of view of Afghans caught on the other side of the conflict—for instance, the perspective of residents of Fayzabad, such as, say, Afghan nurses at the hospital whose daily lives are threatened by mujahideen-inflicted terror. Veterans of the Soviet-Afghan War recall that, during the 1980s, Soviet soldiers dreaded being sent to Fayzabad area—it was considered to be one of the most dangerous provinces in the country.[24] The Soviet troops' main role in the area was to secure the safe passage of trucks carrying provisions, medication, and other vital cargo to the town of Fayzabad from Afghanistan's central provinces, which was no easy task. Located low in the valley, Fayzabad, as well as the road leading into it, were defenseless against mortar attacks and sniper fire from the surrounding mountains, from where Lefèvre takes his picture of the city (150). Soviet soldier memoirs describe having to negotiate daily bombardment from above and numerous IED devices buried in the ground below. Due to the area's geography, pro-government forces never achieved dominance in the area—in fact, Fayzabad only lasted three days before succumbing to the insurgents after the Soviet withdrawal.[25] The MSF team neither sees nor treats the victims of mujahideen attacks—residents of the town who are harassed by mortar and sniper fire from the surrounding mountains—from the very bulwark that the MSF members visit as part of their excursion. This embedded view results in a characteristic mythologization of mountain villages as the "real Afghanistan," while the urban dwellers in the valley down below remain abstract and not even Afghan—"the Russians." Seen from the mountains of Badakhshan, these "Russians" appear to be a vague but powerful threat—indecipherable, and in their vagueness, irredeemable.

Paradoxes of the embedded perspective abound in Girardet's *Killing the Cranes* as well. While Lefèvre traveled to Badakhshan, Girardet describes frequenting another famous province—the Panjshir Valley that was the stronghold of insurgent commander Massoud. MSF teams were present there as well, and Girardet describes his encounters with them. He describes how, on one occasion, MSF doctors had to flee the area due to heavy fighting between Massoud and government forces but left their passports behind. When the government forces discovered the passports, it almost resulted in an international scandal, but since the doctors themselves were not found, the incident dissipated (218–219). While critical of contemporary practices of embedding reporters with NATO-affiliated troops in Afghanistan (*Killing the Cranes* 8), Girardet fails to see that he was an embedded reporter himself. Just like Lefèvre's, Girardet's view of Afghanistan is limited to the mountain ranges and villages held by the jihad fighters and to the path of weapon-smuggling caravans. On one occasion, curious to see the other side—urban life in socialist-era Kabul—but denied a visa, Girardet recalls having bought a ticket to Delhi with a transit via the Kabul airport, which, he had hoped, would permit him to catch a glimpse of life the capital. He does not see much from the windows of the airplane, of course, but one detail he describes is of significance. Specifically, he recalls noticing that the commercial airliner followed a corkscrew trajectory when descending, to avoid mujahideen anti-aircraft missile attacks. Provided by the Reagan administration from 1985 on, anti-aircraft infrared homing missiles made airplanes and helicopters vulnerable to attacks from the ground, making air travel unsafe both for the military and for civilians. To avoid being struck, commercial airliners on descent followed a corkscrew trajectory and were often accompanied by fighter jets firing off fake heat targets to steer infrared-homing missiles away from the aircraft. Seeing the war, briefly, from the other side, however, has no effect on Girardet's romanticization of the insurgency; no sympathy for Afghan civilians follows from this experience. In fact, on another journey into Afghanistan with the group of mujahideen, he takes part, as an embedded journalist, in an attack on the airport in Jalalabad—a major Afghan city one hundred miles south of Kabul. While this particular attack fails to inflict casualties in Jalalabad's airport, the skirmish results in a retaliatory attack by the Soviet forces on the village that served as mujahideen stopover. One almost expects a David Towne moment—a pause, a realization of the author's complicity with the forces that make daily life unsafe for Afghan civilians—but the moment never arrives.

The following anecdote from *Killing the Cranes* is typical, yet telling. During one of his trips across the border, Girardet traveled to the mujahideen-controlled Panjshir Valley to spend time with Massoud, a commander he revered. Once there, Girardet noticed two men—both doctors—who were running one of the three clinics in this insurgent-controlled area. The men, who he presumed were volunteers, revealed to him that they were captives, having been kidnapped from the nearby city by Massoud's fighters. Gigardet then explains to his readers:

> The Afghan doctors had been captured by the mujahideen, who accused
> them of being Khalqis [communists]. They may have been, but anyone
> who worked with the government was considered communist. Active col-
> laboration was common, but for different reasons. Sometimes, this was for
> ideological gain or ideological commitment—or because they considered
> the "progressive" forces of the Moscow-backed factions less abhorrent
> than the specter of the fundamentalist mujahed government headed by
> the likes of Hekmatyar, the nightmare of many educated Afghans. (159)

This passage makes several things painfully clear: The author does not get to
meet many, or perhaps any, so-called "Khalqis" (communists) from Afghan
cities—Afghans who prefer regular work as doctors, teachers, police officers,
firefighters, tradesmen, or businessmen to being in the mountains with the
jihad fighters. He also finds it necessary to explain to the reader—who by
that point in the book is conditioned to dislike the ferocious communists,
and admire, with the author, Islamist commander Massoud (mythologized
as the "Lion of Panjshir" or, paradoxically, as an Afghan Che Guevara)[26]—
the possible reasons for their choice to work in a city as doctors. He also finds
it necessary to put the word "progressive" in quotation marks, to emphasize
that there could be nothing truly progressive about the "Moscow-backed"
Afghan socialists. The United States' leading Afghanistan scholar Barnett
Rubin writes: "Americans and other supporters of the mujahidin admired
the Afghans' resistance to an evil version of modernity, while still sharing,
by and large, the view that the resistance represented ancient ways—perhaps admirable, if doomed—resisting the modern, centralized state" (*The
Fragmentation of Afghanistan* 4). Girardet's captive Afghan doctors therefore
need to be redeemed, rhetorically, for their choice to work for the evil, noncapitalist modernity down in the city rather than joining the "ancient ways"
of the resistance. Their captivity in the mountains, paradoxically, figures
as redemptive, with Massoud restoring them to their proper Afghanhood.
The reporter's embedded point of view, as well as his set of biases—among
them the bias not just against socialism, but against the third-world state—
remains unexamined in this otherwise gripping memoir. This does not mean,
necessarily, that the reporter is an ardent supporter of Reagan's policies in
the region; for instance, he equally admires Massoud and Cuban revolutionaries. Yet the author's dislike for the third-world socialist nation-state
(seen as oppressive, necessarily totalitarian, necessarily barbaric) and his
romanticization of those who choose to subvert it frames his entire account.

1979 and the Aftermath

Earlier in this chapter, I argued that the triumphant narrative of the end of the Cold War in 1989 makes the history of its late era (1979–1992) illegible. It is precisely this problem that *City of Spies* and *The Wasted Vigil* set to engage, recovering in turn muted histories. The long 1979 is dramatized, respectively, through a figure of a Pakistani child who is killed (in Khan's text) and through a figure of the Afghan child who is lost (in Aslam's). While in Khan's novel the truth of the child's death is revealed, in Aslam's, the truth is hidden and part of the evidence withheld from both the characters and the reader. By signaling the limits of the truth-finding impulse, Aslam suggests, perhaps, that the work of memory regarding this shared past is as of yet incomplete. By tracing these histories of violence, both novels inquire into genealogies of the 9/11 wars and the rise of transnational terror along the Afghanistan-Pakistan border. The complex memory ecosystem staged by these two novels offers a striking contrast to the simplistic remediations of the past offered in the texts discussed in chapters one and two.

Why do the stakes of revisiting 1979 rise rather than diminish in the post-9/11 era, and what are these stakes? Literary critic M. Scott Phillips writes:

> The euphoria over the fall of the Berlin Wall, the first Bush administration's declaration of the "New World Order," and the emergence of what Benjamin Barber has referred to as "McWorld" seem naïve now, in the context of post-9/11 events, the recent collapse of the global economic bubble, the renewed hostility toward American economic and political hegemony, and the advent of a serious Islamist challenge to political and social liberalism. (7)

The myth of the spontaneous collapse of the socialist bloc and of the subsequent bloodless triumph of Western liberal democracies unravels when considering the intensity of the late Cold War conflict in Afghanistan. Not only is the end of the Cold War far from being bloodless, but this history reminds us that the socialist project, at least in this part of the world, was defeated not by liberal democratic forces, but by ultraright, extremist forces who challenged it and then came to power in its wake. Moreover, revisiting the long 1979 suggests a coevolution of the covert CIA operations, transnational terror networks, and European humanitarianism—a revision that prompts Western readers to ponder the uncomfortable yet necessary questions of historical responsibility that is shared across the political spectrum. Where *The Kite Runner*—the best-known text about Afghanistan to date—forges a poignant, visceral image of the Soviets as the killers of trees and sexual predators, and where some recent Hollywood blockbusters (such as Ben Affleck's *Argo*, for example) hammer out a clean, heroic image of a CIA operative, one should stop and ask, what is at stake? Is it to, as in Hosseini's case, foreclose the idea of socialism as a viable alternative to capitalist modernity? Is it to absolve the West of any blame, making sure covert and increasingly privatized wars continue into the foreseeable future? By contrast, by examining, via this chapter's texts, the long 1979 of Islamabad, Peshawar, and Badakhshan as casting a long shadow, we get a sense of a convergence of multiple national and transnational histories that must inform our view of the 9/11 wars era. These texts, intentionally (in Aslam and Khan) or unwittingly (in Lefèvre and Girardet), perform important work of remembrance and recovery, not only engaging with a historical archive, but opening up possibilities for a transnational reconciliation process—through recounting traumatic histories from multiple points of view, with the purpose of creating what Aslam calls poignantly "the kinship of wounds" (318).

4

Witness: Modes of Writing the Disaster

Writing the Disaster

In his 2011 memoir, Donald Rumsfeld recalls 1989—the moment that heralds Afghanistan's imminent catastrophic collapse—from an American official point of view:

> As the Soviets completed their retreat, the CIA station in Islamabad, Pakistan, cabled the headquarters in Langley, Virginia, two words: "We won." [. . .] In the chaos of civil war that consumed the country after the Soviet departure, the United States embassy in Kabul closed its doors. [. . .] Few American policy or intelligence officials imagined that they would ever have to concern themselves again with that distant, poor, and abused land. (366)

As evidenced by this passage, Rumsfeld's memoir conveniently sidesteps questions of historical responsibility, divesting, in the same gesture, the ensuing tragedy in Afghanistan of global significance. Reinscribing Afghanistan's tragedy as a world-historical event, in a Hegelian sense—an event whose arrival changed the course of world history—remains an important ongoing task for twenty-first-century historians and cultural producers. The texts discussed in this chapter insist on the need for collective remembrance, safeguarding against the gesture of historical erasure exemplified by Rumsfeld's account. They inscribe the Afghan disaster as an object of memorialization, foregrounding its key role in the late twentieth and early twenty-first centuries' global affairs. Pushing against the limitations of the post-Cold War humanitarian imaginary, they forge new vocabularies for writing traumatic histories. They maintain an interest in documenting suffering; yet, in their attempt to capture long-term political violence, armed conflict, and the resulting loss of life, they decenter the human as well as the humanitarian figure. Ultimately, these authors are interested not only in suffering, but in the human, cultural, and environmental resilience. It is at this juncture that the contours of new Afghanistan writing begin to emerge—texts that stand up to historical scrutiny, serve as a counterpoint to official accounts, and document past and ongoing violence without resorting to victimization. With its focus on tracing these new modes of representation, this chapter is transitional—we move from a critique of the humanitarian imaginary to finding, together with the authors of these texts, a way forward.

The three texts grouped in this chapter—Kamila Shamsie's *Burnt Shadows* (2009), Qais Akbar Omar's *A Fort of Nine Towers* (2013), and Zia Haider Rahman's *In the Light of What We Know* (2014)—share an interest in memory and in literature as a medium of memory. In relation to Afghanistan, they can be said to initiate what Jeffrey C. Alexander calls a trauma process—the work of assessment of a traumatic history in which the victims and the perpetrators of crimes are named, losses counted, and responsibility attributed. Alexander views the trauma process as a creative practice, in which cultural memory is not simply recovered, but conjured anew. He writes: "The trauma process does not simply return to buried memory; it creates new ones. It allows events to be seen in a different way, and repositions roles and responsibilities of actors, and suggests that the present must be repaired in a manner that makes it consistent with the newly remembered past" (154). The aim of this process, therefore, is repair—a kind of truth and reconciliation process that occurs through excavating relevant truths about the past. For the trauma process to occur, Alexander suggests, carrier groups (groups with symbolic capital) have to emerge "with the resources, authority, or interpretive competence to powerfully disseminate these trauma claims" (30). Writers and other cultural producers play a key role in the trauma process—initiating discussions, conducting investigations, or creating fictional characters who become spokespersons for historical ills.

lexander's framework can be viewed as a productive means for con-
ualizing contemporary Afghanistan writing as a work of repair, with
aveat that, in this case, this work occurs in the global, rather than a
national milieu. It must be noted, however, that the language of trauma
has limitations as it has been associated, since Cathy Caruth's major intervention, with fast violence—an unexpected event that then produces gaps
in memory, language, and representation. While scholars have pointed
out that the notion of trauma is capacious enough to include other forms
of violence that are cumulative and recurrent,[1] the view of trauma as a
rupture—an event that rips time apart—remains strong. In 9/11 cultural
production the attacks in New York have been inscribed as a major national
(and occasionally as a global) trauma, with a resulting interest in the failure
of memory and representation, and the nature of the event as a rupture that
signals a complete break with the past is foregrounded. Jean Baudrillard
famously wrote in 2002: "With the attacks on the World Trade Center in
New York, we might even be said to have before us the absolute event, the
'mother' of all events, the pure event uniting within itself all the events
that have never taken place. The whole play of history and power are disrupted by this event, but so, too are the conditions of analysis" (4). This
indictment makes use of Caruth's notion of trauma as a breakdown of one's
analytical and linguistic capacities. Richard Gray in *After the Fall: American
Literature Since 9/11* observes that writers who attempt to engage with the
9/11 tragedy manifest a fixation on the failure of linguistic articulation. He
writes, "If there was one thing writers agreed about in response to 9/11,
it was the failure of language; the terrorist attacks made the tools of their
trade seem absurd" (1). "'Nothing to say,'" he adds, "became a refrain, a
recurrent theme with writers, as they struggled to cope with something
that seemed to be, quite literally, beyond words" (15).

To distance myself from the language of rupture and exception as
prevalent in 9/11 cultural texts, I suggest that Afghanistan's prolonged
strife is better captured by the term "disaster." I propose this term to delin-
eate a crisis that cannot be reduced to any single iconic image of extreme
violence. Unraveling over the course of four decades, it includes both fast
and slow forms of violence—manifesting as loss of life, infrastructure collapse, habitat diminishment, environmental toxicity, hunger, disease, and
proliferation of terror and poppy fields. Involving many global actors and
networks, such a disaster is so distributed in time and space that its contours are hard to grasp. Signaling a crisis that is long-term, continuous,

enfolded into the very fabric of the everyday, such disaster never ends; one is ensconced in the disaster and carried forth by its forces, subjected to the slow catastrophe of its rhythm. "The disaster ruins everything, all the while leaving everything intact," writes Maurice Blanchot (1). What does it mean to make the disaster legible? In his essay "How to Write the Disaster," Joshua Schuster presents the disaster as profoundly enigmatic and ambiguous. "Disaster," he writes, "is the mark of an event that refuses revelation or redemption even if other conditions are made possible in its wake" (168). In contrast to an apocalypse—a catastrophic end that delivers revelation and, ultimately, salvation, the disaster does not offer such closure. Instead, the disaster delivers nothing. It cannot be absorbed into a narrative of either progress or collapse; it cannot be viewed as epiphany, restitution, or productive purge. The disaster is not the end of history: Schuster pronounces that "other conditions are made possible in its wake" (168). To a survivor's dismay and disbelief, historical processes continue unabated in the disaster's aftermath. On the one hand, this tentative continuation testifies to life's resilience as weakened forms of life struggle yet persist in the ruins. On the other hand, it attests to human failure to learn from history. When a survivor looks ahead in search of solace and atonement, she finds the seeds of new catastrophes brewing.

Here, I propose the term "writing the disaster" as better suited to describe global Afghanistan writing than "trauma fiction." The three texts grouped together in this chapter resist the trope of language failure (associated with trauma), conjuring, instead, divergent yet powerful modes of speaking about their crises. While including the 9/11 attacks, these texts contest the motif of exceptionality by decentering the 9/11 events and placing them in the light of other—both prior and subsequent—historical catastrophes. In contrast to Patrick Fuery, who calls 9/11 "a terror unlike any other" (182), they all insist that 9/11 is an event connected with many others, woven into the very fabric of the interconnected world we inhabit.[2] These texts' characters experience the disaster as a process that unfolds. They are depicted as living in the wake of an anterior crisis and in the shadow of another that is already looming on the horizon. To live through the disaster, for Blanchot, is to persist beyond survival, is to lose the grounds for making sense of things, is to lose a world (2). Yet to survive a disaster does not mean to be exempt from history. Carried from the jaws of one catastrophe to the next, these texts' characters survive the end of not one, but multiple, worlds.

The three works grouped here focus on Afghanistan's catastrophic history from a South Asian perspective.[3] Omar's text is a memoir that takes readers into the very heart of the Afghan disaster. It narrates the period of the collapse of the state, dramatizing the country's catastrophic unraveling in the era of the civil war that followed the overthrow of the last socialist government in Kabul in 1992. Following publication in English by Picador, the memoir was translated into twenty other languages and deserves the attention it is receiving. By describing what it meant to have lived through the destruction of Kabul as it was captured by the warring jihadist groups in 1992, the memoir gives us a glimpse into what it means to have survived the sieges of Fallujah, Mosul, Palmyra, Raqqa, or Aleppo in the twenty-first century. In the vast corpus of works that have been written about Afghanistan in recent years, Omar's text is unique insofar as it is a work of a survivor who was an eyewitness to the entire crisis of the 1990s—the crisis that lasted nine long years before the 9/11 attacks, during the time when the larger world, as Rumsfeld's quote reminds us, was not watching.

The other two authors examined here—Shamsie and Rahman—center the Afghan tragedy by placing it in the context of other twenty- and twenty-first-century catastrophes. Both novels write the Afghan disaster by having foreigners drawn into its vortex—a mixed-race polyglot translator in Shamsie's novel and a Bangladeshi human rights lawyer in Rahman's. At first glance, Shamsie's and Rahman's novels are not directly about Afghanistan—their storylines move freely between countries and continents. This movement is symptomatic and is designed to draw attention to the permeability of Afghanistan's borders, as well as its enmeshment with multiple histories—the Cold War rivalry, the War on Terror, the infrastructures of global capitalism, and so on. Yet their main storyline culminates in Afghanistan, as if to emphasize that Afghanistan is a place where things come to a halt, where rival parties finally face a standoff, where various independent lines of flight intersect. Rahman underscores the idea of Afghanistan as a site of such fierce fighting by comparing it to a board game "in which players fight to set down the very rules" (363).

Of the three writers discussed here, Shamsie is the most established figure in the newly emerging canon of South Asian works written during the 9/11 wars era. An author of six acclaimed novels to date, Shamsie was born in Pakistan, yet her trajectory of transnational migration and travel marks her as a novelist of the global age. A dual citizen of Pakistan

and the United Kingdom, she is defined by what we could call transnational trigamy, straddling Karachi, Pakistan, where she grew up, the
United States, where she went to college (Hamilton College, University
of Massachusetts Amherst), and London, where she lives now. In *Burnt
Shadows*, she thrusts into center view the less publicized, non-Western
catastrophes of the twentieth and twenty-first centuries. The novel's four
sections mark four catastrophes: the atomic bombing of Nagasaki in 1945,
the Partition of India and Pakistan in 1947, the intensification of the Cold
War in Afghanistan in 1982–1983, and the War on Terror of 2001–2002
with its epicenters in New York and Afghanistan. The novel's mode of writing the disaster can be called constellational—by putting several historical
catastrophes side-by-side, the author opens each event up in a manner
characteristic of multidirectional memory staged by Nadeem Aslam (as
discussed in the previous chapter). Her method can be called "amplifi-
cation"—gaining an understanding of hidden aspects of one catastrophe
through its echoes and resonances in another.

Rahman boasts a similar transnational trajectory. Born in rural
Bangladesh, he was raised in poverty by immigrant parents in London,
and later studied and worked in both England and the United States. His
ambitious first novel draws parallels between the War on Terror and the
financial crisis of 2008, foregrounding the opaque, distributed, technical nature of both catastrophes. The novel's recursive-digressive structure
foregrounds the nontransparency in the heart of such crises. Afghanistan,
in the book, provides a focal point through which to bring to light the
complexity of contemporary wars, staging Kabul as a site of collision and
confluence of multiple military and nonmilitary networks. With its attention on the question of knowing, Rahman's novel suggests that disaster is
unthinkable, resisting our epistemic thrust. The catastrophic effects—such
as deadly acts of terror—are apparent to an eyewitness, but the causes
remain obscure—not because they exceed the capacity of ordinary language, but because they are massively distributed in space and time, and
ultimately, like the 2008 financial crisis, too technical for any single person
to comprehend.

Taking as a point of departure Debjani Ganguly's assertion that the
world novel offers a mode of witnessing that makes historical events and
traumas legible (as opposed to mass media that make them visible), I
propose that the three selected texts construct three modes of witness,
and therefore three modes of writing, and making legible, the Afghan

disaster.[4] Both Omar's and Shamsie's texts offer a long-term witness as a main device that allows them to document the protracted crises that span years to decades. Shamsie's witness spans sixty years, straddling many countries and continents, dramatizing, through her migrations, the catastrophic history of the long twentieth century. Similarly, Omar's memoir offers a long-term witness, embedded with the enfolding disaster in Afghanistan, providing a continuity necessary to understand the Afghan crisis, its causes and consequences, as well as its long-term global effects. By contrast, Rahman's novel, through both its plot and its formal aspects, argues against the primacy of eyewitnessing, claiming, instead, that, due to its complexity, the disaster is beyond human witness. The disaster, in Rahman, is not a single event or an object, but numerous interrelated events and objects (one can say, it is a hyperobject). It cannot be perceived but can only be accessed through mathematics (computer modeling), and even then, certain things remain opaque. As the indeterminacy at the very core of the world continuously thwarts our epistemic thrust, the disaster, in fact, calls for a nonhuman witness.

While situated in NATO-centric contexts (England and the United States), these diasporic South Asian writers engage in a critique of American imperialism and indict the ruthless profiteering at the heart of the interventionist program. All three writers underscore the enmeshment of the War on Terror with the infrastructure of global finance capitalism—an imbrication that problematizes the moral dogmas of the battle of "good versus evil." "Many of the foreigners who came here [to Afghanistan] claiming to help us left very rich," writes Omar bitterly in his last chapter (375). "Meanwhile," he adds, "the Afghanistan that we had dreamed about during all those years of bombs, whips, and stonings still has not returned to us" (378). In turn, Rahman underscores the greed that drives many humanitarians and developers. He writes, sardonically, that in 2002 no explanation was necessary for why someone would come to Kabul: "There were already numberless new arrivals in Kabul, would-be development wonks, skulking about the city waiting for a Western development agency to throw some meat their way, and they, like all hyenas, needed no explanation when the smell of meat was in the air" (384). In Shamsie, the reader is conscripted into probing and questioning the morality of the shadow infrastructure of private military contracting—a business that "outsources death" (Zinck 50) to third-country nationals (TCNs) in what can only be called a necropolitical business enterprise.

And yet, in spite of these critiques of the continuing Western interference in Afghanistan, the authors resist the paralyzing discourse of us versus them. Instead, they foreground the fact that the lasting legacies of colonial violence that persist in the era of the 9/11 wars create ambiguities and polarizations far more complex than this hegemonic discourse suggests. Shamsie and Rahman feature characters who are caught, to use Harleen Singh's words, "on both sides of the War on Terror" ("Insurgent Metaphors" 36)—becoming, unwittingly, complicit with acts of violence, and although by no means terrorists, cannot be absolved of blame either. Taken together, the three texts illustrate the increasing complexity of global Afghanistan writing as seen over the two decades of the 9/11 wars: by shifting of attention from fast to slow violence, by focusing on infrastructures and conditions that enable it, and by bringing into view the global networks of power.

Reverberations Across Time

The first sentence of *Burnt Shadows* invokes an image that came to define 9/11 writing early on—the image of the clear blue sky[5]: "Later, the one who survives will remember this day as grey, but on the morning of 9 August itself both the man from Berlin, Konrad Weiss, and the schoolteacher, Hiroko Tanaka, step out of their house and notice the perfect blueness of the sky" (5).

The "perfect blueness of the sky" here both summons and interrogates the image that became the trope ubiquitous in 9/11 writing—the clear blue sky out of which the planes came, signifying the age of innocence prior to the attacks. Here, the perfectly blue sky is the sky over Nagasaki on August 9, 1945, minutes before the city would be seared by an atomic bomb dropped by an American pilot, Major Charles W. Sweeney, resulting in 75,000 deaths. The capture of Nagasaki's tragedy through a 9/11 trope forces the reader into a shocking recognition of an earlier catastrophe by way of the more recent one, creating a powerful resonance between the two. Moments prior, the novel's six-sentence-long enigmatic prologue describes a scene in a prison cell, invoking another color—orange—the color of Guantanamo Bay and thus a potent signifier of the War on Terror's many catastrophic failures. The prologue's last sentence, "How did it come to this," implies that the novel will provide a possible answer by writing a genealogy of "orange," illuminating the long trajectory that leads the yet unnamed character to Guantanamo.

One of the most prominent features of *Burnt Shadows* is its architecture. The novel is divided into four sections that mark four catastrophes. Starting in Nagasaki on the day of the atomic bombing, the book then moves to the Partition of India and Pakistan in 1947, the war in Afghanistan in the 1980s, and finally, into the early days of the War on Terror, 2001–2002. These different scenes of violence are connected through the figure of an eyewitness—Hiroko—a Japanese woman who experiences all of these catastrophic events during her life span. Plagued by survivor guilt, she lives across several eras, straddling different countries and continents and incurring many losses. Implicitly, by means of its architecture, the novel makes an argument against the centrality of the 9/11 attacks in the contemporary imaginary, ending with the War on Terror that the book positions as the end result of the catastrophic long twentieth century. Shamsie therefore resists "the mythologizing that has taken place around 9/11 and given it a narrative primacy over all other world events of the last few decades," as noted by Singh in "A Legacy of Violence" (159). Additionally, by embedding the War on Terror into a broader temporal framework, the novel argues against what Georgiana Banita calls "the exclusion of anteriority in the War on Terror"—the erasure of its genealogy in the Af-Pak region in the 1980s (227).

The novel's title invokes the shadows of the incinerated victims of the atomic bomb that were etched into the concrete, evidencing the instantaneity of their extinguishment. Cast by invisible bodies, these shadows are a potent allegory of the disaster that remains unseen, incomprehensible, yet forever imprinted into the landscape. It also evokes the shadow-like radiation burns etched into Hiroko's back—the trace of the bomb inscribing itself for posterity on her body. If someone asked Shamsie whether the book was about writing the disaster, she would probably ask, which disaster, and whose disaster? The choice of historical catastrophes she writes about is significant. All four catastrophes occur in non-Western spaces, spanning several sites in Asia: Nagasaki, Delhi, Afghanistan (with a spillover of the conflict into Pakistan's cities Karachi and Peshawar), and again Afghanistan, which becomes the epicenter of the War on Terror. Sidestepping the Euro-American disasters of the Shoah and the 9/11, Shamsie seeks to assert the significance of the catastrophic events that cross into global mainstream visibility far less often. With this, she attempts to write a history of the catastrophic twentieth century from the point of view of the subaltern—a project that she also pursues in her 2014 novel *A God in Every Stone*, where she brings into view the experience of World War I by a soldier from the colonies (Pakistan) and also describes the long-forgotten massacre that occurred during the anti-colonial riots in Peshawar in 1930. The catastrophes in *Burnt Shadows* are all global catastrophes that pose lasting, unresolved ethical questions that Shamsie interrogates. For instance, she chooses to write of Nagasaki, not of Hiroshima (the first city that was bombed), because of the ethical question *the second bomb* poses. "Why a second bomb?" Hiroko exclaims, "Even the first one is beyond anything I can . . . but a second. You do that, and you see what you've done, and then you do it again. How is that . . . ?" (100).

Similar to centering the ethical question posed by the second bomb, Shamsie seeks to position the unraveling of Afghanistan as one of the main catastrophic events of the twentieth century—one that poses lasting ethical questions as well. It is telling that some critics do not "see" or skip over some of the catastrophes that Shamsie seeks to make central, in spite of the book's very structure foregrounding the resonance between the four events. Singh, in her introduction to the interview with Shamsie, mentions only three events—Nagasaki, Partition, and 9/11, thus omitting the Afghanistan section and replacing the War on Terror with 9/11: "Though Hiroko is not the narrator of the novel, the viewer is positioned to view Nagasaki, Partition, and 9/11 from her perspective" (157). Similarly, Zinck speaks of the bombing of Nagasaki and 9/11 as the two events that frame the novel, thus skipping over both Partition and the Afghan crisis and, once again, substituting 9/11 for the War on Terror. Yet Shamsie is adamant that *Burnt Shadows* is not a 9/11 novel and that it is not one of the four disasters it narrates. After emphasizing that the books in fact "'skips' 9/11 and picks up with the war in Afghanistan and the Indo-Pakistan stand-off," she adds, "I continue to be quite annoyed when people say—and a lot of people say this—that my novel starts with the bombing of Nagasaki and ends with 9/11. It ends with the War on Terror. That is an important distinction" (159).

Shamsie's decision to focus on these non-Western disasters is determined not only by her commitment to writing history from the point of view of the subaltern, but also by her long-term interest in what she calls "the missing pictures"—photographs of atrocities that do not enter into mainstream visibility because of ideological or political constraints or because photographs were never taken in the first place.[6] As a novelist, she believes it is her duty to recover these missing pictures, bringing into visibility the hidden crimes and their unmourned victims. The War on Terror as well as the Afghan jihad of the 1980s are paradigmatic examples of covert wars—long-term disasters of which many pictures, and records, are missing.

The architecture of resonance, the polycentric approach of the novel that has not one but four centers, works multidirectionally, as one disaster informs our understanding of another. The story of a Japanese schoolboy—an adolescent kamikaze pilot who steers his plane into a US warship—invokes, in the first pages of the book, the horrors of the 9/11 attacks that would occur fifty-six years later. And in 2001, the discourse of saving American lives in the context of the War on Terror reminds Hiroko of an American GI who told her that "the bomb was a terrible thing, but it had to be done to save American lives" (61)—a statement that proves to be intolerable (more so than the bombing itself) and makes her flee US-occupied Japan in desperation. By creating an architecture of transhistorical and transborder reverberation, Shamsie seeks to amplify the less visible disasters, giving voice to their victims and critiquing the troubling complicity of the citizenry steered by nationalist sentiment. In doing so, she seeks to counteract Western solipsism and amnesia, both of which are exemplified in the novel by a young American engineer, Kim Burton—for whom the 9/11 attacks is the only world historical event she has ever experienced.[7] The narrative forms a loop from the bombing of Nagasaki that claimed the lives of Hiroko's fiancé and her father, to the War on Terror, in which Hiroko loses her son, Raza, a Pakistani citizen and a US green card holder, to government sweeps, when he is reported to the authorities by Burton and arrested under suspicion of terrorism. Although Raza is not killed, the novel's ending (foreshadowed in the Prologue) conveys the sense that mother and son will never meet again and that Raza will be disappeared, tortured, and lost in the global shadow network of CIA black sites. It is in the context of the War on Terror, with its climate of anxiety and paranoia that Hiroko, the survivor of the atomic bombing, finally finds the answer to the question that haunted her for fifty-six years: Why was there a second bomb? The reaction of wounded Americans who support the invasion of Afghanistan and the rounding up of foreigners exemplifies for the protagonist how citizens buy into the polarizing logic of "us" (whose lives need to be protected) and "them" (whose lives are expendable), and come to support their governments' atrocities committed in their name.

A long-term witness and a survivor of multiple catastrophes, Hiroko
is able to bear witness to fast violence, such as the atomic blast itself, and
to "long dyings," toxic aftermaths, and violent blowback. Nixon notes "the
representational bias against slow violence" (13), especially in mass media
with its short attention span, and the problem slow violence and the resulting "long dyings" pose for memorialization. "In the long arc between the
emergence of slow violence and its delayed effects," he writes, "both the
causes and the memory of catastrophe readily fade from view as the casualties incurred typically pass untallied and unremembered" (8–9). *Burnt
Shadows* is committed to bringing slow violence into view in multiple ways.
Though her bird-shaped radiation burns are numb to the touch, they are
a vehicle of memory, a part of Hiroko that refuses to let go and forget:
"Some days she could feel the dead on her back, pressing down beneath
her shoulder blades with demands she could not make sense of but knew
she was failing to meet" (50). The long-term suffering of the body that
keeps the memory of the disaster in its genes, its tissues, and its bones,
manifests, among other things, in a miscarriage that prevents the birth of
a deformed child. The novel does not describe the extent of the deformity,
but addresses it indirectly: "The doctor never told her precisely what was
so wrong with the foetus, she only said some miscarriages were acts of
mercy" (208). Slow violence also manifests as the mental torment that
drives Hiroko out of her country where she is perceived as *hibakusha*—the
irradiated one—into the unknown world, Delhi, Karachi, and later New
York, making her homeless, a perpetual foreigner. Similarly, the novel
demonstrates that the full extent of the Afghan crisis of the 1980s takes
decades to manifest—in the transnational jihad "blowback," and more
prosaically, as the long-term human cost of the collapse of the Afghan
state—the event that propelled millions of Afghans out of their homeland
into the larger world, condemning them to the bleak prospect of living as
illegal migrants on inhospitable foreign shores, or as perpetual refugees.

In his discussion of post-9/11 writing, Gray describes how American
authors, in the aftermath of 9/11, grapple with "imagining what it feels
like to survive the end of the world" (17). *Burnt Shadows* brings into view
the fact that the twentieth-century crises created countless survivors who
know a thing or two about losing a world. When Hiroko meets an Afghan
man named Abdullah in the public library in New York, there is an instant
recognition of such shared experience of loss. As Abdullah shows Hiroko
the book he is looking at, she recognizes the yearning for a homeland that

no longer exists. "'Kandahar. Before the wars.' He ran his palm across the photograph, as though he could feel the texture of the ripening pomegranates pushing up against his skin. [. . .] Hiroko nodded, touching the page as reverently as Abdullah had. It was difficult to find photographs of Nagasaki that preceded the bomb" (317). She sees in him "a man who understood lost homelands and the impossibility of return. He had looked at the photographs of Kandahar's orchards as Sajjad used to look at pictures of his old moholla in Dilli" (319). Sajjad, Hiroko's Muslim Indian husband, was ejected from his beloved Delhi (he calls it "Dilli") after the Partition of 1947, having the family resettle in Karachi, Pakistan, where they gradually rebuilt their lives as refugees.

Centering the unraveling of Afghanistan as one of the key disasters of the twentieth century, examining its legacy—the legacy made manifest during the War on Terror—is the main trajectory of the book's two last parts. Shamsie dramatizes this long conflict through three characters who reside in Pakistan in 1982–1983: Harry Burton (English American), Hiroko's son Raza (a Japanese Pakistani "bomb-marked mongrel" [194]), and Abdullah (an Afghan boy growing up in an Afghan refugee neighborhood in Karachi). Shamsie traces their stories into the post-9/11 era, making audible the reverberation of the American-assisted Afghan jihad of the 1980s in the US-led War on Terror of 2001–2002. Harry Burton—Hiroko's family friend—is an allegory of Anglo-American interference in South Asia, and also of colonial legacies of privilege and power. He is a son of James Burton, a colonial administrator in British India at the time of the Partition. Having attended an elite boarding school in England, Harry later immigrates to the United States and becomes an instant convert of the American dream. A passionate hater of communism, and due to his colonial education, a fluent speaker of Urdu (Hiroko's husband was his childhood Urdu teacher), he joins the CIA, returning to Pakistan in 1983 to assist with the Afghan jihad against the Soviets. A figure reminiscent of Aslam's CIA operative David Town (*The Wasted Vigil*), Harry supervises a complex operation of weapon smuggling via the port city of Karachi into Peshawar and the adjacent jihad training camps along Afghanistan's border.[8] The novel shows that the Burtons, ultimately, are a destructive presence in Hiroko's and her family's lives. Harry becomes indirectly responsible for the death of Hiroko's husband in 1983 (he is killed by one of Harry's local CIA assets). Post-9/11, he draws her son, Raza, into the murky world of military contracting—an endeavor that in time will

seal Raza's fate resulting in his arrest as a terror suspect (he is reported to
the authorities by Kim Burton, Harry's daughter). Harry's world is one
of "lies and manipulation" (Singh, "A Legacy of Violence" 161); Harry's
most problematic feature is that he does not hold himself responsible for
the tragedies unfolding in his wake. Like Aslam's David Town, he is an
ardent believer in American hegemony: "Communism," he says, "had to
be crushed so that the US could be the world's only superpower" (175).
In his pursuit of this goal, he is pragmatic, strictly utilitarian in relation
to the means of conducting war: "rape is off limits, children are off limits,
but aside from that, whatever works, works" (289).

The "Afghan" jihad Harry supervises is a complex, transnational affair;
although somewhat skeptical about foreign recruits (and anticipating blowback sometime in the future), he welcomes the internationalization of the
infrastructure of terror. Weapons that arrive to Karachi docks in Pakistan
in shiploads come from all over the world, and so do the recruits in need
of training:

> [N]ow, the war was truly international. Arms from Egypt, China and—
> soon—Israel. Recruits from all over the Muslim world. Training camps
> in Scotland! There was even a rumor that India might be willing to sell
> some of the arms they had bought from their Russian friends—even
> though it might prove to be little more than a rumor, Harry couldn't help
> enjoying the idea of Pakistan, India, and Israel working together in an
> American war. Here was internationalism, powered by capitalism. (207)

By referring to the Afghan jihad, throughout the book, as an American
war, Shamsie seems to suggest a causal relation between Afghanistan's
catastrophic unraveling and the actions of the United States, exemplified
by Harry Burton. Yet, her argument in the end is more complex. To assign
such a causal relation would be to sidestep complex questions of coagency
and responsibility, as well as to blur the difference between actions and
conditions for action—a distinction outlined by Judith Butler in *Precarious
Life*—a book written shortly after September 11. In this text, Butler argues
against an explanation that links the rise of global terror and the attacks
of 9/11 to US actions by ways of direct causation:

> No doubt, there are forms of Left analysis that say simply that the United
> States has reaped what it has sown. Or they say that the United States

has brought this state of events upon itself. These are, as closed explanations, simply other ways of asserting U.S. priority and encoding U.S.
omnipotence. These are explanations that assume that these actions orig-
inate in a single subject, that the subject is not what it appears to be,
that it is the United States that occupies the site of that subject, and that
no other subjects exists or, if they exist, their agency is subordinated to
our own. (9)

In other words, Butler warns the reader against seeing the United States
as a direct (and only) cause of the spread of transnational terror—a move
that ultimately leads to a deterministic view and contributes to the fantasy
of Western omnipotence. Other parties, she underscores, extremist networks among them, were also responsible for the rise of terror. Offering
a distinction between actions and conditions for actions, Butler proposes
that the United States' imperialism bears responsibility for setting up the
conditions, without being the sole cause, for the spread of terror—the acts
of terror, nevertheless, committed by independently "acting and deliber-
ating subjects" (11).

This distinction between the conditions (the infrastructure of war, the
political groundwork, media coverage, destabilization, and other activities that pave the way to war) and individual agency is central to the
way in which Shamsie unpacks the Afghan jihad as it arrives to Hiroko
and her family's doorstep in Karachi. While Harry, along with his CIA
colleagues, works to put in place the infrastructures of terror, it is up to
the Afghan refugees who live on the outskirts of Karachi to make use of
them. The fate of Abdullah—a fourteen-year-old Afghan boy—dramatizes personal agency and the power of structural conditions. It is made
clear that Abdullah is expected, but not coerced, to join the jihad once he
turns fourteen. In fact, he hesitates and tells Raza, his friend, of his doubt:
"Afridi is going to Peshawar next week. My brother Ismail said I should go
with him, and he'll meet me and take me to the camp. But I don't know.
You said once, there are other ways to fight the Soviets. Maybe I'd be more
useful here, with Afridi" (214). And yet, Abdullah's individual agency is
circumscribed—both by the lasting legacies of colonial subjugation and
powerlessness that limit his choices in the world, and by the new structural
conditions, among them gun trade, jihad training camps nearby, the prospect of well-paid work as a fighter, and religious indoctrination embedded
with the refugee community. These infrastructures make Abdullah's path

to jihad seamless, just as the infrastructures of elite British and American education, as well as racial privilege, carry Harry into a successful career at the CIA and his becoming a formidable agent of the new Empire.

Raza, in particular, dramatizes the enduring legacies of colonial privilege and power. An intellectual and a polyglot, coveted for his multilingual translation skills in a transnational job market, he remains marked by his race (as Pakistani Japanese), which leads to his downfall in 2002 when he is arrested as a terror suspect. Having been recruited by Harry Burton into the lucrative business of private military contracting, Raza finds himself in Afghanistan in 2002, on a military contract firm payroll, assisting in the US-led operation. His fate illustrates, once again, the power of structural conditions; once the post-9/11 infrastructures of suspicion are put in place, detection will inevitably follow. Following a shooting at the base, during which Harry and several TCNs are killed, Raza is "detected" by a hypervigilant CIA agent on the military base, realizes that he cannot prove his innocence, and has to flee. A Pakistani citizen with links to the Afghans (while in Afghanistan, Raza attempts to find his childhood friend Abdullah), he is seen as a terror suspect, his phone conversation with an Afghan man days prior to the shooting serving as proof of his guilt. Raza's entrapment in the post-9/11 global terror hunt parallels his earlier journey along the shadow military infrastructures of the Afghan jihad when, as a seventeen-year-old boy, he unwittingly travels with Abdullah to a jihad training camp in Peshawar, even though he is not an Afghan and has no reason to join the war. While young Raza is quickly uncovered by an ISI agent (Pakistani intelligence) supervising the camp and sent back home to his worried parents, his journey illustrates how easy it is to follow the infrastructures of terror once they are put in place. The last pages of the novel have him on the run from the CIA, smuggled by human traffickers out of Afghanistan and across the world, and finally arrested in Canada. Thus, the figure in the Prologue—a naked prisoner waiting in his cell for an orange suit turns out to be Raza. Raza's arrest exemplifies "the potential of the War on Terror to cause miscarriages of justice by vilifying the innocent" (Banita 31), his extraordinary rendition adding to his mother's long list of losses incurred during the catastrophic twentieth century.

The figure of Abdullah—whose story the novel picks up again in its concluding pages—exemplifies the ambiguous position of the Afghan mujahid in the post-9/11 American imaginary. Having joined the terror force against the Soviets as a fourteen-year-old boy and having driven "the last Soviet out of Afghanistan" (210) by means of jihad (as Raza and Abdullah fantasized in their youth), Abdullah inherited not a free and independent Afghanistan, but a ruined country, weakened, first, by a decade and a half of mujahideen-inflicted terror and government retaliations, and, destroyed, finally, by the victorious mujahideen factions fighting each other for spoils. In the end, Abdullah inherits a ruined world; having lost his country, he has lost everything. An overthrow of the socialist government heralds the country's joining not the free, liberal First World, but the army of dispossessed in the Third World readable to its former benefactors as a disposable army of cheap labor. Reduced to an expendable body without the means of subsistence and a passport that bestows no privileges yet marks his belonging to a failed state, he travels to America illegally, smuggled by human traffickers in conditions that invoke the horrors of the middle passage. The reader gets a glimpse into the shadow geography of human trafficking—another infrastructure in place in today's world—when Shamsie describes Raza's journey from Afghanistan to Canada while on the run from the CIA. When Raza crosses the Gulf of Oman—a short trip in comparison to crossing the Atlantic—in a small wooden boat packed with countless other bodies in the searing inferno of the hidden compartment, he cannot but think of the mass graves he had seen in Bosnia. Illegal and effectively stateless, Abdullah then settles for a precarious life as an illegal immigrant and a taxi cab driver in New York city, yearning for his lost homeland, missing his family, and dreaming of the gardens of Kandahar as they existed before the war. To add to all this, the political winds in America have changed; in the climate of the War on Terror, the former Afghan jihad fighters are no longer viewed favorably, as exemplifying "the invincibility of the ideals we in this country hold most dear, the ideals of freedom and independence" (Reagan), but as terror suspects to be detained, tortured, and disappeared. As the FBI knocks on Abdullah's door, the circle is complete. Having escaped through the window, he is destined for another passage across the Atlantic, back to Afghanistan, that is, if he survives the journey's horrors.

Long-Term Witness

"Could a grave be as big as a whole city?" the narrator of *A Fort of Nine Towers* asks himself (21). While Shamsie's novel ends with the story of a former Afghan mujahid who left the country after the mujahideen victory, Qais Akbar Omar's memoir tells the story of someone who stayed in Afghanistan to witness the horrors of the "victory's" aftermath. Omar's memoir is, in fact, one of the very few texts that tell this story, taking us into the very heart of the Afghan disaster. Published in 2013, the text reflects upon the legacies of the mujahideen and the Taliban, suspending judgment about the ideologies that fuel them and focusing instead on the real-life consequences on people's lives in Afghanistan.[9] The early years of the civil war are seen through the eyes of a child whose father tries to protect him and his siblings from the horrors of that war, moving them from one place to another to save their lives, "like a cat carrying kittens in its mouth" (231). The memoir provides a gripping account of a country ravaged by fighting, yet manages to deliver unforgettable scenes of human kindness and heroism, bringing into relief people's ability to care for each other while in the jaws of the disaster. In its desire to understand what has happened, the memoir seems surgical in its work of dissecting the crisis, as compared to the generalizations and myths perpetuated by many of the human rights best sellers discussed in earlier chapters. For someone interested in teaching a text on Afghanistan's epoch-defining crisis, this would be a powerful and accessible source.

An insider's account, it is nevertheless an example of global writing. Written in English and for the Western audience, the memoir assumes a didactic approach, proffering its Boston University MFA-adorned author as a bridge between cultures. Omar's personal trajectory is unique: Having survived the civil war, the Taliban rule, and the War on Terror, he became an exile in the late period of the American intervention era, while completing his MFA degree in Boston. "I wrote an op-ed for *The New York Times* [in 2014] about ghost money that the CIA was giving to President [Hamid] Karzai at the time," he explains in an interview with WGBH News. "As soon as that one came out, we got a lot of visitors coming to our shop [in Kabul] trying to take me to lunch, and of course you go to that lunch and you never come back."[10] Omar's memoir, although based on the events he witnessed and experienced, reads like fiction. Its gripping plot is guaranteed to keep readers on the edge of their seats while offering an array of colorful characters—both Omar's family members and people he meets while the family flees the war in their old Soviet-made Volga.

In contrast to Shamsie, whose protagonist straddles different continents during her lifetime, Omar's memoir offers a witness who is trapped in warring Afghanistan and witnesses the entire era, in fact, multiple eras, thus providing continuity of memory from the early days of the conflict well into the era of the 9/11 wars. In contrast to many other diasporic Afghan texts that are stories of escape and exile, Omar's witness is embedded with the unfolding disaster, submitted to the agony of its monstrous pulse. The book is fueled by the testimonial imperative in which to narrate the disaster means to open pathways toward redress, reconciliation, and healing. "While this book focuses on my family's experience, every Afghan family has stories similar to ours," writes Omar in his Author's Note. "They all need to be told. They need to be heard. They must not happen again" (393). In an interview, Omar confesses that the memoir is a personally therapeutic work that allowed him to mitigate the long-term effects of PTSD—recurring nightmares and flashbacks that used to haunt him—through sharing his story with others.

Omar further underscores the importance of testimony and witnessing through his poignant address to the reader in the postscript, where he hails the reader as a witness: "I have long carried this load of griefs in the cage of my heart. Now I have given them to you. I hope you are strong enough to hold them" (postscript). Here, the author is aware that the consumption of his text might turn toxic—or, as Banita puts it, "the eye of the spectator [. . .] may be damaged in the process of witnessing" (35). He thus expresses hope that the reader is strong enough to "hold" his grief, showing care for the reader as witness—an act of reciprocity that is routinely sidestepped in humanitarian writing, where the victim is seen as having nothing to give back, except for the story of his or her suffering. Importantly, this act of care for the reader is supplemented by Omar's set of qualifications that indicate the nature of witnessing desired—compassion without victimization of the survivor of the crisis. Expressing a desire to be seen as an Afghan who suffered, the author also talks of loving being an Afghan, of loving Afghanistan (4). Early pages of the memoir speak of the joy of growing up in a tightly knit Afghan family in 1980s Kabul. A sense of joy permeates descriptions of his childhood, serving as an antidote to victimization. Even later, when the violence of war makes the family flee Kabul, Omar talks about experiencing the pleasure of seeing various parts of Afghanistan, road-trip style, of the elation of learning (such as learning how to weave traditional Afghan carpets), and finally, of the joy of teaching others (teaching Kuchi nomad children to read and write while seeking shelter with the Kuchi caravan). The statement about the happiness of being an Afghan contrasts with Yasmina Khadra's problematic declaration in which he asserts that his novel—*The Swallows of Kabul*—is supposed to incite "the joy of not being an Afghan."[11] Where Khadra's novel constructs a victim, setting up the conditions for assistance and intervention, Omar's book shirks such a gesture. Rather than proffering his memoir as an appeal for external aid, he assumes agency for his country's future by saying, "I am the embodiment of this world-spanning mixture of peoples we call Afghan. . . . I want to help rebuild what so many others destroyed" (4). In short, the memoir's emphasis on Afghan self-determination, agency, and access to happiness signals Omar's awareness of, and opposition to, the literature of victimization, best exemplified by the human rights best seller.

The historical moment that marks the advent of the disaster in Omar's text is the cry "Allah-hu-Akbar" that permeates the city on one dark night circa 1990, a year after the Soviet's withdrawal from Afghanistan. The haunting howl is a spontaneous manifestation of collectivity united by the expectation of imminent change; composed of many voices, it announces the inevitability of the coming of the mujahideen to Kabul. The howl is accompanied by a failure of electricity, which drowns Kabul in darkness, prompting Omar's mother to say, prophetically: "Oh, it's as dark as a grave" (21). The darkness that enveloped the city that night heralds the forthcoming eclipse of Afghan modernity: "I had never seen it before," remarks the narrator. "Kabul always had electricity" (21). The memoir thus starts one year after the end of the Cold War, after the demolition of the Berlin Wall, in short, after the spectacle. The story provides a counterpoint to the triumphalist NATO-centric visions of 1989. It is also in tension with the clichéd view that Afghanistan, in the aftermath of the Cold War's end, simply returns to its "natural state," so to speak—an insular, archaic place that presumably it had been before becoming a Cold War hot spot.[12]

It is true, in fact, that the suffering that followed was to be globally invisible. What happened in Afghanistan after 1989 was not considered a world-historical event; it was to be viewed as a local tragedy in a distant zone of suffering—until September 2001. This attitude is exemplified not only by Rumsfeld (as quoted in the beginning of this chapter), but by other American officials as well. Consider, for instance, Zbigniew Brzezinski, who in a 1998 interview said: "What is more important to the history of the world? The end of the Soviet empire or the Taliban? The end of Soviet control of eastern Europe and a free Europe, or a few disgruntled Muslims?"[13] To this day, the Afghan tragedy has remained unmourned and insufficiently memorialized by all involved parties.

As I've already discussed in chapter two, the dating of the Afghan crisis by both fiction and nonfiction writers reveals their ideological investments and global positioning. Hirsh, for instance, dates the beginning of the crisis from 1973—the overthrow of the monarchy—speaking of the pre-1973 era as "the Golden Age of Afghanistan."[14] Khadra points at the vices and excesses of the Taliban's theocratic regime (starting in 1996) as a chief culprit. Hosseini in *The Kite Runner* points to the Soviet invasion of 1979—the Russians—as the single defining cause of the disaster, capitalizing on the long-standing anti-Soviet sentiments of his American readers. By providing yet another genealogy of the crisis, Omar reveals his own set of investments. Free of an anti-statist bias, he is more invested in having a well-functioning state system rather than in a particular set of ideological beliefs (royalist, communist, capitalist, Islamist, etc.). While Hosseini in *The Kite Runner* paints socialism as unnatural and predatory by creating a strong set of associations between socialism and rape, socialism and failure, socialism and the assault on nature (as in the image of the ruined trees in Kabul), Omar associates socialism with a functioning state and improvements to infrastructure. Notably, he also associates it with fecund gardens and the natural rhythms of nature.

Prior to the civil war, he writes, "[w]e lived well. Time moved graciously with the pace of the seasons, and nudged us gently through the stages of life. But then one night the air was filled with the unexpected cries of '*Allah-hu-Akbar*,' and nothing has ever been the same since" (20). For Omar, Afghanistan is a joyful place until 1992, until the last socialist government is deposed and the power is taken by "men with big turbans and long beards" (27). This difference in periodization is important, for Omar's temporality is not NATO-normative. Socialist government, well in place at the time of his birth, does not spell disaster, brainwashing, or economic ruin in the form of expropriation of his wealthy family's property. Instead, they "live well," enjoying the fruits of their prospering businesses, the opportunities provided by the state, and the cosmopolitan mentality resulting from being a part of a multinational socialist world. Omar's father, a schoolteacher, a businessman, and a professional boxer, frequently travels to boxing championships in other socialist counties. His mother wears short skirts and works at a bank. His grandfather—a beloved patriarch—is a successful, respected businessman and an intellectual who equally enjoys reading Freud, Dostoyevsky, and Rumi. This is how Omar describes his childhood in an interview to CBC:

"I was born in year 1982, three years after the Soviets invaded Afghanistan."

"So tell us about life in Kabul for you as a little boy."

"Oh, it was really joyful, you know, this is one of the things that people don't understand is that Kabul was a small city, a city of 200,000 people—now it is a city of 6 million people—and it was like a garden, the whole city was like a garden with tall trees along the roads, with parks, people having a normal life—I mean, it is exactly what you have in this [American] part of the world."

[. . .]

"So when you were growing up, when the Russians were in charge, where did you live, what was your house like?"

"Oh, it was in Kote Sangi, which is in the newly developed part of Kabul; our courtyard ran for three acres, we had about one hundred and twenty Macintosh apple trees in our courtyard, there were fields of grass everywhere, and flowers, we used to grow vegetables, and sometimes we had so much that we shared with all of our neighbors—that was the kind of a community we had."

In his memoir, Omar documents the early months of the mujahideen rule with a sense of humor, the following anecdote capturing the paradoxes of Islamization of the country overnight, after the socialist government falls:

Two months before the arrival of the Mujahedin, we had been taught in school that we are related to monkeys.

Our teacher said, "Humans are a kind of animal, and animals were created by nature."

"Who created nature?" I asked.

"Nature was self-created," our teacher said.

[. . .] After the Mujahedin came to Kabul, our same teacher now taught us from a new textbook called *The Creation of Adam*. It did not say anything about monkeys. [. . .]

Our teacher started saying things like, "The history of humans started from Adam and Eve, and the earth existed long before them. Do not let Shaitan [Satan] be your guide; he misled Eve and Adam and drove them out of paradise."

I was confused. "What happened to the monkeys?" I asked our teacher, "And nature?"

The teacher sat on the edge of the desk, and for a minute he did not say anything. "The monkeys and nature are Communist perceptions." (29)[15]

Omar's narrative also differs from numerous NATO-centric accounts with respect to how the Taliban era is assessed. The author resists the wholesale demonization of the Taliban, examining their contested legacy and posing questions about what would have happened had the Taliban been allowed to stay in power. The "strange peace" (359) brought by the Taliban as they evicted the warring jihadists from Kabul is welcomed by Omar's family who use this time to recover and rebuild from the carnage of war; yet the plight of women—especially widows and orphaned women who are not allowed to work under the Taliban law—is exposed by Omar as one of the chief ills of the Taliban theocracy. His astute observations about life under the Taliban illustrate the distinction that Mahmood Mamdani makes between "lawful dictatorship" (such as the Taliban) and "terror outside the law" (such as the era of the warring mujahideen [176]).[16] There is a strong suggestion in the memoir that the Taliban could have become acculturated and profoundly changed through its members' long-term encounter with the worldly, urban culture of Kabul. To no small degree, the success of Omar's memoir is attributable to his commitment to ideological neutrality (he does not condemn any of the regimes on ideological grounds) and to the fact that it is narrated by someone who stayed in Afghanistan throughout the entire era of conflicts, thus being attuned to the minutia of survival and recovery.

The memoir's title, *A Fort of Nine Towers*, summons the image of the tower—a poignant symbol in post-9/11 writing. A figure of both resilience and shattering, it instantly evokes the 9/11 attacks, resonating with iconic post-9/11 texts, such as Art Spiegelman's *In the Shadow of No Towers*. Richard Gray notes the mythologization of the tower in the post-9/11 imaginary, stating that "[t]he fall of the towers [. . .] and, for that matter, the fall of people from the towers—has become a powerful and variable

visual equivalent for other kinds of fall" (7). The fort of nine towers in
Omar's memoir is a paradoxical image. Serving as a refuge for Omar's
family after they flee their home in Kabul in 1992, the fort is both a
shelter and an image of disfigurement: Out of nine towers invoked by
its name, only one tower remains standing. The fort thus signals not the
catastrophic fall that is sudden, but references the catastrophic *longue durée*
history of Afghanistan—a land crossed by many imperial armies causing
much destruction. The image of the last tower is particularly poignant; it
represents a hope for salvation and betokens stubborn resilience amidst
unfolding catastrophe. Although many rockets fall in the fort's courtyard
during the periods of heavy bombardment by warring mujahideen factions, the last tower remains intact. The tower also represents the site from
which to observe and survey the terrain, signaling the role of the writer
as a chronicler of a catastrophe. If to write of an atrocity means to initiate
a form of a nonjudicial hearing, making the villains accountable for their
crimes, Omar's memoir does it particularly well.

The memoir's first seventeen chapters document the collapse of the
Afghan state and the downward spiral into a full-fledged urban war. Set
in the four years between the fall of the last socialist government (1992)
and the arrival of the Taliban (1996), the main part of the memoir offers
a macabre look into the deadly cartography of urban warfare, aimed at
dissecting the anatomy of violence and naming the perpetrators. The crisis takes the family and thousands of other families in Kabul off guard.
Having spent weeks in one room of the house while rockets rained on
their neighborhood, the family uses the few hours of ceasefire to flee to
the Fort of Nine Towers—a walled compound two miles away from their
home—and the residence of a family friend. Situated on the other side of
what becomes known to Kabulis as "snipers' hill," the fort is sheltered from
most of the rockets and from sniper fire. As they leave the house for the
first time in weeks, the family sees firsthand their city disfigured by war:

> What we saw, I will never forget. Thousands of people like us were tak-
> ing advantage of the ceasefire to flee from our part of the city. Thousands
> and thousands of people, all walking in near silence. [. . .]
>
> For the first time in two months since the fighting had started, all
> of us were seeing the destruction it had caused. [. . .]
>
> There were big craters in the road where rockets had fallen. This
> was the best road in Kabul. There were still many half-exploded rockets

standing in the middle of the road, like nails that had been banged half-way through a piece of wood.

Hundreds of dead bodies were scattered all over the pavement, on the sidewalks, and in the park in the middle of the road. Some looked like they had been there for a long time. Blood was matted all over their bodies. Most were on the main road. Maybe they had been hit by a rocket while they were trying to cross it. But many of them had been shot with bullets to the head, chest, or back. This was the work of the snipers. I could not believe my eyes; I thought I was seeing an American horror movie, especially when I saw parts of bodies, like arms and legs or even heads, lying by themselves. (40)

The main part of the memoir is a narrative of entrapment, the family learning to survive as refugees in the Fort, while their city is being destroyed. The family's predicament recalls Nixon's term "displacement without moving" (19)—a displacement that occurs not via migration but via a destruction of the conditions that sustain life in one's environment. This term, Nixon argues, is

a more radical notion of displacement, one that, instead of referring solely to the movement of people to their places of belonging, refers rather to the loss of the land and resources beneath them, a loss that leaves communities stranded in *a place stripped of the very characteristics that made it habitable*. [. . .] Such a threat entails being simultaneously immobilized and moved out of one's living knowledge as one's place loses its life-sustaining features. (19, emphasis my own)

Omar's family's immobilization and entrapment is accompanied by the removal of the very infrastructures that sustain life *beneath* them. As intense fighting continues, the family's wealth is looted. Hundreds of carpets warehoused by Omar's father in their family compound are stolen by armed militias (it takes days and multiple truckloads for the looting to be complete), and the compound itself is mined by a Hazara faction that controls the neighborhood. Macintosh apple orchards are destroyed by rocket-propelled grenades. Trees are cut and wooden beams are taken out of houses for firewood. Streets are emptied and littered with corpses by snipers who terrorize the city from the hills. Water pumps, telephone lines, electric supply infrastructure, banks, schools, and everything else that makes their neighborhood livable is destroyed.

Set in 1992, the memoir might have its reader recall the siege of
Sarajevo (concomitant with the battle over Kabul) and the unraveling of
Kashmir, another concomitant catastrophe, dramatized vividly by Salman
Rushdie's *Shalimar the Clown*. When considered in the context of the second decade of the 9/11 wars era, marked by the siege and destruction of
many cities, the memoir is chilling and timely; it gives the reader a glimpse
into what it means to be trapped in a city overcome by warring militants.
Fallujah—a city occupied by militants for two years—became a death trap
for the residents who did not manage to flee. On June 9, 2016, three weeks
prior to the city's liberation by the Iraqi army, an *Independent* correspondent reported on the population's plight:

> Families fleeing Fallujah have told how they were forced to eat animal
> food to stave off starvation during a brutal siege of the Isis-held city. A
> woman who managed to reach a refugee camp with her children said
> they moved from one home to another to avoid battles until they were
> caught in the crossfire. "We have witnessed tragedies that no one should
> ever witness," she said in an interview with the Norwegian Refugee
> Council.[17]

Omar's memoir reverberates with news reports from these cities—besieged,
occupied, utterly destroyed during the 9/11 wars era—Mosul, Raqqa,
Palmyra, Tikrit, Tripoli, Aleppo, and many others. Memory becomes multidirectional as remembering Kabul resonates with remembering Mosul,
casting a new light onto the Middle East destabilization in the aftermath
of the wars in Iraq, Libya, Syria, Afghanistan, and Yemen. Omar's account
of the siege of Kabul becomes especially gripping when he recalls three
failed missions from the Fort to the family compound to retrieve family
gold buried in the courtyard. Being the oldest son, Omar accompanies,
first, his grandfather, and on subsequent two missions, his father. Each
mission provides a glimpse into what it means to be caught in a gridlock
of urban warfare—a window into the horrors that, to use the words of a
woman from Fallujah, "no one should ever witness."

  During their first mission, ten-year-old Omar and his grandfather
are captured by Hazara fighters and brought into a courtyard of the house
that used to belong to their neighbors—a site where, Omar recalls, he
once attended a party with musicians playing. Omar recalls a chilling,
Conrad-esque sight:

In the center of the courtyard where the platform for the musicians had been, there was now a ditch filled with the heads of men and women. Dozens of them. I looked at them with their eyes open, staring at me with their shabby hair matted with blood. I started to vomit but controlled myself. (77)

The Hazara commander explains the slaughter to the horrified witnesses—an old man and a boy—who are frozen in anticipation of their own death:

"I want revenge." He said those words very slowly. His voice was getting higher and higher. "I want revenge! My whole family has been killed by Gulbuddin, Masoud, and Sayyaf [rival mujahideen commanders]. Their commanders raped my sister and my mother before they killed them. Do you know how I know that? They made me watch them! . . . [B]efore I die, I'll kill as many people as I can. I will rob them, rape them, and murder them," he said, getting even louder. (86)

Although Omar and his grandfather are unexpectedly released after the Hazara commander realizes he used to be Omar's father's boxing student, the memories of that day will haunt the narrator forever. The second failed mission to retrieve the family gold buried in their courtyard—an asset that would allow the family to get smuggled out of Afghanistan—results in an even more bone-chilling experience. As the brief ceasefire draws former residents of the neighborhoods to their houses to retrieve their possessions, or simply into the streets, they are captured and enslaved by another sadistic commander who uses their slave labor to build an underground tunnel to fortify the positions of his faction that controls the area. Omar and his father are caught and enslaved for several weeks, digging the earth in the darkness of the tunnel, chained to other captives, witnessing, day after day, scenes of unspeakable violence that Omar narrates in the calm, controlled voice of someone who gives testimony at a tribunal:

Days passed. The routine was the same every day. The commander and his men used the women during the night in the presence of all of us, and forced the men to work as slaves in the day. . . . Those who did not work were whipped like donkeys. . . . By the end of about two weeks, only seven men and two women were left besides us. (106)

The last surviving slaves are eventually liberated by another commander, who kills the sadistic militiaman, explaining that he was a convicted criminal, released when the mujahideen opened all the prisons in the city. Having returned to their family after several weeks of absence, Omar and his father do not share their experience with their loved ones. Omar, once again, hails the reader as the first witness to his story of the atrocity. He writes: "[My cousins] had no idea what had happened to me, and until now I have never told them, or anybody" (115).

Looking back at his childhood experiences of war, Omar calls this period in his life "living in the time of Shaitan, the devil" (227). Displacement without moving turns into actual dislocation as the family decides to flee Kabul and seek shelter in the countryside or smaller towns that are still free of war. Temporarily palliating the family's suffering, this road trip in the time of violence is eventful, terrifying, but also joyful, as the parents do their best to shield their children from seeing violence. The road trip offers a repertoire of positive, life-affirming images painting a breathtaking panorama of Afghanistan's ethnic and cultural diversity, and its natural beauty. The trajectory of the journey spans half a country—from Kabul to Mazār-i-Sharif to Tashkurgan to Bamyan to Kunduz back to Mazār-i-Sharif and Kabul—as the family flees war that continuously threatens to catch up with them. One of the journey's highlights for Omar is an experience of "living inside the Buddha's head"—in a cave made by ancient Buddhist monks behind the great Buddha statue in Bamyan (169).

During the long months of flight and homelessness, Omar recalls his family history of nomadism, framing their uprooted existence as the return to and a reenactment of their ancestral ways, embedding the idea of itinerant lifestyle as a new identity core—"[we were] modern nomads with a beat-up old car" (157). Exemplifying Banita's claim that a nomadic subject is a permanent "human contact zone," Omar finds that he is enriched by experiences of encountering others with lifestyles dramatically different from his own (223). While in Bamyan, the narrator befriends an old Buddhist monk living in one of the caves behind the great Buddha's head. Later, in Mazār-i-Sharif, he learns how to design and weave traditional carpets by spending time with a Turkoman family—knowledge he makes use of during the Taliban era as he starts a carpet-weaving factory. The family's modern nomadism eventually morphs into actual caravan-style travel when their car unexpectedly breaks down. As the family has no money left, they join a Kuchi caravan, staying with them for the next two months before returning to Kabul. Kuchi hospitality, aside from saving Omar's family from peril, offers them a glimpse into the lifestyle of their ancestors, some of whom were Kuchi nomads:

> We ate Kuchi bread-cake, spiced rice, kebab, and thick Kuchi-style yoghurt. I could see that my new uncles and cousins were very fond of meat. Amir Khan said a Pashto proverb as his mouth was full of kebab: "Even burnt meat is better than vegetables." And the rest laughed. After dinner we drank green tea and ate dried melon until midnight. In every sentence they used a proverb. Some of them started their sentences with a verse or two from a famous poet. (203)

As the war strips away the thin layer of modernity, a traditional Kuchi nomad lifestyle—one that follows the seasons in a slow-paced migration tried by centuries—proves more resilient than modern life. Through this experience, nomadism becomes incorporated into the narrator's identity: "we [are] Kuchis and wanderers by nature," Omar announces to his father toward the end of the book (358).

The time of Shaitan comes to a close unexpectedly with the arrival of the "strange" Taliban to Kabul in 1996 (281). Omar attends high school and later the Faculty of Journalism at Kabul University during the Taliban era. It will, no doubt, take decades to process the legacies of the mujahideen takeover and the Taliban rule. As Adam Klein writes in his Introduction to the collection of stories written by Afghans under age thirty, "The Taliban and the mujahideen are more prominent in this collection, more problematic than Americans or Russians, their legacies more contested" (xiii). Omar's account of the Taliban era is fascinating as he points to both the further losses incurred by the family ("We have no photos [because they were burned]" [9], and "I buried the ashes of my beloved books under a mulberry tree in the garden" [319]) and gains ("Now we had peace in Kabul, and we did not see blood and corpses and body parts on streets anymore" [286]). As Omar observes, Taliban-era Kabul was "strange, but stable" (359)—filled with the paradoxes brought forth by a theocratic rule, as well as the cultural difference between the ruled (residents of Kabul) and the rulers (graduates of rural madrassas, unaccustomed to city life). For the narrator's family, the Taliban brings a chance to recover from the poverty and strife brought on by the four years of war. Eighteen-year-old Omar divides his time between the small carpet-weaving factory he founded in the Fort and his studies at Kabul University:

For the next two years, I studied hard and worked hard. The credits I needed for my degree slowly accumulated, as did the profits from my carpet factory. The strange peace brought by the Taliban made it safe for foreign buyers to return to Kabul, and my sales increased. A woman might be beaten for leaving her home alone, but in other ways the Taliban regime provided a sense of security. Many things worked. The banks. The mail delivery. Offices. Safe transportation all over the country. (359)

The coming of the Taliban, in spite of their installment of an oppressive theocratic state system, thus marks the winding down of the disaster. The narrator seems to suggest that by 2001, the Taliban, by virtue of their day-to-day interactions with Kabul's residents, may have started to transform, perhaps losing some of their most radical traits. Omar describes teaching his Taliban classmates to read and write, to use the gym, and to play basketball:

A few of them quit being Taliban. They were not bad guys after all. They were just guys who wanted to have a chance in life. They wanted to marry Kabuli girls and to continue living in Kabul. We told them that they would have to share all the housework with their wives. At first, they thought we were making fun of them. Then they realized that we were serious. (363)

The memoir ends with a brief description of the 9/11 attacks—news that shocks Omar's family and puts a halt on their plan to leave the country. The memoir decenters the 9/11 attacks, presenting them as a gravitational wave that reaches New York nine years after the destruction of Kabul and the disaster of Afghanistan's complete implosion. The narrator observes:

Now the horrors that had filled our lives for so many years were happening even in America. We felt as if something had been taken away from us. "What hope can we have for Afghanistan if this is what is happening in America?" we asked each other. (364)

While Omar's family is deeply saddened by the global spread of violence, they see the attacks as a continuation of a tragic history rather than the beginning of a new era, unlike Giovanna Borradori's "the first historic world event in the strictest sense."[18] When the Taliban leave the city in anticipation of the American invasion, Kabul erupts into a party, with dancing and music. Omar writes: "Winter was approaching and the weather was turning cold. Daily life went on. We were so used to war. There was little left to be disrupted in Afghanistan" (369).

Nonhuman Witness

While Shamsie's and Omar's texts make ample use of an eyewitness (specifically, a long-term witness), Rahman's debut novel dramatizes the limits of eyewitnessing by staging its protagonist's incapacity to comprehend the events in which he takes part. The novel divests the human subject of its authority and import, suggesting that contemporary disaster has no eyewitness—is beyond what we conventionally refer to as witnessing—not because of its horrific nature, but because of its tremendous complexity and distributed qualities. Using analogies drawn from mathematics, theoretical physics, and finance, the novel dramatizes epistemological uncertainty, pointing to the limits of individual agency within an ambiguous moral universe where responsibility is widely distributed among not only individuals, but numerous overlapping systems and networks. The financial crisis of 2008 is placed in proximity to the War on Terror, bringing into relief the infinitely complex, dispersed, technical nature of both crises. Attempting to understand the disaster, Rahman seems to propose, is the task of a gifted mathematician trained in complex systems modeling—that is, if she knows all the facts. And all the facts, of course, are not known.

The novel's basic structure centers on a multi-week conversation between two friends—an unnamed narrator and his friend, Zafar, in the narrator's house in London. As Zafar is trying to process the events that took place when he was in Kabul in 2002, the narrator—an investment banker—is coming to terms with the financial crisis of 2008. It is Zafar—an Ivy league-trained mathematician-turned-human rights lawyer—who most poignantly exemplifies the insufficiency and the inadequacy of the eyewitness as he unwittingly gets drawn into the War on Terror in 2002 Kabul, indirectly causing loss of life yet emerging from it having understood nothing. The conspiracy he gets inadvertently conscripted into is orchestrated by at least two networks working in tandem—the American military and ISI (Pakistani intelligence agency), and although Zafar is able to reconstruct some of its logic in retrospect, the entire conspiracy, along with its contingencies, causes, and consequences, remains opaque. Both characters' personal lives are deeply affected by the events they take part in. Zafar's career and personal life, upon his return from Kabul, appear to be in shambles; similarly, the narrator's life is unsettled by the financial crisis—turned into a scapegoat by his partners in the firm, he is requested to appear in front of the congressional committee to be questioned about subprime mortgage industry protocols. Both characters ponder what personal responsibility means at a time when individuals function within complex networked systems that exceed their understanding; in doing so, they try to decide whether to condemn or absolve themselves of guilt. *In the Light of What We Know* has a distinct post-9/11 flavor, in that it communicates a sense of widespread crisis and emotional fatigue radiating from the novel's multiple centers of gravity. 9/11 itself is an event described only circuitously; similar to Shamsie's and Omar's texts, the novel evokes the attacks only to decenter them by focusing on other crises, such as the War on Terror and the 2008 financial crisis, which in turn frame the characters' personal unraveling. Instead of domesticating these crises, the novel intensifies them through defamiliarization, slowly and painstakingly rendering them more and more opaque.

The novel's formal aspects foreground epistemic uncertainty and ambiguity. Its maze-like structure is purposefully confusing, as it is composed of citations, flashbacks, fragments of Zafar's narration and excerpts from his journal, footnotes, and meandering dialogue between the two central figures. The novel's recursive-digressive structure leads the reader down many false paths. At the end, the text does not cohere into a plot that delivers all the answers, probing and thwarting the reader's expectations of finding out the truth. The basic story of Zahar's involvement in a conspiracy is reconstructed post factum by the narrator (who is also a mathematician), foregrounding the opacity in the heart of the disaster, and suggesting, perhaps, that mathematics is one of the tools that may give us an insight into the complexity of the contemporary condition. The novel itself is conspicuously featured as a technical construct—an obscure, unwieldy artifact that underscores its own constructed nature, at times offering too much (too many details to keep in mind, too many clues to follow, too many footnotes) or too little (not providing the answers in the end). The text includes an intimidating array of facts and data—on finance, law, mathematics, quantum physics, and world history—as if comprising an assemblage that forms a miniature model of the contemporary universe. The reader is conscripted into data mining and pattern recognition—for instance, into seeking a pattern among several long quotations that serve as epigraphs to each chapter—to deduce the possible meaning of what is to come. The vicissitudes of the reader's journey through the book parallels the strife of the protagonist, who, despite having a shrewd technical mind, cannot follow the permutations of his own journey.

Central to the text is the issue of knowing—what can and cannot be known—its evocation of "the unknown unknowns" referencing Donald Rumsfeld's famous epistemological exertions. In the post-9/11 context of the War on Terror, Rumsfeld distinguished, famously, between known unknowns and the unknown unknowns: "The idea of known and unknown unknowns recognizes that the information those in the positions of responsibility in the government, as well as other human endeavors, have at their disposal is almost always incomplete" (Rumsfeld xiv). The novel's epigraph—a quote from Sebald—announces the concern with truth-finding, as well as the truth's elusive nature: "Our concern with history [. . .] is a concern with preformed images imprinted on our brains, images at which we keep staring while the truth lies elsewhere, away from it all, somewhere as yet undiscovered" (1). This concern with truth, especially the hidden nature of it, is similarly signaled by Zafar's own sentiment: "In order to catch even a fleeting glimpse of the world, we must break with our familiar acceptance of it" (196). To journey into the realm of truth, one has to abandon the domain of the customary, routine, intuitive forms of comprehension. Further probing the limits of our epistemic drive, the novel returns, over and over, to Zafar's obsession with Gödel's Incompleteness Theorem. The Incompleteness Theorem brings into view the limits of mathematical reasoning: "[w]ithin any given system, there are claims which are true but which cannot be proven to be true" (11). The truth remains withdrawn; the world would remain nontransparent even to an omniscient mind (there are truths that cannot be proven). The Incompleteness Theorem resonates in powerful and problematic ways with Rumsfeld's assertion of the same point when formulating his preemption strategy: "[it is wrong to think that] if something could not be proven to be true, then it could be assumed not to be true" (xiv); "[instead we] need to prepare for the likelihood that we would be attacked by an unanticipated foe in ways we may not imagine" (xv). This resonance brings into view the interconnectedness of mathematics and contemporary warfare (a fact also emphasized by forensic architect Eyal Weizman).

These epistemological issues are woven into the novel's discussions of postcolonial history—such as the history of Bangladesh, where Zafar was born. Zafar is a postcolonial subject marked by the traumatic story of his conception. He is a child of rape that occurred during the Bangladesh Liberation War of 1971, during which, as the novel explains, many Bangladeshi women were raped by Pakistani soldiers. This traumatic origin story marks Zafar as a subject in search of personal redemption, as well as in a search for belonging. Brought up by adoptive immigrant Bangladeshi parents in a rat-infested basement apartment in England, Zafar's world is from the very beginning a migratory, nomadic one—the pattern he perpetuates in his adulthood defined by intercontinental travel and multiple migrations, becoming "a human being fleeing ghosts while chasing shadows" (16). The events of 2001 find Zafar in Bangladesh, where he works as a human rights lawyer. He gets conscripted into coming to Kabul where, he was assured, he "could make such a difference" (32), and he agrees in part because his British ex-girlfriend—now a prominent humanitarian worker in Kabul—insists that he come there. On his flight to Islamabad, he is assigned a seat near a Pakistani army colonel whose generous offer of hospitality in Islamabad he cannot refuse. Through tracing Zafar's experiences in Islamabad and Kabul, the novel weaves together postcolonial histories and the global War on Terror, illustrating Zafar's unique set of vulnerabilities that make him an easy target for Pakistani intelligence. The guests at the colonel's house party—all Pakistani military—earn Zafar's trust by complaining about the British and their imperialism, hint that Zafar is a "coconut" (a "South Asian who has become white in all but skin color" [321]), tease him for having a soft spot for the British elite, while at the same time hailing him as one of them: "You're one of us, dear boy. You're one of us. Welcome home" (321). Zafar's position in the world—his homelessness—makes him particularly vulnerable to both their benign criticism and the offer of instant belonging, to the extent that this makes him obey the colonel's enigmatic request before Zafar leaves for Kabul: "Find out what's in the envelopes" (328).

Both a privileged transnational knowledge worker and a postcolonial subject imperiled by his traumatic origin, he wants to do good but ends up following the infrastructure of the military-humanitarian networks laid out for him. Zafar's notebook suggests persistent anxiety about identity. He felt he belonged to "that buffer class of native informants" (375) and "lived beyond his psychic means" (358). His is a divided self; Zafar lives in a state of "continuing civil war" being "a man going forward as many selves contained in the same, shoulder to shoulder," "partitioned into people who hated each other, and to side with one was to scorn the other" (379). A part of him feels affinity with the British elite (his ex-girlfriend, Emily, belongs to a prominent aristocratic family), while another part feels that by associating with these elites, he is betraying his origins. In Afghanistan, these tensions become unbearable. Condemning the humanitarian workers whom he compares to hyenas who come to Kabul as if they smell meat in the air, he feels affinity with the residents—people who, like his mother and his adoptive parents, suffered personal injuries and historical injustice: "Something was gathering in me, as if armies had been summoned from all corners and the ground bore the first tremors of their approach. Now I might call them armies of injustice, humiliation, and defeat, but at the time I felt them as only the beginning of a kind of end" (388). Further, he writes, "I felt I wanted to apologize to someone, to the Afghanis [*sic*] here and there, the drivers waiting by the gates, the attendants, the cleaners and cooks, the staff, the servant class" (379). As it turns out, Zafar's psychic unraveling, his mounting hatred for Westerners in Afghanistan, and his bonding with the locals is predictable, and calculable, something that the Pakistani agents expect and know how to capitalize upon. He plays exactly the part written for him by the military, the script culminating in the bombing of the Café Europa minutes before his arrival there for a meeting with Crane, a military contractor and a minor player in the conspiracy, who is summarily eliminated through the bombing.

If on his way to Kabul, Zafar believed he understood a few things about Afghanistan and its tragedy, recasting in his mind some of the well-worn facts about the history of clashing imperialisms in the region, on the way back from Kabul he concedes that he, in fact, understands nothing.

> In the mess of Central Asia there are as many sides as there are opportunities to steal a match. There are no sides to tell us who is doing what, for whom, and why. There are only exigencies, strategies, short-term objectives, at the level of governments, regions, clans, families, and individuals: fractals of interests, overlapping here, mutually exclusive there, and sometimes coinciding. (481)

In Islamabad, the Pakistani army colonel explains some of the conspiracy plot details to Zafar, retrospectively filling in some of the blanks that Zafar had already deduced. The colonel emphasizes that he, Zafar, will not be harmed. However, many people *have been* harmed—specifically, a collateral damage in the Café Europa bombing orchestrated by the agencies to eliminate US contractor Crane. Zafar is aware of these deaths because he was in the proximity of the bombing, delayed by a few minutes by coordinated actions of the intelligence agency's proxies. He describes the scene:

> First came the sound. People crying, not women but men, a wailing, the sound of cries for God, *Hai-Allah* groans, and American voices on megaphones. [. . .] I felt sick, my gut convulsing like a caught fish. But what I remember most vividly is the sensation behind my eyes, an extraordinary pressure pushing my eyeballs out, as if they were no longer mine, as if my body were rejecting them. Did I want to cry or did I want to keep myself from crying? I wanted both. (473)

Through Zafar's unwitting involvement in the conspiracy, the novel dramatizes the degree to which an individual is exposed to military and paramilitary surveillance systems, while at the same time being oblivious to the complex infrastructures of control that track (and predict) one's actions in the post-9/11 universe. An individual's hyperexposure to these surveillance systems is at odds with her or his ability to comprehend the networked world—one that becomes progressively more opaque and impenetrable. Zafar is monitored and closely followed, all the minutia of his movements, all of his conversations transparent to the Pakistani military (and, likely, other military and intelligence networks as well). Once Zafar gets a glimpse of the complexity he is entangled in, he is overcome by an intellectual vertigo. Failures to know and understand—epistemological failures—result in events that cannot be remedied through individual action.

This nontransparency in the heart of the disaster is made even more poignant through a parallel Rahman draws between the War on Terror and the global financial crisis of 2008 triggered by the subprime mortgage crisis. The level of abstraction at the core of the contemporary finance system requires highly specialized, expert knowledge. Rahman explains the prehistory of the 2008 crisis expounding, for pages on end, how the very specific financial innovations going back to the 1989 Exxon Valdez environmental disaster (the oil spill in Alaska) laid the foundation for the contemporary crisis. Credit default swaps, synthesized securities, hedge funds, special investment vehicles, collateralized debt obligations, security tranches, equity tranches—"that stuff is so esoteric," says Zafar, "that the only people who understand it are in the business" (263). Within this system, the responsibility is widely distributed. The narrator says: "I feel no guilt for what I did in finance. [. . .] People will lose their homes, their jobs. But tell me how I can feel guilt for something that was not only legal but actively encouraged by governments everywhere" (38). With multiple individuals, firms, institutions, and governments implicated, how would one weigh one's own contribution to the disaster that ensued? In the narrator's own words, "How much *should* one foresee the consequences of one's own actions? And how much do other cases that combine with one's own actions, and thereby muddy one's role, exonerate one?" (51, emphasis in original). The novel then draws the War on Terror in Afghanistan and the infrastructure of global capitalism into an even tighter loop, noting the connection between the global financial system (the real estate bubble) and war financing: "[Suleiman] pointed out other houses, formerly belonging to Talibs but that had been acquired by Westerners for their rocketing market value, including diplomatic missions and their staff, whose real estate purchases had boosted Taliban funding. Property in 2002, even in Kabul, was booming, as it was the world over" (34). By bringing the two crises into proximity, the novel brings into view a tension between manifest violence and hidden terror, echoing Slavoj Žižek's distinction between subjective and objective violence: "The subjective violence of the real world, the violence that takes the form of mass murders, genocide, and rape, masks the underlying objective violence of capital, systemic, anonymous, that informs real-life developments and catastrophes throughout."[19] Subjective violence, such as a mass murder in Café Europa or the tragedy of a family losing a home, is observable by an eyewitness. Objective violence—the truly obscene violence—remains hidden, the visible disaster just a screen for larger subterranean processes that an individual cannot imagine or know.

To sum, the three texts in this chapter offer three types of witness—each of them serving as a lens through which to narrate and memorialize the Afghan crisis. Shamsie's long-term witness creates resonances between multiple historical catastrophes to amplify them, bringing the Afghan disaster into the orbit of global history. Omar's lasting entrapment in the very heart of the disaster offers another long-term witness—one able to provide an insightful take on the Afghan tragedy, foregrounding the importance of the functional state as the value most of us take for granted. Rahman underscores the permeability of Afghanistan's national borders, inscribing the Afghan disaster as one of the global crises that is opaque, resisting our epistemological thrust. In doing so, he exposes the limitations of eyewitnessing. Rahman's text suggests that a nonhuman witness, such as a mathematics that "like Spinoza's God, won't love us in return" (195), is an imperfect but valuable tool that gives one an insight into the nature of twenty-first-century catastrophes. All three texts offer powerful alternatives to the humanitarian mode of writing traumatic histories. They draw attention away from a human figure to infrastructures, conditions of possibility, and long-term and distributed processes. Shamsie and Omar foreground slow violence as processes of ruination that unfold over decades. Rahman's nonhuman witnessing, with its attunement to the complexity of contemporary warfare, decenters the human figure entirely. In the next chapter I will discuss Nadeem Aslam's work as further decentering the human by invoking the trope of deep time (as opposed to the short time span of human life) and by extending the notion of witness to nonhuman species and, ultimately, to the earth itself.

5

The Deep Time of War: Nadeem Aslam and the Aesthetics of the Geologic Turn

The Deep Turn

In a 2013 interview, Nadeem Aslam, a Pakistani British writer, explains that he prefers to write in multiple stages, with the entire first draft of each manuscript written by hand: "Words seem to be flowing from my mind into my hand, then down the pen, and onto the page—blood becoming ink" ("An Interview," par. 9). This statement exemplifies a complexity that characterizes his writing. Traversing the mind-body dualism by connecting together mind and hand, the sentence then converts blood into ink, the image of a reverse transubstantiation gesturing toward Aslam's magical, alchemical aesthetic. Moreover, the image of blood and ink summons Islamic history, specifically, the inscription in the House of Wisdom in Abbasid Baghdad that once read, "The ink of the scholar is holier than the blood of the martyr." This reference embeds Aslam's writing within the *longue durée* of the Islamic intellectual tradition. His writing's fluid movement between divergent realms and timescales positions him as a writer of the era of the Anthropocene—a concept that calls for vertiginous shifts in scale and binds humanity with the planet's history.[1]

The term "Anthropocene" was introduced in 2000 by Paul Crutzen and Eugene F. Stoermer to signify an era in which humankind becomes a geological force in its own right (17). It designates the era of large-scale human impact on Earth's ecosystem as well as the blowback that will result in the form of unforeseen consequences and future risks neither calculable in advance nor preventable in the long term. Tobias Boes and Kate Marshall observe that the term "Anthropocene" brings attention to the presence of human traces in Earth's stratigraphic record as a form of "writing," the unique geological signature of human presence on Earth (62). In turn, the Anthropocene and the public debates surrounding it influence literary production in numerous ways, placing a premium on what Adam Trexler calls climate change fiction (5). In this chapter, I extend the line of Boes and Marshall's inquiry by asking, what would it mean to write about humanitarian disaster in the new geologic era? How does the new Anthropocene aesthetic inform and influence the writing of traumatic histories? In what follows, I return to Aslam's work as exemplifying what I call the aesthetics of the geologic turn—an aesthetics that draws on the sensibilities and imagery that have emerged in the era of the debates about the Anthropocene. More specifically, I address how Aslam stages a new mode of writing traumatic histories by examining, in his two post-9/11 novels, the four decades of war in Afghanistan, dramatizing the proximity of human and nonhuman suffering as well as bringing into focus the geological signature of contemporary warfare.

At first glance, the rhetoric of climate change and the documentation of human suffering in distant zones of conflict seem entirely unrelated. Yet, the new set of concepts, images, metaphors, and frameworks that developed around issues of climate and environment are bound to change the way we see warfare from our post-anthropocentric, post-9/11 moment. Contemporary warfare must be addressed as a dramatic instance of terraforming, a force that changes habitats for both humans and nonhumans: redefining inter- and intraspecies relationships, affecting established ecologies, and enabling new forms of slow and fast violence.[2] The multispecies ecology of war must become a field of study and concern. The hunt for Osama bin Laden revealed how birds can become instruments of warfare. When birdsong was heard on a bin Laden video released after September 11, 2001, ornithologists were consulted to determine his location.[3] Birds threaten planes and are themselves threatened during the time of war when the skies fill with fighter jets and bomber aircraft. Bountiful orchards (as in the case of Jalalabad orchards in Afghanistan) and entire forests are cut down to provide heat for refugees fleeing zones of violence.[4] Aslam's work in particular exemplifies how the new mode of writing war in the era of the Anthropocene must also reframe the questions of witnessing and the mediation of suffering by drawing in the nonhuman as witness to the disaster, mediating our knowledge, and providing evidence that adds to established forms of witness, such as testimonial and forensic modes.

Born in Pakistan, Aslam moved to England when his father—a communist—had to flee Zia's dictatorship in 1980. Bilingual and bicultural, Aslam has devoted his career to exploring South Asian Muslim identities and histories. Having emerged as a postcolonial writer with his first novel, *Season of the Rainbirds*, Aslam has grown into a global novelist with his midcareer *Maps for Lost Lovers*—a novel that traces the shifting landscape of radicalism, memory, and trauma in South Asian immigrant communities in England. Drawing on a planetary dimension while writing about localized histories of violence and conflict, *Maps* testifies to its author's commitment to exploring traumatic histories as exemplifying and inseparable from larger global processes. Yet, it is Aslam's two latest novels, *The Wasted Vigil* and *The Blind Man's Garden*, that make visible his impact in forging a new vocabulary for writing about the conflicts of the post-9/11 era, which is, coincidentally, the era of the debate on the Anthropocene. United by a set of common themes and aesthetic sensibilities, both novels trace the lives of characters caught in the mayhem of war in Afghanistan some time after the beginning of the coalition-led operation of 2001. Refraining from victimization of their characters, the novels depict human suffering and violence as part of a larger geological and social landscape defined by human and nonhuman forces. In *The Wasted Vigil*, Aslam's portrayal of the conflict in Afghanistan is refracted through the prisms of geology and archeology, with the overarching motifs of earthwork (excavation, unearthing, burying) dominating the plot. Characters' interactions with the earth bring into view the earth as a medium of memory where it serves as a conductor of messages from the deep past and into the deep future. *The Blind Man's Garden* continues the project of writing by way of the earth, further incorporating the geologic and the lithic into the story of the war. While *The Wasted Vigil* is set entirely in Afghanistan, *The Blind Man's Garden* is a cross-border novel set in an area spanning northwest Pakistan and southeast Afghanistan, which effectively suspends the boundaries of nation-states by revealing the two countries' deep historical, cultural, and ecological connections.

These novels' attention to the earth as a medium and a witness exemplifies a larger set of sensibilities that I call the aesthetics of the geologic turn. The geologic turn designates the surge of interest in geology and earth sciences that has recently swept through many disciplines in the humanities.[5] More specifically, the geologic turn crystallized around the idea of deep time, "a domain of inquiry that extends millions of years into the past" (Shryock and Smail ix). Key works by Wai Chee Dimock, who proposed the deep time framework for the study of literature, and media theorist Siegfried Zielinski, who offered a vision of deep media studies in the *longue durée*, have been followed by a multitude of texts that use the concept of deep time to open up new perspectives or reinvigorate established fields. In media studies, Zielinski's concept of deep media was extended by Jussi Parikka to carve out a new area of study—the geology of media—that takes interest in the geological substratum of media (the rare earths and metals that are used to make it) and the geological "afterglow" of e-waste (60). Similarly, the deep turn in sound studies bolstered the field through the study of "long sounds," as well as by drawing attention to the earth and the ocean as material mediums of sound conduction (Khan, *Earth Sound, Earth Signal* 162). Andrew Shryock and Daniel Lord Smail extend the study of human history into deep time by proposing a distinction between recorded history and deep history. In contrast with text-based recorded history, deep history requires working with nontextual forms of evidence. Bones, genes, and the brain become deep history's data: "Histories can be written from every type of trace, from the memoir to the bone fragment and the blood type" (13). Moreover, the study of deep human history makes obvious that it is intertwined with the deep past of other species, whereby human-nonhuman "coevolutionary spiral[s]" (19) expose what Thomas R. Trautmann and colleagues have called "deep kinships" that complicate our notions of the boundaries between species (160).

The deep turn in the humanities takes advantage of the new geological sensibility of the Anthropocene while also incorporating and extending the idea of *longue durée*, a framework proposed by Fernand Braudel in 1958 for the study of history. Working within the *longue durée* frame in world-systems analysis allows a historian to detect patterns emerging over centuries and sometimes over millennia instead of focusing on rapidly changing events occurring within a short chronological span.[6] For Zielinski, who describes the history of media as unfolding over thousands of years, deep time is largely synonymous with the *longue durée*.

By contrast, Parikka—who is interested in the geological substratum of media—extends the term "deep time" into geological time, incorporating the slow geological scale in the study of fast-paced contemporary media. In his *A Geology of Media*, recorded human history (thousands of years) is placed into dialogue with immeasurably long geological cycles (delivered through layers of rock) spanning millions and billions of years, provoking imagination by triggering, as Jeffrey Jerome Cohen puts it, "the vertigo of the non-human scale" (24). Dimock similarly positions deep time as recessional frames or scalar expansions ranging from the scales traditionally associated with the *longue durée* to geological timescale. From the geological standpoint, deep time is seen as a vertical compression—its dominant image being not the timeline, but the stratigraphic column. As Shryock, Trautmann, and Gamble observe, geological time is "neither linear nor cyclical but vertical and layered. It must be dug into rather than traced with a finger or walked as a timeline. Deep time presents itself as sequentially compressed slabs composed of different materials, both organic and inorganic; it is compacted, oppressively heavy, and impenetrable; it is hidden from public view" (26–27). A vertically presented layering of organic and inorganic deposits, geological time extends human history into the history of the earth and the universe. Deep time in the geological sense requires a dramatic scaling up—more intense than in studies concerned with the *longue durée*—but involves more than just the issue of scale. The dug-up vertical slab reveals a partial, deeply flawed record that appears to be nonlinear (with older layers folded into or intruding on the newer layers), containing fissures and breaks with entire eras missing altogether. It can thus function as a figure for a nonlinear model of time resonant with many contemporary interests in the humanities (parallel modernities, history as recurrence, multiple temporalities embedded within each historical moment, and so on).

What does it mean to write about human-made catastrophes and traumatic histories in a deep time framework—a framework that brings attention to the recursive cycles of acting and being acted on, the interlacing of geological, evolutionary, and recorded histories? What kind of optical shifts does this transition entail? First and foremost, this new framework brings into focus the issue of material memory, in which envisioning new forms of memorialization and recovery must go beyond the language-mediated therapeutic model—a model prevalent in conceptualizing traumatic histories since Cathy Caruth and Dori Laub. In Aslam's novels, excavation is not just a metaphor for truth-seeking, but a material practice that resists translation into psychological work (or psychoanalytically informed terminology). Second, describing humanitarian crises often involves representing fast violence that takes place within the short chronology of war. By contrast, writing traumatic histories in deep time should incorporate slow violence, "a violence that is neither spectacular nor instantaneous, but rather incremental and accretive, its calamitous repercussions playing out across a range of temporal scales" (Nixon 2). Finally, as this chapter will demonstrate, accounts of witnessing and mediation must extend into nonhuman traumatic histories, thus decentering the human figure. War must be viewed as impacting not only humans or nations, but multispecies habitats, too—it is a multispecies ecology.

Imagining Afghanistan in Deep Time

More often than not, Afghanistan is featured as a landscape of extinction. What is old (that is, what was destroyed a long time ago) and what is new (that is, what has been turned into rubble and dust only recently) are not easy to distinguish. Shortly after the start of Operation Enduring Freedom in the fall of 2001, then-Secretary of Defense Donald Rumsfeld described Afghanistan as "not a 'target rich environment,' either militarily or symbolically."[7] In contrast to the war in Iraq that would follow, with the images it produced of toppling monuments and stunning air strikes, Afghanistan crossed into mainstream visibility as a land that was impoverished to such a degree that there was nothing to apply a spectacular act of violence to, nothing left to destroy. To paraphrase Freud, who discusses the "horror of nothing to see" in relation to femininity (Irigaray 26), Rumsfeld, it seems, was presented a similar horror: a war with a country with nothing left to bomb. Preempting Rumsfeld by less than a year, Lynsey Addario, a war photographer who traveled to Taliban-ruled Afghanistan in 2000, wrote, "Afghanistan looks bombed out even when it hasn't been bombed" (103). Similarly, texts discussed in chapter one featured the country as a depleted terrain that serves as a stage for the loss of humanity, a landscape so dark that Joseph Conrad would have been envious. In *The Swallows of Kabul*, Yasmina Khadra writes, "Kabul! Hidden amidst the wreckage of her avenues, she seems at best a tragic joke" (110), and later, "There's nothing to see, except for utter dereliction, and nothing to hope for" (112). In *Homebody/Kabul*, Tony Kushner echoes: "The streets are as bare as the mountains now, the buildings are as ragged as mountains and as bare and empty of life, there is no life here only fear" (23). To these onlookers, Afghanistan appears to be a land without history, flat Earth containing nothing but rubble, minefields, and shallow graves, capable of producing nothing but dust. Discussing the Taliban's detonation of the Buddha statues in the Bamyan Province—arguably, the last "target rich" locale—Zahid Hussain observes that Afghanistan is a land with no past (38). Afghanistan is similarly evoked as a signifier of negative heritage by Pakistani writer Hasan Altaf, who exclaims, "At least we in Pakistan are not yet blowing up our Buddhas."[8]

Yet could it be that the lack of visible targets—for a bomber plane or a photographer—conceals the wealth of submerged history, perhaps inaccessible to militarized cultural optics? Could it be that, by presenting an agglomeration of images of desolation, these onlookers fail to properly register and decipher the evidence these ruins contain of long histori- cal processes of fast and slow violence? In the context of recent writing about Afghanistan, Aslam's approach is unique as it undoes the discourse of impoverishment by summoning the land's hidden riches. Aslam's writing—lyrical and infused with geological and archeological details— produces new optics for regarding landscapes of loss and a unique way of writing the disaster. In contrast to the flat-Earth imagery—flat because it has no landmarks and no history—Aslam works with depth, excavating the deep memory stored in the land's stony archive. If stones for Addario and Rumsfeld are silent and poor, for Aslam the stones are expressive and eloquent. His lithic cartographies trace destinies of Afghanistan's famous gems and uncover the deep meaning of insignificant rocks. Engaging trau- matic stratigraphy as a mode of excavating memory, Aslam's deep time framework renders simultaneous the deep past and the present, modern fossils and ancient relics. His books argue, ultimately, against a narrow national focus that foregrounds Afghanistan's material and symbolic pov- erty as a nation-state devastated by half a century of war in favor of a deep time approach that excavates inter- and intracontinental connections. They make visible the dense enmeshment and interlacing of human and nonhu- man histories, and restore Afghanistan to its role as a rich, inexhaustible node in planetary interconnection.

In *The Wasted Vigil*—a novel that I already discussed, briefly, in chap- ter three—Aslam examines Afghanistan's history through four central characters from different corners of the world: Marcus, an elderly British doctor; Lara, a Russian widow in search of her brother who went missing during the Soviet-Afghan War; David, a retired CIA agent; and Casa, a young fundamentalist and orphan who grew up in an Afghan refugee camp. This international cast of characters allows Aslam to draw attention to the global nature of the conflict in Afghanistan and, especially, to the often overlooked role of the West in the Afghan tragedy. Marcus, who has been in Afghanistan longer than the other characters, says, "But, you see, the West was involved in the ruining of this place, in the ruining of my life. There would have been no downfall if this country had been left to itself by those others" (64). The novel abstains from assigning blame, however; each invasion, in Aslam's narrative, inflicts trauma both on the Afghans and the intruders—a trauma from which recovery is difficult—creating, as I mentioned, a "kinship of wounds" (318).

The Blind Man's Garden extends the project of examining Afghanistan's conflict by shifting attention to the areas on both sides of the contested Durand Line spanning southeast Afghanistan and northwest Pakistan.[9] Known as FATA (the Federally Administered Tribal Areas), the region has a long history of being represented as ungovernable and prone to violence, having been the site of a massacre of 16,000 British troops during the first Anglo-Afghan War of 1838. The novel explores Afghanistan's tragedy as seen from Pakistan, as the book's multiple Pakistani characters are drawn into the quagmire of the post-9/11 war in Afghanistan. The story centers on Mikal, who is trying to find his way home from Afghanistan to the town of Heer, Pakistan. His journey takes on epic proportions, mapping the landscape of Operation Enduring Freedom—a landscape defined by the fleeing but still dangerous Taliban, the warlords regaining power, American detention camps and torture, bombed-out valleys, weapon-trading villages, and other paraphernalia of war—all of which is placed in the horizon of deep time, both deep human history and geological history. Throughout the novel, Mikal's character in particular is framed by the deep time of liberal Islam—the Islam of the golden age—with its love of science and, in particular, astronomy. The slow gyration of the sky that Mikal knows how to read, and the deep geological time of the landscape he inhabits, makes him appear larger than life, giving him an aura of invincibility. During the last part of his journey, he has two fellow travelers whom he rescues—a wounded US Navy SEAL and a snow leopard cub—signifying the interlacing of US and Pakistani national histories as well as bringing into focus interspecies connections.

Memory as Material Excavation

Dimock proposes that deep time be understood as "a set of longitudinal frames, at once projective and recessional, with input going both ways, and binding continents and millennia into many loops of relations, a densely interactive fabric" (3–4). Deep time is thus presented as a connective tissue and a medium of lasting attachments, nonlinear as well as constitutive of many asynchronous nodes of association. Dimock proposes "restoring" American literature to deep time (4); we should ask, in turn, what does the term "restoring" entail? And what would it mean to restore Afghanistan to deep time? Deep time, Dimock maintains, "nourishes a politics as well as an aesthetics: a devotion to ancient beauty that can lend itself to the charge of treason" (123). The charge of treason, no doubt, is a result of the unfaithfulness induced by the vertigo of deep time—unfaithfulness to conventional chronology and unfaithfulness to the nation. One of the consequences of Aslam's restoring Afghanistan to its deep past is doing away with the recent boundaries of the nation-state. Nations have not only spatial but also temporal borders; as we move back in time, these borders eventually disappear and there emerges a world of blurry boundaries, shifting alliances, the movements of conquering and conquered armies, and radiant centers of power.

Disinterested in the logic of the nation, Aslam develops a vision that is both paleoscopic and syndetic, attuned to the logic of interconnectedness that exists in deep time. "At any given moment," he writes, "we are entangled in all the past of mankind. Our hearts encircled by the echo of every word that has ever been spoken" (*Blind Man's Garden* 190). In the two novels, Aslam works with several vast archives that constitute Afghanistan's deep past, incorporating them into the narrative of its recent history dramatized through the characters and plot. The first "recessional frame," or archive, is one of tricontinental Islam with its great cities (Dimock 3). To use Dimock's words, it is an "archive dating back a millennium" (1). In fact, the Islamic world system emerged between 1000 and 1500 AD, although one can also trace its advent to the glorious days of the eclectic and cosmopolitan Umayyads, who moved the capital of the Muslim world from Mecca to multicultural Damascus around 685 AD.[10] In *The Blind Man's Garden*, the house in north Pakistan (which also serves as a school for boys) figures as a material signifier of the deep time of Islam. Before building the foundation, Rohan, the school's founder, collected the soil from the six great cities of Islam—Mecca, Baghdad, Cordoba, Cairo,

Delhi, and Istanbul—and planted it in the garden, each room thus built on a mixture of Pakistani soil and the soil of one of the six cities. The mixing of the soils, the act of transplanting, signifies interpenetration and the crosspollination of cultures (which each of these cities also, in fact, represents). Rohan's house in the novel is an unstable metaphor of belonging but also of exile and violent displacement, a contested site connoting both roots and uprootedness. Envisioned by Rohan as a house of knowledge (representing the ink of the scholar), the school later becomes the breeding ground of militant Islamism (representing the blood of the martyr). Rohan, the school's founder, is evicted from its grounds.

The multiple temporal scales in Aslam's work can be compared to discrete orbits. The slow orbit of the *longue durée* time of Islam draws the characters into its gyrational movement, imbuing them with gravity. Behind each character there is a multitude of relevant pasts; in fact, each character is a host of stories and lives lived before him or her. While some, such as Rohan, draw strength from Islam's cosmopolitan history, others dream of martyrs and armies. Rohan's son, Jeo, who travels to Afghanistan in the aftermath of 9/11 to help the wounded only to be killed in an anti-Taliban raid within days, remembers hearing stories of martyrs as a child: "the ghostly thousands stretching back through the generations [,] and as he slept they imparted things to him not just of life and death but of eternal life and death" (*Blind* 12). Beyond tricontinental Islam, there is yet another orbit and an archive of even deeper histories: the archive of Eurasia. Drawn into the orbit of Eurasian history, Afghanistan's past enters a new recessional frame, within which it appears as a node in the network of ancient merchant economies, such as the history of the Silk Road. While the previous frame is indifferent to Afghanistan's pre-Islamic past, drawing it into the orbit of Mecca, this new frame brings its pre-Islamic past into relief, drawing Afghanistan into the orbit of the Ganges and ancient Tibet. In *The Wasted Vigil*, Marcus—in the process of digging up an underground chamber for his perfume factory—uncovers a fifteen-foot-tall carved head of the Buddha lying on its side. Too large to move, the head is left where it was found; the life of the factory simply happens around it, installing a "face from another time" into the fabric of the present (17). The Buddha gestures toward the region's Buddhist heritage (second to seventh centuries)—the past that came under attack in the Taliban's war on stones in 2001 when the ancient, 150-foot-tall Buddha statues in the province of Bamyan were dynamited in an act of iconoclastic violence. The Buddha's head discovered underground is a portal to Afghanistan's history in the *longue durée*, a signal received from a pre-Islamic era—an asynchronous bond between distant eras reasserting itself during the time of the Taliban-induced strife. Buddha's head signifies a part of the past that is indestructible; it comes alive when the Taliban attempt to destroy it, gold rays of light streaming from the bullet holes, chasing the attackers away. The Taliban's war against the stony archive, their desire to extinguish the material traces of the past, gestures to the agency of such found remnants, their function as doorways into alternative historical paths not taken yet still possible. The opposite of the ideological foreclosure induced by the Taliban's iconoclasm, these remnants open up the past. Afghanistan's Buddhist heritage heralds the potentiality of Buddhism-to-come, a Buddhist path neither exhausted nor diminished by the subsequent layers of history, being still active and vibrant with energy. Extending Bergson's theory of duration, Elizabeth Grosz theorizes deep time as an energy reserve of a sort, never depleted. She writes that

> every actual present is subtended by the virtual entirety of the past. So deep time, the time of the universe's unfolding, the construction of the earth and all that appears on it, the eruption of life forms, all the momentous and unpredictable emergences never cease; they function both as an historical horizon but also as *unspent forces*, forces whose effects have not been used up by all the time that has separated the present from its primordial past. (133, emphasis my own)

The deep time of Afghanistan arrives intact through the wreckage and debris, revealing a landscape of riches testifying to its remarkable history as a node in a trans-Eurasian network spanning many thousands, even millions, of years, dating back to the great migration of ancient humans from Africa into Asia and beyond.[11]

Although Aslam's Afghanistan is, unmistakably, a land after mass extinction—a ruined place—the images of depletion and exhaustion are juxtaposed with images of agency and potency stored in the remnants of the past. The past is presented as an active potentiality, imbued with energy—sometimes toxic or deadly (as when one uncovers a landmine or a water source contaminated by depleted uranium) or sometimes nourishing and vibrant. Forging a form of memory that is palimpsestic, the novels' ethos calls for the incorporation of all the preserved layers, from the very old to the very recent.[12] *The Wasted Vigil* presents Afghanistan's recent history as a vertical column with historical layers sitting compressed on top of each other (a stratigraphic column of a sort): "Afghanistan had collapsed and everyone's life now lies broken at different levels within the rubble. Some are trapped near the surface while others find themselves entombed deeper down, pinned under tons of smashed masonry and shattered beams from where their cries cannot be heard by anyone on the surface" (29). Afghanistan's history, for Aslam, thus needs to be handled through a process of excavation—through the unearthing of material objects and bodies trapped at various levels. Such excavation is an ethical imperative (that is, the cries from the deep layers need to be heard); excavation and restoration here take the place of testimony as a mode of handling traumatic history. The layer of deposits associated with Taliban rule contains buried art and media objects—audiotapes, books, paintings, family photographs—everything prohibited by the iconoclastic regime. Aslam refers to buried audiotapes found in Marcus's garden as "sound fossils" (16), thus insisting, rhetorically, on a certain simultaneity of the recent and the deep past. The Taliban's era is best presented and understood through what the regime has buried and tried to render extinct. Memory has to be recovered from the fossils, which entails the material labor of clearing earth and caked mud to reveal the objects underneath. Such work in Aslam's novels is done with great attention and focus. A layer of mud that conceals the murals on the walls of Marcus's house (he covered them up during the Taliban era) is now being slowly removed, piece by piece; it will take years to perform this work with a level of care that does justice to the concealed past. The Soviet-Afghan War era left its own residue of fossils: rusting tanks, scraps of metal identifiable by their Cyrillic inscriptions, landmines, and contaminated land. In a striking scene in *The Blind Man's Garden*, Mikal, hypothermic and near death as he struggles to find his way home, stumbles on a field of abandoned Soviet fighter jets: a sea of rusting carcasses resembling prehistoric birds, a burial ground of extinct technology. In a moment of ingenuity prompted by his survival instinct, Mikal then turns the airplanes into fuel by setting them on fire, one by one, their rubber interiors providing him temporary warmth as they go aflame. Remnants of the extinct war, these rusted jets literally become fossil fuel, their unspent bits of energetic value extracted by fire.

Aslam shows how the US-led invasion is creating its own deposits—an archive of deadly media—in the form of unexploded cluster bombs, depleted uranium contaminants, and more prosaic traces in the form of American footprints in the mud, recognizable by their large size: "the soles of several boots have left deep imprints on the muddy ground of the bend. America is everywhere. The boots are large as if saying, 'This is how you make an impression in the world'" (*Blind* 129). The progress of Operation Enduring Freedom is made visible as well through the shaved-off beards of escaping Al-Qaeda militants as they appear in the water many miles downstream—woolly messages sent down the river. In *The Wasted Vigil*, as if attempting to counteract the toxic deposits of war by leaving something of value, David begins building a Native American-style canoe (a technology 14,000 years old) on Marcus's property: a gift from American deep time, an image of transplantation. To preserve it Marcus drowns the canoe in the lake, hiding it from view and instantly fossilizing it for future Afghan generations to discover.

Lithic Cartographies

Aslam's aesthetics of the geologic turn is most visible in his use of imagery that draws on the petrous, creating vast cartographies of human-lithic enmeshments. The writer refers to historical processes as "[r]ivers of lava emerging onto the surface after flowing many out-of-sight miles underground" (*Wasted* 272). Lava is a paradoxical image: rock in its liquid state, actively forming (and terraforming), creating conditions for the formation of emeralds and rubies as it cools down[13]—objects that are then capable of setting in motion artisanal miners, instigating envy, and financing wars.[14] In *A Thousand Years of Nonlinear History*, Manuel DeLanda attests, similarly, "From the point of view of energetic and catalytic flows, human societies are very much like lava flows; and human-made structures (mineralized cities and institutions) are very much like mountains and rocks: accumulations of materials hardened and shaped by historical processes" (55). For both DeLanda and Aslam, geology is not simply a source of metaphors for writing about human life; geology, whether it is understood as a landscape, a source of energy, or the process of mineralization, is an active force that contributes to shaping human history—nonlife forming alliances with life.

Both novels feature stories of gemstones that, having originated in the depths of the earth hundreds of millions of years ago, have rich pasts that both precede humans and overlap with human history. Through these gems, multiple epochs are bound together. Cartographies that trace the life of a gem uncover multiple relations distributed in space and time. This relation-generating capacity of stones has been noted by Cohen, who observes that stones can lead to a "proliferation of relations most obvious over long distance" (24). *The Wasted Vigil* invokes a story of the famous diamond Koh-i-Noor ("Mountain of Light" in Persian)—a gem so precious it warranted its own name. Having originated in India, the fabled diamond changed hands many times. Its owners include Babur, an empire builder who conquered Afghanistan and India and established the Mughal Empire in 1526; a Persian shah, Nader Shah, who captured Koh-i-Noor and brought it to Persia in 1739; and later an Afghan emir, Ahmad Shāh Durrānī, who came into possession of the stone in 1747. As Durrānī is credited with founding the Afghan state that same year, Koh-i-Noor can be viewed as the foundation stone for Afghanistan as a modern state. Eventually ending up in Queen Victoria's crown, the diamond remains in England, weaving together the multiple forces that ruled over and passed through the land that is now Afghanistan.[15] A witness to interimperial rivalries and conquests no single human could witness, the gem did not emerge from this turbulent history unscathed, its size diminished from the original 793 to 105 carats due to multiple cuttings and polishings to increase its luster. Having invoked Koh-i-Noor, Aslam then introduces his own equivalent of the legendary gem: a miniature spinel attached to one of the metal plates inside David's watch. Similar to Koh-i-Noor, the spinel is a stone that travels; weaving distant continents together, it recalls and reveals the cartographies of the Cold War era. Having originated in Afghanistan, the spinel was brought to Vietnam inside the watch that belonged to David's brother, who had been drafted and killed in the Vietnam War. Having inherited the watch, David brought it back to Afghanistan during his CIA days. Posing as a gem merchant, he sought to avenge his brother's death by helping to organize the anti-Soviet jihad (the Soviet "Vietnam"), while also tracing the history of the precious stone. A material medium of memory, the lasting gem thereby ties David's family history to geopolitical history and to the deep geological time of the earth's productivity.

Stones thus become vehicles of communication between asynchronous generations, as well as mediating distant epochs. A gem exhibits an especially strong binding force because of the particular qualities that enable it to enter into human history, becoming an integral part of it: "A diamond becomes a precious gem because its rarity, lucidity, and density can sustain strong confederation with human and inhuman forces, tools, economic and aesthetic systems—coalitions friable stones cannot support" (Cohen 33). In *The Blind Man's Garden*, larger lithic landscapes frequently are invoked to reframe our understanding of the post-9/11 moment in Afghanistan. In the passage below, Peshawar Valley figures as a vertiginous landscape, a petrified signifier of the maelstrom of the post-9/11 universe. Elderly Rohan travels through it with the ancient ruby in his pocket, grieving for his son lost to war just days prior, and thus willing to help a stranger whose son has just been kidnapped and held for ransom by an Afghan warlord. Serving as a stage for contemporary human tragedy unfolding in real time, the landscape also reveals traces of a remote catastrophe—one that predates humans— the changing of places of land and water: "The valley of Peshawar has the appearance of having been, centuries ago, the bed of a vast lake, whose banks were bound by the cliffs and peaks of the surrounding Himalayas, and Rohan has the feeling of being submerged within that vast inland sea" (111). The lithic landscape is a time machine, transporting Rohan into the prehistoric times when the valley was underwater. The valley is not just a human cemetery, but also a graveyard for other life-forms, plants and animals, now extinct in this area—an ancient seabed, rich in fossils. The present is rendered simultaneous with the past via a rock, submerging and drowning him, the two catastrophes appearing concurrent. The passage then draws the reader into an even thicker agglomeration of lithic imagery focusing on the shapes of the rocks as cocreated by natural and human forces, the immemorial effort of currents echoed by the engravings of the Quran:

> He crosses the road and enters the graveyard that contains about a hundred souls, a few decaying tombs and thorn trees. The mountains loom overhead vertiginously, the land and slopes marked with evidence of the lost sea, the effort of currents, waves, springs, streams and rivers. Verses of the Koran are on every headstone—as though the graves are quoting them, carrying on a conversation with one another using nothing but holy words. (111)

Rohan's personal tragedy (the loss of his son) is mirrored by the landscape, which contains vestigial memory of many catastrophes—the eternal dance of ocean and land as they change places over millennia. Extinctions and erosions are followed by periods of recovery, in which the landscape is reclaimed by life:

How did Mikal's body end up here? The mayhem and chaos of war. He looks up at the cliffs. The vegetation everywhere is profuse; after the level of the sea decreased this was a tropical marsh, the resort of rhinoceros, flamingo and tiger, thick with reeds, rushes and conifers. Under his breath he reads the verse of the Koran that is etched onto the ruby. Wealth and offspring are transitory adornments of the nearer life. (113)

Repeatedly, and with great insistence, the passage moves from a description of landscape to linguistic inscriptions and back again, making obvious that language achieves its lasting quality by entering an alliance with a stone; this renders it a material part of the landscape, a palimpsestic plate in its own right. Quranic verses are carved into stone just as the streams and rivers carved passageways through the rock: both an intricate calligraphy, both a material presence capable of affecting, as well as being affected by, the humans entering the landscape. The catastrophe that shaped the landscape a long time ago rendered extinct many life-forms; the contemporary catastrophe creates a new layer of extinction over the ancient one, insignificant by comparison. The inscription on the ruby is ironic; while gesturing toward the impermanence of wealth represented by the ruby, it mocks the human life span. It is Rohan who is a transient adornment of the gem, not vice versa; the ruby, whose luster speaks of the deep time of the Himalayas, will soon change hands, continuing its journey through human history, while Rohan will perish, his gravestone his only durable mark. A lasting mode of memory and an object of multigenerational attachments, stones are ancient media forging connections, creating kinship across time and space. A wondrous palimpsest of three forces—earth's work, divine creativity (the Quranic verse), and human craft—the ruby creates a kinship between Rohan and the poor man whose son he saves with his precious stone.

Aslam's lithic cartographies are deep maps—contemporary characters follow ancient routes of migration, travel, and trade, disregarding recent borders as mere fictions. Rendered simultaneous in deep time, the past and present are placed in conversation with each other. Seen from the scale afforded by the stone, Afghanistan emerges not as modernity's failure, but as a source of worth, enabling a lasting economy of stones and creating continental connections. Uniquely rich in rocky matter, Afghanistan's land produces rubies, spinels, diamonds, and lapis lazuli, among others. This productivity is only visible when the scale is large enough to both incorporate societies that developed their economies along the Silk Road and include the geological time of the earth's productivity. The two nonhuman registers—the slow timescale of the earth (the time it takes to produce gems) and the rapid regrowth of flowers—frame the middle register of the human in Aslam's world, the register that is seen as particularly vulnerable to the mayhem of accelerated destruction that is contemporary war. In fact, the stones and the flowers are what remain in the aftermath of catastrophe. Flowers flourish as they recolonize minefields abandoned by humans, war technology impeding one life-form while enhancing another. The mountains register the aerial attacks as a brief moment in their immense history. These scales of the rapid and the very slow in Aslam frame and protectively envelop the human characters whose environment is destroyed, presented as a source of strength and nourishment for these humans whose present is impoverished. Just as stars become visible during an eclipse of the sun, deep time resurfaces during the eclipse of modernity produced by war.[16] The multiscalar aesthetics forged by Aslam not only reflects the Anthropocene-era turn to multiscalar thinking, but in the context of writing about Afghanistan's tragic history, restores worth to exhausted lives and depleted landscapes. Although it decenters human tragedy via a scalar change, it also signals a possibility of healing for humans by way of the earth.

Earth-Witness

In *The Writing of Stones*, Roger Caillois proposes that "in a stone the image . . . is an immortal witness, recorded for a long period of time: forever, measured against the brief human season" (100). The stone's longevity, beyond being a medium of communication between asynchronous generations, is here imbued with the authority of a witness who can be called to testify in some remote future, asked to provide a record of epochs long gone. Beyond the purely metaphoric dimension or the assumption of panpsychism, how can the idea of witnessing be extended to the nonhuman domain? What kind of witness may be commensurable, for instance, with the deep time of environmental destruction, a scalar process occurring beyond the human mode of perception? Recent discussions of witnessing suggest the possibility of expanding the figure of the witness beyond the human observer. More specifically, there has been considerable interest in extending the notion of witness to technological apparatuses that are capable of bypassing the human observer.[17] For instance, Eivind Røssaak writes: "If witnessing has to do with seeing and insight of some sort, then the figures of the eye and the technologies of the eye become important. . . . Human optics are increasingly being extended and even replaced by technological instruments of seeing and measuring devices . . . [producing] visions and surveillance systems of such complexity that they are readable by computers only" (224). Here both the work of recording and interpreting/reading bypass the human altogether, with technology producing a record to be read by a nonhuman interpreter. Contemporary popular culture is attuned to this shift that incorporates nonhuman witnessing. A *Black Mirror* episode titled "Crocodile" is set in a near future in which the police can tap into nonhuman animal memory to solve crimes. And yet, as Ulrich Ekman, the editor of *Witness: Memory, Representation, and the Media in Question,* points out, "[in regard to witnessing,] we seem quite a bit more willing to consider ourselves technical or technological than animal and animistic" (19). Ekman continues: "Could an animal, could a machine do what I do here in welcoming myself as host and witness at once?" (20). Here I propose the term "earth-witness," or "geo-witness," to capture the nonhuman witnessing described by Aslam—a type of witnessing registered by an ecosystem, as nonhuman (insect) perception, as a deep species-memory (the species-memory of demoiselle cranes), or as a geological trace. This type of witnessing and registering the disaster is different from both human eyewitnessing and witnessing mediated by technology.

The motif of the earth or landscape as mute witness to a human-borne catastrophe is a relatively common feature, including the writing set in zones of conflict and humanitarian suffering. For instance, Nelofer Pazira, in her memoir about the Afghan wars, exclaims as she gazes on the terrain outside of Kandahar, just after the Taliban have been driven away from the city by coalition forces in 2001:

> Could this place have looked the same more than a hundred years ago, in July 1880, when the British and Afghan armies fought here? Could this place have been the same twenty years ago, in January 1980, when the Russians tried to fight their way into this bastion of resistance to foreign invasion? How did this place look a year ago, in December 2001, when the Arabs, Pakistanis and their Afghan allies— the Taliban—were running for their lives under the American B-52 bombers? (333)

Here, Pazira invokes the idea of a landscape as a silent witness to wars fought by humans. Yet her vision of such witness differs significantly from the one provided by Aslam; this difference is important if we are to register what is new in Aslam's aesthetics of geo-witnessing. It is significant that, in Pazira, the landscape described goes through an imagined immobilization—indeed, an abstraction—as a result of which it is positioned as a stable, unchanging signifier against which the agency of humans, capable of both violence and suffering, is brought into relief. The rhetoric of the passage, with its structure of repetition and its foregrounding of the words "the same," insists on the earth's immutability, foregrounding its presumed immemorial presence and constancy. Intriguingly, while potentially bringing the earth-witness into view, this rhetorical move reinscribes the division between nature and culture, seeking in immutable nature a respite from the drama and strife of human history.

Dipesh Chakrabarty's "The Climate of History: Four Theses" famously undercuts such separation, insisting on the inseparability of human and natural history. In Aslam's novels, the earth-witness is the very site of such interlacing. Instead of a signifier of mute stability, the landscape in Aslam's novels is a dynamic force—acting, as well as being acted on—a full-fledged participant in, and not just an immobile observer of, human history. Even geologic landscapes are imagined by Aslam as both affected by human action, and in turn, affecting the human witness who arrives, belatedly, at the site of a catastrophic event. And humans, in line with Anthropocene-era discussions, are depicted as a geologic force:

> [T]he journey to the destination in Afghanistan takes seventeen hours. In deep twilight they cross a broad flat valley with a river and river flats in it, every bit of it scorched black where a Daisy Cutter bomb had been dropped, reducing everything to ash, pumice, lava, the sides of the hills torn up into segments, and scattered over it all is the yellow haze of the unrisen moon, the cold night falling on them out of the east, the stars beginning their slide through the black slopes. It looks like the site of a cosmic incursion such as a meteorite, not the work of men. The US casualties number twelve in the two-month war, whereas countless thousands of Afghanistanis have perished, fighters as well as bystanders, and Rohan doesn't know who will speak the complicated truth, and he watches with attention as though at some point in the future he himself will be asked to tell what he has seen. (*Blind* 112)

This passage stages an irreconcilable tension between eyewitness and earth-witness. Ironically, Rohan is an elderly man who is almost blind and thus unlikely to carry the memory of the disaster into posterity. His fragility and sensory inadequacy is juxtaposed with the landscape's ability to record and carry forward its own memory. The geologic agency of humans whose conspicuous act of terraforming through warfare is equated with "a cosmic incursion" here is registered by the landscape itself. Evocatively called "a Daisy Cutter," this 15,000-pound bomb—the largest nonnuclear weapon in the US army inventory—was used in Vietnam to clear forests for helicopter landings and has been referred to as a "mammoth" bomb due to its size and impact force (Spitzer). In Afghanistan, Daisy Cutters have been used to penetrate Al-Qaeda's underground cave complexes in Tora Bora. The astronomical scale invoked by the passage is telling. Here Afghanistan figures not as a nation-state, but as a geo-body struck by an extraterrestrial force. That force turns solid rock back into the quagmire of lava, pumice, and ash, reversing the natural processes that originally created the landscape and thus bringing into the foreground the scalar consequences of human actions. A semi-blind human witness is rendered trivial compared to the cosmic forces he struggles to comprehend—forces that, by changing the valley's geological history, create a nonerasable record of their own violence.

Moreover, earth-witness in Aslam's novels is not just rock, but a dynamic ecosystem, inhabited—aside from humans—by multiple life-forms and technological objects. Aslam's plots incorporate vegetation, insects, birds, and animals, adopting a multispecies approach that brings into focus "the host of organisms whose lives and deaths are linked to human social worlds" (Kirksey and Helmreich 545). Demoiselle cranes, whose migratory paths have been severely affected by decades of war in Afghanistan, are often featured in *The Wasted Vigil* as not just part of the setting, but as a nonhuman witness whose gaze is contrasted with and frames the agency of human protagonists.[18] These nonhumans are revealed as actors who have a stake in the ongoing war in Afghanistan. In one striking scene, the two characters most defined by the shallow chronologies of war—David (ex-CIA) and Casa (the young Afghan militant)—are placed in the vicinity of a flock of migrating cranes, "the million-year-old gaze of the demoiselles watching them from far away" (*Wasted* 187). This faraway gaze from a long-gone epoch—from deep time—beckons and accuses, testifying to migratory histories a million years old—histories that have been disrupted by aerial warfare. The demoiselles' gaze contests ideological boundaries as well as the boundaries of nation-states, calling into view a length of Eurasia as experienced through history by a particular species. Connecting Siberia and India, the cranes' migration calls for a peaceful Afghanistan—a land that serves as a connecting node, a locum of respite and nourishment during the arduous journey across the Himalayas. Stored in the birds' muscle memory, genes, and brains, this deep species memory—threatened by contemporary wars—once again reveals the scalar, incalculable, long-lasting consequences of individual actions. David, who has been fueling the fire of the Soviet-Afghan War, is cast as accountable not only for human, but also for these nonhuman casualties, his legacy extending into the deep future summoned by this nonhuman gaze.

If the nonhuman gaze of the cranes speaks from the depths of millennial time, another form of nonhuman perception—insect perception—exemplifies nonhuman witnessing at the microtemporal register. Contemporary media theories bring into focus the microtemporality of a machinic sensorium.[19] Yet microtemporalities predate the contemporary digital universe as they also are found at the level of microbial evolutions, viral replications, insect perception, and particle time. In Aslam, human perception appears slow in comparison to insect sensing—a type of creature-witness occurring at a swarmic microregister. *The Blind Man's Garden* features a scene where a swarm of flies signals the arrival of Jeo's (Naheed's husband's) body to the gate of her compound. A few moments before hearing the knock at the gate, Naheed notices a sudden stop to the buzzing of a swarm of flies around a bird carcass to which she is tending; the flies' attention has been redirected to a larger human body. The flies' disappearance remains illegible to Naheed until, having heard the knock at the gate, she steps outside her walled compound and sees the decaying body that attracted the flies. The multiple ways in which Aslam's writing incorporates nonhuman witness thus situates this witness as neither mute nor immutable, as in Pazira. Rather, it comprises multiple forms of registering and perception: from memory stored in landscape to the swarmic perception of flies to the changes in the muscle memory of migrating birds. Depicting the war as a multispecies ecology serves the purpose of uncovering multiple forms of environmental violence (such as habitat destruction) that affect both humans and nonhumans. By decentering the human figure, its temporal scale, and its mode of perception, such a view reveals that the destinies of human and nonhuman actors are deeply interlinked.[20] The snow leopard cub—who is rescued by Mikal and then travels with him as Mikal navigates his way home—becomes a metaphor of a historical journey shared by two different species. Ultimately, Aslam's writing of the nonhuman witness promotes what Cohen calls the ethics of scale: "a cautious *living with* that looks deep into time, that stresses enduring ecomaterial affinity and rejects the devaluation of matter as self-evident asset, inert commodity, or resource for extraction" (41, emphasis my own).

Aslam's mode of writing the disaster in the era of the Anthropocene brings to the foreground what Grosz calls "an excess of life over death in the existence of species" (137)—a multitude of unspent forces and vitalities found in landscapes commonly seen, as in the case of Afghanistan, as landscapes of depletion and loss. Such excess becomes visible when these landscapes are restored to multiple recessional frames of deep time: the deep time of Islam, Eurasian time, and geological time. Moreover, such a view forces us to consider the ethical implications of warfare through the prism of the deep future, bringing into view the long-term geological and environmental aftermath of contemporary warfare. Aslam's writing thereby exemplifies the benefits of the geologic turn for writing traumatic histories in the era of the Anthropocene, the era in which human actions have consequences that span well beyond their terrestrial temporal scale. Those benefits, as well as the aesthetics of this mode of writing, are most noticeable when contrasted with humanitarian mode of representing Afghanistan—one that foregrounds Afghanistan's symbolic and material poverty and focuses on extreme forms of spectacularized human suffering. Aslam's works emphasize systemic and slow violence, habitat diminishment, and ecosystem degradation while upholding the earth and human resilience in the *longue durée*, insisting on planetary fragility and, simultaneously, highlighting the earth's persistence. In a striking gesture at the end of *The Blind Man's Garden*, Aslam takes advantage of the astronomical perspective opened up by the narrative and compares Afghanistan not to Earth, but to Jupiter—the brightest planet in the solar system, characterized by violent surface storms that can rage "for hundreds of years" (367). This astronomical inscription offers a paradoxical vision of hope—that the lasting storm will eventually subside—and affirm the undepleted potency of planetary depth as compared to the inevitable passing of every surface disturbance.

6

The Kabubble: The Humanitarian Community Under Scrutiny

In the opening pages of her 2015 memoir *Farewell, Kabul,* Christina Lamb, a seasoned British reporter with decades of experience in Afghanistan, describes the closing of Camp Bastion in the Helmand Province in 2014. It was a billion-pound British base, the largest since World War II, with an airfield that had become "Britain's third busiest airport" (4). The withdrawal of the British forces, who had failed to achieve their mission in the unruly province, signaled the end of Britain's fourth war in Afghanistan. It was marked by a somber mood and did not compel a celebration. Having lost the hope of defeating the devious Taliban; weary of endless, pointless clashes with the local narco-barons and their private militias; demoralized and losing public support at home, the British forces retreated quietly. "Lofty aims of transforming Afghanistan were forgotten," Lamb writes, "Now it was about damage control" (6). The year 2014, the end of the NATO-led large-scale operation in Afghanistan, no doubt, marked a moment of reckoning—a quiet one, because no one wanted to publicize the failure of the so-called peacebuilding and "reconstruction." The year was further tainted by the advent of the Islamic State—a horrific consequence of the US war in Iraq. Lamb's memoir's subtitle, *From Afghanistan to a More Dangerous World,* captures her assessment of the state of the world in the aftermath of the War on Terror. Both Afghanistan, the subtitle suggests, and the larger world, have become less stable and more (rather than less) dangerous. Assessing the early days of reconstruction in Kabul from the perspective afforded by the war's inglorious end and NATO forces' retreat, Lamb, like others, tries to figure out what went wrong. In the memoir, she condemns the West for double-dealing, the secret services for propping up the widely hated Afghan warlords with cash, thus allowing them to spring back to power, the expats for partying senseless in houses rented for astronomical sums of money from the Taliban leaders (400), and the aid community for "helping itself rather than Afghans" (146).[1] The era of enchantment with humanitarian-military interventions that were supposed to liberate and transform target societies ended with vast disillusionment and a profound loss of faith in such projects.

In this chapter, I discuss a trio of cultural texts that reflect, from Kabul, on the era of the humanitarian wars—Tina Fey's 2016 film *Whiskey Tango Foxtrot* (directed by Glenn Ficarra and John Requa); Kim Barker's 2011 memoir *The Taliban Shuffle* that served as an inspiration for Fey's movie; and Nicolas Wild's graphic novel series *Kabul Disco* (2009; 2013). In their assessment of the Western presence in post-9/11 Afghanistan, they use comedy to capture the idiosyncrasies and the overarching absurdity of the foreign-led "Afghanistan Reconstruction" project. Their comedic pedagogies prompt laughter—a reaction to the farcicality contained in the very concept of humanitarian wars. Henri Bergson writes, in his book *Laughter*, that a "humourist is a moralist disguised as a scientist"; humor, he contends, is "the more emphasized the deeper we go down into an evil that actually is, in order to set down its details in the most cold-blooded indifference" (127). These three cultural texts are designed to entertain their audiences through humor; yet they also are critical projects that expose the sinister side of foreign presence in Afghanistan—"the evil that actually is." They offer up a repertoire of anecdotes, comedic situations, absurd images, and impossible characters, giving us a vocabulary in which to talk about the encounter between Afghanistan and the international community tasked with rebuilding it in its own image. Their narrators are self-deprecating and lack the hubris that permeated the early Afghanistan-based fictions discussed in chapters one through three. As such, they index a long journey from the early years of the War on Terror—from the era when foreigners viewed and portrayed Afghanistan as a site of oppression, destitution, and female captivity—to the war's second decade, characterized by a sense of the West's exhaustion, impotence, and cynicism. This sense of cynicism can be captured by Costas Douzinas' pronouncement about humanitarian interventions in the twenty-first century: "Whatever the ideology," he writes, "humanitarianism has become a job opportunity" (64). In all three texts, Kabul is reimagined as "Kabubble"—a paradoxical site of transnational career building, an inflated economy zone, and as a new kind of ruin—a ruin of late neoliberalism.[2]

Weary of the clichéd portrayals of Afghanistan that precede them, these texts are remarkably self-aware; engaging stereotypes only to mock them, they rewrite conventional geographies of power and privilege, and by doing so, manage to dislodge the coordinate system by which we map the differences between the global South and the global North. These texts are most notable because of what is absent in them—first and foremost, absent is the trope of rescue of the suffering Afghans by a benevolent subject from the West—the likes of *Kandahar*'s protagonist Nafas, *The Kite Runner*'s Amir, or the heroic leaders of the MSF team in *The Photographer*. These newer works show no interest in deploying the humanitarian imaginary to justify Westerners' presence in Kabul; instead, the clichéd narrative of Western-borne salvation is repeatedly ridiculed. In all three texts, the narrators move to the Afghan capital in search of a career opportunity, driven primarily by economic forces. Self-serving and opportunistic, the narrators are "good subjects" not in the moral but in the Althusserian sense, insofar as they embody the spirit of neoliberalism that requires properly interpellated individuals to constantly reskill, improve, and reinvent themselves—in their case, by relocating to a conflict zone. In these texts, corporeal vulnerability becomes a symbol of late neoliberalism; bodily wounds index other injuries and risks that affect subjects of globalized market economies in crisis. Collateral damage proliferates, producing new ruins—ruined bodies, bankrupt companies, busted economies, and failed states. Geographies of victimhood—economic violence, physical and military violence—here are not limited to Afghanistan, but span the globe.

These texts also push back against the convention of turning Afghan cultural difference into a spectacle for Western consumption. They do not traffic in images of Afghan insularity and backwardness (unless they want to mock them); they also keep the pseudo-ethnographic impulse to document and explain Afghan cultural difference to their Western audiences firmly in check. Instead, these texts turn their gaze on the members of the international cohort of expats who gathered in Kabul after 9/11. In doing so, they scrutinize the lifestyle, habits, dietary preferences, and

mating practices of these folks, as well as question their motives and make
fun of their "humanitarian" endeavors. In sum, they examine these expats
with the curiosity of a trained anthropologist, treating them as if they
were members of an exotic tribe. In all three accounts, raucous parties are
presented as the international community's prime habitat and thus become
a particularly rich source of "data." Such parties represent the true face
of the humanitarian project in reconstruction-era Afghanistan: Western
professionals, many of them middle-aged, like Barker or Fey's protagonists,
become intoxicated, literally, by consuming large quantities of booze and
drugs, and figuratively, by being transported into a carnivalesque space[3]
where cultural norms are suspended. Barker writes:

> Often, the reality of Afghanistan interrupted the fun. A security guy
> shot up a bar; an attention-seeking journalist tossed a stun grenade at
> a party, blowing out all the windows. A consultant company threw a
> dance and trampoline party with camels and actual Afghan nomads—a
> measure of authenticity, I guess, that had become legendary with Afghan
> nomads, who spread rumors across the region of a foreigner trampoline
> orgy. . . . The brothels and over-the-top parties were only a symptom of
> the absurdity that this war had turned into by the fall of 2005. (73–74)

Here, westerners in Kabul are called out on their exploitation of Afghan
traditional culture (hiring Afghan nomads to pose as exotic props at a
party) and on their reckless behavior, such as throwing a stun grenade at
a party. What is more notable, however, is the reversal of the direction of
the gaze in which the westerners themselves are repositioned as objects of
scrutiny—examined by both Barker and the Afghans who marvel at the
misbehaving foreigners and then spread rumors of "the foreigner trampo-
line orgy." The Afghans in Barker's passage are well aware of their status
as exotic objects in Western media; westerners, however, are not cognizant
of their own status as being observed, and judged, in multiple ways, by
culturally more competent Afghans, who are used to having foreigners in
their environment. And this is where the irony lies. Set in Afghanistan,
Barker's memoir is an ethnography—not of Afghans, but of transnational
workers of the late-neoliberal era, a class to which she herself belongs.

This comedic reversal, where Afghans are situated as self-aware objects
of exploitation, and simultaneously, as the subjects of the gaze, while the
expat humanitarian community, lacking self-awareness, is put on display,

disrupts familiar representational frames and causes anxiety in some critics. Tina Fey's film, which generally follows Barker's assessment of the expatriate community in Kabul, has been subjected to a harsh criticism in the liberal-leaning media. Feminist reviewers condemned the film for focusing too much on its white protagonist's trajectory (a forty-plus-year-old journalist played by Fey herself) and thus for using Afghanistan as a mere setting. Stephanie Abraham, for instance, contends that the film "champions a white, middle-class American feminism that sees Western women as free and other women, in this case Afghan women, as oppressed" (par. 2). Anne Helen Petersen condemns the film's treatment of race in her review, concluding that "*Whiskey Tango Foxtrot*'s racism and exoticism are not novel. . . . It's neither the worst nor the best of its genre" (par. 1). In similar vein, reviewer Glen Dunks bemoans the shortage of scenes depicting Afghanistan and Afghans. The film, he argues, is not interested "in the race relations on screen, which is odd considering where it's set. The locals are mostly secondary to Barker's story" (par. 10).

Some of that criticism is fair: A Hollywood production, the film indeed suffers from flaws not found in the memoir that inspired it. Most significantly, the film raises immediate concerns about the widely criticized Hollywood practice of whitewashing; the two main Afghan characters are played by Caucasian actors, Christopher Abbott (a white American actor) and Alfred Molina (born in Britain, of Spanish and Italian parentage).[4] As such, the film lacks cultural authenticity. No native speakers of Dari or Pashto are featured. Barker herself, upon visiting the set outside Santa Fe, New Mexico, observed that, while the dusty-beige, windswept terrain reminded her of Afghanistan, the actors proved less realistic: "[T]he extras playing Taliban members . . . seemed to be mostly of Mexican heritage, their turbans were tied like Christmas bows and they were eating Kind bars. This was definitely not Ghazni Province" ("My 'Kabubble,'" par. 7).

On the level of the plot, the film modifies the memoir's storyline in at least two significant ways: It adds the romance between the protagonist named Kim and the male lead (played by Martin Freeman), and ends with Kim achieving career success as a news anchor in Washington. The film's upward trajectory is at odds with the storyline in the memoir where Barker starts her assignment in Afghanistan fully employed and in a relationship and ends up single (her relationship cracks under the pressure of a foreign assignment) and jobless (as her job is eliminated by the newspaper in the aftermath of the 2008 recession). Regrettably, an inscription of the romantic

and career success in the film positions the film as a personal empowerment
story for a white American woman—a problematic trope that has not gone
unnoticed by critics. To make matters worse, Fey's own interpretation of
the film likely added fuel to the already raging fire—in a *New York Times*
interview, she told Melena Ryzik: "I just found it fascinating, the weird mix
of Kim having this freeing, wild experience privately, in the middle of a
place where women are so oppressed" (par. 7). Fey's uncritical deployment of
an opposition between the white American protagonist's growing freedom
and Afghan women's lack of such is, however, a misreading of Barker's story,
which works against such an opposition by bringing into view Kim's depression, disenfranchisement, loneliness, and extreme burnout by the end of her
stay in Kabul. Moreover, Fey seems also to be misreading the very film she
stars in. The film, in fact, follows the memoir in carefully navigating away
from the tropes of female oppression in the Muslim world, which is most
notable in its treatment of the contentious burqa issue.

During the first wave of writing/screening Afghanistan (treated in
chapters one and two), the burqa functioned as a material instantiation of
Afghan women's extreme oppression under the Taliban rule. The burqa
repeatedly has been inscribed as tomb-like, suffocating, pinching, stifling,
and violating the innate human dignity of women.[5] Accordingly, the trope
of unveiling, ubiquitous in these early texts, signaled liberation and restoration of human dignity. Consider, for instance, the significance of the
trope of unveiling in the film *Kandahar* (chapter one), which begins and
ends with the protagonist lifting the burqa to reveal her face. Feminist theorist Malini Schueller recalls the ritualistic unveiling performed on Zoya,
an Afghan women's rights activist, by Oprah in 2001 as designed to stage,
for the American-based audience, "the transformation from archaism to
modernity, objecthood to subjecthood" (par. 19). As NATO troops entered
Kabul in the fall of 2001, Western media outlets were awash with stories
of jubilant unveilings. A *Newsweek* reporter wrote, in November 2001, "as
soon as she heard about the Taliban's defeat, Azimi joyously burned her
burqa at home. 'I felt so depressed wearing the veil,' she said. 'Now I see the
sunlight and it's so beautiful.'"[6] This obsession with Afghan women's dress
and, correspondingly, a focus on saving these "women of cover" (as George
W. Bush called them) has been subjected to feminist critique early on, most
famously in Lila Abu-Lughod's 2002 article "Do Muslim Women Really
Need Saving?" and also in numerous other texts.[7]

In Fey's film, the two scenes that feature the burqa signal a playful, self-conscious reversal of that early trope. The first scene takes place in the context of Kim's embed with a group of marines tasked with repairing a village well that has been destroyed by an improvised explosive device (IED). As a burqa-clad village woman signals her wish to talk to Kim privately, away from the soldiers, Kim follows her into a house where she is met by a large group of women who lift their burqas to greet her. At the moment of unveiling, the film cuts to Kim's surprised face instead of revealing the faces of the women. These women, then, enlist Kim as a mediator. They wish to instruct the marines to stop repairing the well as its presence in the village prevents the women from enjoying their daily hike to the stream in each other's company, away from the men. They also reveal that they have been destroying the well, each time it was rebuilt, using IEDs they had created using old Soviet-era land mines. The scene thus not only interrupts the viewer's voyeuristic desire to look underneath the veil, but also endows Afghan women with rebellious agency, autonomy, and technological skill needed to manufacture IEDs. The second burqa scene features Kim herself donning the garment to conceal her identity on a trip to a dangerous assignment. Invoking, and immediately reversing the connotations between the burqa and Afghan culture's repression of female sexuality, the scene depicts Kim being liberated by the burqa to greater sexual expression. In contrast to her usual awkward, inhibited self, Kim turns flirtatious and seductive as she walks across the courtyard of her expat compound, turning the gaze of all her male team members. In this scene, white expat men are, paradoxically, hailed by the burqa into responding to fully covered Kim—who commands attention—as a sexual, and empowered, being. Their faces reflect awe rather than a predatory response, further inscribing the donning of the burqa as Kim's taking charge of her sexuality. To argue, as the reviewers above do, that Fey's film is simply a repetition of the old "racism and exoticism" perpetuating tropes of Afghan women's oppression, is to misrecognize the film's work of evading and subverting these tropes.

That said, we can now turn to what I believe is the film's key contribution. While I am sympathetic to the feminist critique of some of the film's flaws, I believe that these initial polemics failed to register precisely what is new in *Whiskey Tango Foxtrot* (and in Barker's memoir): a critique of the Western-led humanitarian enterprise in Kabul and a desire to expose the preposterousness of its mission. As in the memoir, Fey's protagonist does not have her experiences privately, but is portrayed as part of a habitat of international development workers and foreign correspondents—a habitat that is toxic and exploitative both of westerners and their Afghan helpers. Her personal liberation begins when she manages to extricate herself from this toxic community. To decipher the film's place in the conversation about Afghanistan and US-led humanitarian wars, we need to situate it within an ecosystem of similar works—the memoir that inspired it as well as other texts written by transnational knowledge workers as they reflect on the era of massive foreign presence in the aftermath of the 2001 invasion. These texts focus on the crowd of expats, mostly, though not exclusively, white; however, it is not to celebrate their achievements, but to expose their irredeemable shortfalls. Unlike early post-9/11 texts, these newer works are not concerned with examining—or delivering to western audiences— stories of Afghan cultural difference, which explains the relative paucity of scenes depicting Afghans in their own environment. These texts' prime object is not Kabul—an Afghan city—but the "Kabubble"—an incubator of a specific kind of expatriate microculture. In all three texts, Afghans who are featured are multilingual, cross-culturally competent, sometimes quirky, but overall well adjusted; they are not in need of rescue or pro- tection. These Afghans bring into further relief the cluelessness of the monolingual transnational "humanitarians" as a group. It is the reckless, clueless foreigners with no prior training or knowledge of Dari who need to be protected from the dangers they do not know lurk in the environment. The trope of rescue characteristic of the first wave of writing and screening Afghanistan is also reversed. Afghans featured in these texts—even in Fey's film—are no longer victims: cross-culturally competent and effective, they observe, assist, lust after, or take care of the floundering foreigners who make a provisional home in the Afghan capital.

While it is important to continue to be vigilant, critiquing narratives that "champion middle-class white feminism," it is equally necessary to acknowledge the trajectory of self-learning and self-critique indexed by the cultural texts written in the second decade of US-led war and recon- struction in Afghanistan. This crop of texts offers "Kabubble" as a mirror for diagnosing the pernicious problems of our shared neoliberal present characterized by the universal precarization of labor, increased competi- tion for resources, the prevalence of short-term thinking and short-term contracts, and the diminishment of state and community support sys- tems—both in Afghanistan and in the global North. The failures of

Afghan reconstruction, these texts suggest, are not accidental but embedded in the neoliberal project itself. Their characters embody its spirit and faithfully act out the roles that are offered to them. The expatriate failures are the failures not of individuals but of systems—the neoliberal regimes imposed, in the aftermath of the invasions, in Afghanistan and Iraq. These regimes involve the dismantling of existing infrastructures of community sustenance and protection with nothing to offer in exchange, except for the opening of these vulnerable communities to volatile global market forces. And the massive project of neoliberal revamping of these invaded economies, as Michael Schwartz explains, required a "robust civilian presence" (215), a large cohort of western professionals, in these sites. Fey's, Barker's, and Wild's texts show what this robust civilian presence looked like.

Life Is a Party

Whiskey Tango Foxtrot opens with a scene at a party. Half-naked bodies, loud music, people of all ages drinking, snorting cocaine, smoking hashish, making out, and scream-singing in and out of tune frame our first view of the main character—news reporter Kim Baker, played by Tina Fey. A forty-something professional woman, she is shown jumping up and down in a crowd of bodies, drinking hard liquor from a bottle (Figure 6.1). The raucous party is then interrupted by the sound of a nearby explosion. The music stops as the explosion reaches the dancing crowd in the form of dust shrapnel that comes down from the ceiling. A moment later, some party members—reporters—rush to their cell phones to file a report to their news agencies, and Kim, on her cell phone with her editor, hurries to the site of the bombing. This opening scene, which takes place in 2006 Kabul, presents reconstruction-era Afghanistan as a site of extreme partying and, simultaneously, a site of violence. The visual-sonic resonance between descending shrapnel and a mad chorus of ringing cellphones is evocative; shrapnel invokes corporeal injury, while cellphones connote connectivity and globalization. The focus on the international community carousing in a conflict zone sets the tone for the critique offered in the film: It will focus on this group's predictable failures. The film then flashes back to 2002, the time when Kim—a cubicle-bound news writer for a television network in Chicago—is offered the opportunity to go to Kabul as a correspondent. Feeling stuck in a rut and even "moving backwards" in her life, she sees this as an opportunity for adventure and positive change.

Figure 6.1. A foreigners' party in *Whiskey Tango Foxtrot*.

Quite similarly, Wild's *Kabul Disco*—named after a party mix CD—foregoes the theme of Afghan cultural difference and focuses, instead, on the party scene, expatriate life, and the extravagant habits of international community members. In book one, Nicolas, a comic book artist and illustrator residing in France, is hired by an international communications company based in Kabul to work on the Afghan election awareness campaign. The company, we are told, has humanitarian roots—it is a former NGO that grew rapidly in post-9/11 Kabul, prompting its founding members (two Frenchmen and one Argentinian) to turn it into a private communications and public relations firm. The book follows Nicolas as he relocates to Kabul, initially for a three-month term, describing what it means to be a foreigner working in post-9/11 Afghanistan. Images of Afghan culture play a modest role in the first book. Mostly, Nicolas's life is limited to his guesthouse, the office, and the expatriate scene, with a French restaurant, La Joie de Vivre, at its center. Nicolas is surprised, upon his arrival to Kabul, to find a vibrant Western community there. The reader is conscripted into both admiring and detesting his bosses who are prominent fixtures on the expatriate scene. World-savvy enterprising socialites with designer sunglasses, they boast an impeccable sense of fashion, a taste for foie gras, and a knack for making money in a war zone (Figure 6.2).

Upon arrival, Nicolas feels out of his element not because of his unfamiliarity with Afghan culture, as one would expect, but because he does not quite know how to behave around the so-called "bobos"—French

Figure 6.2. Graphic designers and their boss Valentin.

bourgeois bohemians—abundant in Kabul. "They miss the high society so much," Nicolas's politically savvy and ascetic fellow designer Tristan says, "they've rebuilt parts of Paris in the middle of Kabul. La Joie de Vivre, it's appalling" (*KD*1 38). By contrast, Nicolas and Tristan call themselves "momos"—moneyless morons (38), a term that indexes class difference between the precariously employed pair of graphic designers and their successful entrepreneurial bosses. Tristan's condemnation of the international community eventually causes him to leave Afghanistan. He says, "I think what we are doing here sucks. We are taking the piss out of the Afghans. It's worse than neocolonialism" (*KD*2 56). Nicolas, by contrast, is more than ready to be seduced by the little privileges afforded by the expat life, and at the end of his term he asks for a contract extension (Figure 6.3). After all, he has no other prospects.

Barker's memoir—published in 2011 as *The Taliban Shuffle*—is the most nuanced and the most direct of the three texts in its critique of the "Kabubble." She gives reconstruction-era Kabubble other nicknames too, calling it terrordrome, Kabul High (74), and Hotel California (72) to capture the state, and the mood, of the expat community. The memoir is rich in detail, chronicling the various depravities incubated in the community that is supposed to secure neoliberal peace and prosperity by ensuring the "robust civilian presence" of westerners in Afghanistan. Barker brings into relief a sense of excitement, opportunity, and risk that permeate the international scene, painting an unforgettable picture of a community of foreigners out of touch with the culture and people they are supposed to be helping. Barker underscores the ruthless opportunism of the group. For most, humanitarian aims are part of their job description; yet the motives and the behavior of these humanitarians are at odds with their organizations' aims. She writes:

Figure 6.3. Nicolas expressing happiness at the sight of a new short-term contract in a war zone.

> For most [foreigners], Afghanistan was Kabul High, a way to get your war on, an adrenaline rush, a resume line, a money factory. It was a place to escape, to run away from marriages and mistakes, a place to forget your age, your responsibilities, your past, a country in which to reinvent yourself. . . .
>
> How out of touch were they? Employees of the Department for International Development (DFID), the British equivalent of USAID, decided it would be a good idea to throw a going-away party just before the election, with the dress code specified as "INVADERS—Alexander the Great, Hippies, Brits, Mughals, Russians, and general gratuitous fancy dress. Gorillas welcome." . . . Well, at least it wasn't the Tarts and Talibs theme party, thrown the year before. (284)

The image of a prominent humanitarian agency throwing an "Invaders" or a "Tarts and Talibs" party in a city that struggles to rebuild itself after decades of horrific wars captures the essence of Barker's critique. The cultural appropriation here is more than scandalous—it is so outrageous that it becomes comical, absurd. It calls for an ethnographer to document it, an anthropologist to explain its logic.

Such scenes suggest that the international community in Kabul does not coalesce into a collectivity with a political or moral consciousness of any kind. Transnational nomads, these members of the creative, humanitarian, and paramilitary class behave like invaders insofar as they enjoy the spoils of a neoliberal "conquest" of Kabul, rebuilding the city in their own image, yet unaware of their large footprint. They bring with themselves bars, brothels, and gated communities, as well as short-term thinking, a lack of cultural memory, and a lack of investment in or a vision for the future. They are post-utopian, capitalist-realist, competitive, and homeless, belonging neither to Afghanistan nor to their home nations. Geographer Jennifer Fluri, in her study of the post-9/11 expatriate community in Kabul, found that short-term assignments were indeed the norm: "Short-term assignments (i.e., three months to one year) provide workers a crucial line item on their resumes as part of longitudinal career trajectory" (990–991). This short-termism, she argues, explains these international workers' sense of impunity: "behavior, desires, and personal freedoms are chosen and are often determined by the temporality of their assignments and the inability of local governance to enforce the rules of law on internationals who engage in illegal activities" (991). In short, this community, by its very design, acted as an extraterritorial force that was not subject to any law; instead of helping to support the weak Afghan state, they made evident its lack of real power. In fact, like the European humanitarians two decades prior (MSF and the like), these twenty-first-century Western civilians establish a system that runs parallel to, and often in competition with, the Afghan state.

By describing the over-the-top parties in guesthouses, the over-the-top prices in restaurants and bars catering to foreigners, the inflated rent tags, and the overheating economy swelling up with reconstruction money, Barker mines the disconnect between the humanitarian community's lofty aims and their largely destructive economic and cultural footprint in Afghanistan. Instead of attempting to close the gap between foreign helpers and locals, the international community revels in their own bubble, not noticing that the gap eventually turns into a major rift. Again, Barker turns to extravagant parties as a symptom of this disconnect:

> More than a hundred people crammed into the house and the yard outside. We had Marilyn Monroe, a pirate, Death, the Quaker Oats guy, Cat Woman, a convincing Kim Jong Il, and a belly dancer, along with various sexy witches. Tom bought all the bandages from various pharmacies in Kabul and wrapped himself like a mummy. We danced in a large group, until Tom started to sweat through his bandages, which produced a stench similar to either an antibiotic paste gone bad or dead people. A shady Afghan American with an Elvis hairdo showed up at about 2 am—the month before, he had crashed a barbecue at the Fun House and peddled toothpaste tubes full of cocaine for $150 each, snapped up by many foreigners who judged it bad cocaine but minty fresh. (129)

The bandaged partygoer here allegorizes international aid—instead of offering it to the ones in need, the humanitarian community uses it up on itself, wastefully—an act that results in the stench of death. While the humanitarian imagery discussed in chapter one relied on the incommensurability of (immense) need and (insufficient) aid, here the aid does not reach its destination, but is wasted in an act of extravagant expenditure, by the helping community itself.[8]

I Am Extraordinary

Barker's, Fey's, and Wild's critical focus on the expat community indexes the trajectory of learning from 2001 to the second decade of the 9/11 wars. To make this trajectory even more obvious, in this section I revisit, briefly, two early post-9/11 Afghanistan travelogues—*The Places In Between* (2004) by Rory Stewart and *The Bookseller of Kabul* (2002) by Åsne Seierstad. These works indulge, without self-irony, in the tropes of exceptionalism and benevolent humanitarianism, showing none of the self-awareness or self-critique that characterizes Barker's, Fey's, and Wild's works. Instead, authors of these widely known travelogues deploy neocolonial fantasies and position themselves as lone explorers of a territory that is both uncharted and exceptionally dangerous (as if there were no international community present). In *The Places In Between*, Stewart, a British citizen and now a Tory MP and Minister of State, describes his three-week journey on foot from Herat to Kabul shortly after the ousting of the Taliban by coalition forces in 2001. In the book's opening paragraphs, he presents his journey as a one-of-a-kind solitary experience in a place that is perilous and wild: "I was alone and a stranger," he writes, "walking in very remote areas; I represented a culture that many of them [the Afghans] hated" (from the book's dedication). Invoking colonial tropes of exploration, this framing bestows an aura of exceptionality upon the narrator, who appears to have exclusive access to an extraordinary experience. Throughout the book, Stewart continues to portray himself as an exception by quoting Afghans who either marvel at his endeavor or ridicule it: "[You are] the first tourist in Afghanistan," Stewart reports being told by an Afghan government official in Herat, "You will die, I can guarantee. Do you want to die?" (3).

Susan Kollin, in her analysis of travel writing, proposes the term "redemptive unmapping" to capture a neoimperial fantasy that prompts contemporary travel writers to present the landscapes they journey through as in some way uncharted, as terra incognita. This imaginary unmapping allows travel writers to present themselves as first-time explorers rather than simply tourists. Collin reads this desire as "a response arising in the era of late imperialism when the West began to perceive that new global conquests were no longer available to be claimed" (14). Having been closed to westerners from 1979 to 2001, post-9/11 Afghanistan presented a perfect opportunity for such unmapping. In *The Places In Between,* the reader is conscripted into seeing Stewart as a brave, solitary, Western explorer of an exotic, Eastern country, where he acts as a self-fashioned anthropologist and a collector of unique experiences and facts. "Every night, in over five hundred villages, I interviewed people about their possessions, communities, and history," he writes. "My notebooks were filled with facts about places I could rarely find again on the map" (73). Later in the book, Stewart quotes an Afghan village elder comparing him to Dr. William Brydon—the famed survivor of the 1842 ambush outside Jalalabad that wiped out the entire British Army during the first Anglo-Afghan War, an event that sent shivers throughout the Empire, prompting the myth of Afghanistan as unconquerable. "Do you know Dr. Brydon?" the elder says. "He was English. We killed you all but we left him alive to ride into Peshawar. . . . I think Afghans shall send you alive like Dr. Brydon" (131). Here, Stewart unabashedly positions himself alongside a heavily mythologized historical figure who witnessed an unspeakable atrocity and lived to tell the world about it.

In *The Bookseller of Kabul,* the author creates a similar narrative persona—solitary and heroic. She opens her book with the following:

> I had spent six weeks in Afghanistan with the commandos of the Northern Alliance—in the desert by the Tajikistani border, in the mountains of Hindu Kush, in the Panjshir Valley, and on the steppes north of Kabul. I have followed their offensive against the Taliban; I have slept on stone floors, in mud huts, and at the front; I had traveled on the back of trucks, in military vehicles, on horseback, and on foot.
>
> When the Taliban fell, I made it to Kabul with the Northern Alliance. (ix)

In these early post-9/11 texts, the solitary "I" of an adventurer figured as a legitimizing fiction that gave credence to the extraordinary-experience claim. The themes of courage, danger, solitude, and unique access are

interrelated; claims to extraordinary experience can be viewed as trust-
worthy only if the reader believes that the author is the only one with
access to this experience. Correspondingly, the claim to unique access is
substantiated by painting the terrain as extremely dangerous, which would
prevent others from traveling there. To bring into view, by contrast, the
existence of a vast, entrepreneurial, opportunistic, international community in post-9/11 Afghanistan is to undermine such claims. Stewart's and
Seierstad's texts skirt the topic of a massive international presence in post-
9/11 Afghanistan, the presence that made it possible, and relatively safe, for
the first time since 1979, for westerners to travel there. Lamb, in her own
memoir, restores some of this context; she recalls, for instance, Stewart as a
memorable fixture on the expatriate scene in Kabul, referring to him as an
eccentric old Etonian who roamed Kabul "in a long velvet coat" and "was
always entertaining company" (407).[9] A former tutor to Prince William
and Prince Harry, she writes, Stewart "was living in a mud-walled fort
running a foundation inspired by Prince Charles to revive traditional craft.
In 2010 he would be elected to Parliament as a Tory MP" (399–400). In his
memoir, Stewart is vague about his reasons for traveling to Afghanistan,
implying, however, that the trip was prompted by his love for Afghan
history and archeological heritage. To bring into view, as Lamb does, the
author's elite connections, his extravagant lifestyle in Kabul, and possibly,
his opportunism, is to undermine his claims of exceptionality, courage, and
selflessness. Seierstad, whose memoir became an international best seller,
selling more than 1.2 million copies worldwide (it was translated into 29
different languages), was sued for defamation by the Afghan book salesman whose life story she dramatized in her text. The bookseller claimed
the book violated his privacy, exposed his family to threats, and ruined his
reputation. In 2010, Seierstad lost her case in the Norwegian court and
was required to pay 250,000 kroner (about $32,000) to the bookseller's
second wife for privacy violations.[10] Yet, in spite of the moral controversy
surrounding her book, in the epilogue Seierstad positions herself not as a
beneficiary, but as a benefactor of Afghanistan as she talks about donating
$300,000 from her book's royalties to an Afghan development fund. "I
have seen so much misery," Seierstad says. "That's why I donated so much
of the money from the book back to Afghanistan. It's not that it makes me
feel good, but it makes me a bit happier that now hundreds of boys and
girls are going to school because of the book. Many babies are being saved
because I'm supporting midwives and nurses, who are needed because

the birth mortality rate is so high" (5). In sum, Steward and Seierstad are deeply invested in their own image as benefactors; as such they skirt the topic of themselves having *benefited from* the opportunities provided by traveling to Afghanistan after 9/11.

In sharp contrast to these early works, Barker, Wild, and Fey do not boast about their generous donations to Afghan funds, do not position themselves as especially courageous, and make no claims to an extraordinary experience. Instead, they use humor to portray their incompetence; foreground their lack of uniqueness, special skills, or courage; and highlight their embarrassing belatedness to the country that has been in the epicenter of many global wars for nearly half a century. Barker emphasizes, right away, that Kabul in 2002–2006 was not a place of danger. She explains that when she first arrived to Kabul in 2002, the war seemed over, people flocked to the streets, the Taliban had retreated into Pakistan, and the insurgency was not yet a problem. This calm period lasted, she explains, until 2006. She writes, for instance:

> In Kabul that spring of 2005, the lack of war was as obvious as the bikinis at the pool of L'Atmosphère, the restaurant of wicker chairs, glass-topped tables, and absurdly priced wine that had become the equivalent of the sitcom *Cheers* in the Afghan capital. How quiet was it? It was so quiet that an award-winning correspondent would spend the summer filming a documentary about a Kabul school for female drivers. . . . It was so quiet that I went to a brothel for fun. (47)

Journalist Jason Burke echoes Barker's assessment in his own recollection, referring to this period as "happy early days in Afghanistan" (77). Reassured by the rapid retreat of the Taliban and by the presence of international troops, émigrés and refugees returned to reclaim their homes. Bolstered by the international crowd, businesses flourished. Schools for girls reopened. Kabul, almost overnight, turned into a rapidly globalizing city. Burke thus recalls this era:

> Journalists filled the coffee-shot-cum-bar at the Mustafa Hotel in Shar-e-Nau, watching DVDs of Russell Crowe in *Gladiator* on a new flat-screen brought from Dubai, and held impromptu parties on the roof that provoked complaints about late-night noise from the newly refurbished Interior Ministry. NGOs poured in international staff. . . .

Thousands of often young, usually highly educated, largely white
Western people arrived. Many were experienced, serious, and highly
qualified; others were not. . . . One new adviser cheerfully complained of
being hired on a Tuesday, and arriving to Afghanistan, a country he had
never visited before, on a following Sunday. . . . One evening in 2002,
as off-duty Italian soldiers, Dutch and French NGO workers, British
anti-narcotics experts, American journalists and a gaggle of recently
hired consultants to the newly created ministries drank and danced, the
author was offered ecstasy by a development specialist who had flown in
that day from Frankfurt. (79–80)

These accounts mock the trope of extreme danger by explaining that
these early years (2001–2006) were the safest for travel to Afghanistan,
safety afforded by the presence of NATO troops and the general support
of the civilian population.[11] Moreover, instead of deploying neoimperial
explorer fantasies, Barker, Wild, and Fey go through great pains to show
that the territory they arrive to "discover" has not only been thoroughly
charted, but extensively colonized by the hordes of other expats, among
them humanitarians and NGO workers, advisers, troops, military contractors, entrepreneurs, sex workers, and genuinely seedy characters. They
introduce many side characters to paint a fuller picture of the milieu as
well as to reveal the absurd. Consider, for instance, an American vigilante
in Barker's book (also mentioned by Lamb) called Tora Bora Jack who, as
she explains, pretended to be a US special services agent, set up a makeshift
jail, kidnapped Afghans off the streets, and locked them up on suspicion
of terrorism (he was later convicted, spent some time in prison in Kabul,
and was then quietly released and allowed to go back to the United States).
The change of focus—from a lone westerner to the habitat she shared,
inevitably, with thousands of other do-gooders and fortune-chasers, paints
a portrait of a community whose cultural and economic impact was significant and whose moral compass was flawed. It prompts us to ask new
questions—not about Afghan cultural difference, but about what brings
all these expats to Kabul, and about the culture that they create there.

Anthropologist Barbara Heron, in her book-length study of white
female humanitarians, is critical of what she sees as her subjects' investment in the image of themselves as moral subjects; she also notes the
pernicious presence of the savior trope in their autobiographical stories
(110). She writes that "virtually all participants tell stories of our overseas

experiences that inevitably, and to some degree inadvertently, have the effects of casting ourselves as heroic figures" (107). This, however, is not true in the narratives discussed here. From beginning to end, Barker's, Wild's, and Fey's protagonists are critical about their own role and positionality in the Afghan reconstruction project; they are not at all sure they are making a difference, not at all certain they are making things better, and not at all convinced their behavior is ethical. In fact, they are ready to condemn themselves. Heron's "[c]laim to goodness and a moral self" (98) does not exist in these stories; also missing is "the 'know-better' development worker stance" (102). Barker, for instance, describes a moment of self-consciousness and shame when she finds herself in a Chinese-run brothel getting drunk, singing karaoke, and watching monkeys copulate in a cage on the eve of Eid—an important Islamic holiday marking the end of Ramadan. Reflecting upon this evening in her memoir, she says: "I was no longer just observing the bad behavior of the foreign community. Within weeks of my breakup [with my boyfriend], I had fully signed on" (78). Not only do these texts dislodge the belief in development workers' moral integrity, but there is also something important about the way in which these texts bring attention to their own status as commodities and to their authors as entrepreneurs. As cultural products, they lack innocence—the 9/11 wars created a worldwide market for stories from Kabul and Baghdad. These texts are the result of their authors' entrepreneurial efforts as they try to amass cultural capital in a struggle for survival in the cutthroat race for ever-diminishing resources in the austerity-era first world. *Kabul Disco*, for instance, both mocks itself and brings attention to itself as a commodity by noting that westerners writing about their Afghan experience are a tiresome cliché. On a flight from Kabul to Herat, coworkers tease Nicolas who is scribbling in his journal: "Are you writing a novel? . . ." "Most foreigners who live here write about their lives. As if the air in Kabul gives them writing skills" (84).

Further bringing into relief and mocking the trope of exceptionality deployed unabashedly in Stewart's and Seierstad's texts, Barker, Wild, and Fey use self-deprecating humor to highlight their narrators' lack of extraordinary qualities, cross-cultural competence, or even basic training in the international milieu. Traveling to Kabul in the aftermath of Operation Enduring Freedom, all three suggest, required no exceptional skills. Barker remarks that, in 2002, to go to Kabul, one needed only to be single, without children, and therefore "expendable" (16). She is explicit about her complete lack of qualifications to be a foreign correspondent, and instead of foregrounding courage, paints herself as being risk-averse: "I was convinced that death lurked behind every corner, perhaps the most unlikely foreign correspondent ever born" (16). She also admits to an utter lack of cross-cultural training: "I was hardly qualified to go anywhere, even Canada. I had never been to Europe. I spoke only English. I knew little about Al-Qaeda or Osama bin Laden. I knew about as much about Islam as I knew about Christianity, given my hippie infidel upbringing" (18). Kim Barker (Fey's character), similarly, is sent to Afghanistan because all experienced correspondents have gone to Iraq, and because she is unmarried and childless—"no one will sue if I die," she explains to a fellow passenger on the flight to Kabul. Kim's monocultural identity, her whiteness, and her lack of international experience is a source of comedy throughout the film. "'Kim' is American for 'white lady,'" she says, introducing herself to a world-savvy Lebanese correspondent. In this dialogue, whiteness indexes a monocultural identity rather than privileged status.

The lack of training or prior knowledge of Afghanistan that all three narrators manifest exemplifies the paradoxes of neoliberal development. *Kabul Disco*'s Nicolas receives no instruction, either prior to or upon his arrival to Afghanistan. Yet his first assignment is to draw an illustration of the Afghan parliament, and the deadline for the project completion is fast approaching. As he scrambles to find images of the Afghan parliament to imitate, he is baffled to discover that none exist, since the parliament itself does not yet exist. His boss explains that the illustration should be a symbolic representation of what the parliament might look like in the future. He advises:

> Make it symbolic by respecting the ethnic balance: 45% are Pashtuns, 36% are Tajiks, 12% are Uzbeks, 14% are Hazaras. And then there are a few Nuristanis, of course. Draw some wearing shalwar kamiz with turbans, patoos, and pakol. Then others wearing three-piece suits. Out of the 300 members, 25% are women. (48)

Nicolas walks away only to return after a few minutes. He asks, sheepishly:

> Sorry for my stupid questions but I just wanted to know, what do Pashtuns, Tajiks, Uzbeks, Hazaras, Nuristanis, a shalwar kamiz, a patoo, a pakol and women look like? (48)

The incompetence and lack of training of the arriving foreigners position the reconstruction project as a morally questionable enterprise that is destined to fail. As one reviewer puts it, "what really struck me about *Kabul Disco* is Wild's ambivalence about his role as a Westerner teaching Afghans about their new Afghan reality when he can't quite grasp it either" (*"Kabul Disco* by Nicolas Wild"). This comedic portrayal of clueless foreigners trying to educate the Afghans and transform the Afghan culture is supported by research that suggests that the overwhelming majority of foreigners (nearly 98 percent in one study) had no prior knowledge about Afghanistan prior to their arrival.[12] The irony is further compounded by the fact that out of the remaining 2 percent many mentioned reading fiction, mainly *The Kite Runner*, as their only cultural background training (Fluri 993).

From Tragedy to Comedy

Martha Lauzen notes that "comedy requires the comic to call attention to one's self" (107). The self-deprecating comedy of Barker, Fey, and Wild stands in sharp contrast with scenes of tragedy, terror, and humanitarian crisis that permeate early post-9/11 global Afghanistan writing and film. What necessitates this turn to comedy in the second decade of the 9/11 wars? Barker writes: "[A]bsurdity was the only frame that helped me make sense of what I saw: a military operation dubbed Operation Turtle, a Tarts-and-Talibs-themed party" ("My Kabubble"). Perhaps, the move from tragedy to comedy in the wars' second decade is prompted by the need for self-reflection and self-critique. Comedy, like the Owl of Minerva, arrives at dusk, offering a sense of detachment from which to examine one's actions.

Aside from foregrounding the absurd, comedy in these texts might have another purpose—disturbing familiar frames of reference by bringing together elements that seem to not belong together. It thus becomes a pedagogy that prompts us to rethink what we consider self-evident—providing a mirror that distorts familiar shapes to foreground an important detail by exaggerating it. Lauren Berlant and Sianne Ngai suggest that "comedies help us figure out distances and differences. . . . In the comedic scene, things are always closer to each other than they appear. They are near each other in a way that prompts a disturbance in the air" (248). In all three texts, distances and differences between phenomena that we regard as separate are blurred, as objects are brought into uncomfortable, laughter-inducing proximity. Perhaps the most notable of such unexpected proximities is the one between Afghanistan's socialist past and the new Western neoliberal present. In *Whiskey Tango Foxtrot*, during Kim's first embed with the US Marines, she travels with them to an Afghan village to repair a village well. As the military convoy arrives to the village in their Humvees to examine the well that has been damaged by explosives, an elder approaches an African American marine to ask if they were Russians (or "shouravi," communists, to be precise). The baffled soldier responds, with indignation: "The Russians? No sir, that was, mm, 20 years ago." "We are here to help," he offers after a pause. Upon considering it further, he chooses to add: "And I am black." The elder goes back to the villagers and says: "The Russians are black now" (Figure 6.4).

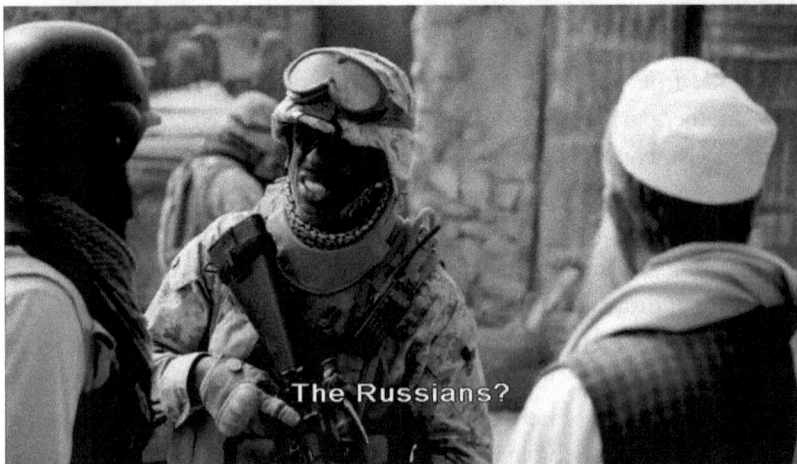

Figure 6.4. A village elder talks to a US Marine via an Afghan translator.

The expression on the elder's face suggests a possibility that he is simply messing with the soldier. The elder's question, while perplexing to the marine, isn't out of bounds, however, as the socialist government twenty years prior quite similarly tried to improve the infrastructure of villages and towns by building wells and water supply systems. Comedy material is derived from the fact that the foreigners seeking to liberate and civilize the Afghan population are mostly unaware of the long history of development and modernization efforts behind them.

A similar case of unexpected, laughter-inducing proximity between the disavowed socialist past and the neoliberal present is found in Wild's second book in the series. During his second term in Kabul, Nicolas is tasked with drawing a series of posters for the Afghan campaign against opium production, tentatively titled "Opium is bad" (19). Upon brainstorming, the team of designers settles upon the key message of the campaign: "Opium is an insult to the values of Islam" (*KD2* 42). Weeks later, billboard signs are produced and distributed. Nicolas feel tremendous pride as he sees the poster he designed—one that features Shaitan (the Devil) holding poppy stems in his hand—on a billboard in the city of Jalalabad (Figure 6.5).[13]

However, his feeling of success is short-lived. Soon after, Nicolas spots another image—a wall-sized fresco featuring an Afghan man and an Afghan woman with a sickle and a hammer, trampling poppy plants—a remnant from the socialist era (106). The caption, the Afghan translator explains, reads: "Opium insults the values of Islam" (Figure 6.6). A laughing fit that follows the discovery is Nicolas's reaction to two disparate things brought, uncomfortably, into unexpected closeness: the communist efforts to rid the country of narcotics and the team's present-day PR campaign. It is laughter-worthy that a team of precariously employed creative workers, laboring under the pressure of three-month contracts, employment uncertainty, and back-breaking deadlines in a war zone comes up with an "innovative idea" to brand opium production as un-Islamic only to discover that images such as theirs already exist in the Afghan landscape as remnants from the communist era. This discovery disturbs the comforting sense that the new international community is better equipped than the former socialist community to transform Afghanistan. It also directly contradicts Nicolas's understanding of Afghanistan's socialist past that he recasts for his readers' benefit in the first book, in which the communist government is depicted as banning Islam in Afghanistan (26).[13] Significant, also, is the difference in the iconography. The image from the

Figure 6.5. "Opium is an insult to the values of Islam."

socialist era provides an alternative to what it condemns: It is confident in its orientation toward a better future where a strong society based on the values on gender and economic equality, in Islam, trumps the opium production enterprise. The neoliberal-era poster, by contrast, emphasizes the harm (the Devil is foregrounded), while offering, iconographically, no alternative to the economies of inequality and exploitation powered by poppy cultivation.

Precarity: Contesting the Privilege Hypothesis

Fey's, Barker's, and Wild's accounts suggest that the humanitarian community in reconstruction-era Afghanistan should not be understood exclusively as a community of privileged first-world consumers. While many researchers and lay observers paint an image of the dramatic asymmetry between the expats and the locals in post-2001 Afghan cities—and that asymmetry, no doubt, existed—I would like to push against the privilege hypothesis somewhat by drawing attention to the fact that not only privileged members of global humanitarian and business elites, but also members of the global precariat are drawn to zones of conflict in the

Figure 6.6. "Opium insults the values of Islam."

advanced neoliberal economy. In current research on reconstruction-era Afghanistan, the privilege hypothesis predominates. In her insightful article "'Foreign Passports Only': Geographies of (Post)Conflict Work in Kabul, Afghanistan," Fluri distinguishes between citizens of sovereignty (expats from the global North) and citizens of exception (such as local Afghans). Citizens of sovereignty are defined as "individuals who may live and work in spaces marked by a continual state of exception, while retaining benefits associated with their legitimate and 'acceptable' sovereign citizenship (confirmed by one's passport or visa)" (987). Such benefits include transnational mobility, including the ability to leave Afghanistan and access to state protection in the case of an emergency. Citizens of exception, however, do not enjoy such protection. Kabul's post-2001 neoliberal economy, Fluri argues, was marked by such global inequality and worked to reinforce rather than ameliorate it. Extreme inequality, indeed, is a hallmark of neoliberalism—and all three texts, but especially Wild's and Barker's, bring into view the eccentric consumption practices of the expatriates, contrasting them to the endemic poverty that surrounds them in Afghanistan. At the same time, however, they also make visible their narrators' economic precarity, and by doing so, insert some nuance into the privilege claim and thus problematize a clear-cut divide between the global North and the global South.

Wild's narrator, a French creative professional (a graphic designer and illustrator of children books), unemployed and without a permanent living arrangement, in the opening chapters of the book, bemoans his inability to come up with an idea for a graphic novel. Aspiring to greatness but unable to make ends meet, he temporarily stays in the house of his more successful friend—an entrepreneurial comic book author who works incessantly and has published thirteen books. In the book's opening frames, Nicolas opens an email with an ad forwarded by a helpful acquaintance that says: "Afghan communication agency needs comic book author to work in Kabul" (6). Having dismissed it quickly—"Kabul? You have to be desperate to take a job like that" (6)—Nicolas is then confronted by the roommate who reminds him that it's time for him to move out and get his own place. The scene concludes with Nicolas feigning enthusiasm and long-standing passion for Afghanistan as he promptly applies for the advertised job. The economic precarity established from the beginning marks Nicolas as a transnational nomad not entirely by choice—his relocation to a conflict zone is prompted by a lack of economic opportunities in France. His economic and career prospects are bleak enough (as he himself admits, "one must be desperate to apply for a job like this") to chase a three-month contract in a distant country about which he knows nothing.[14]

Along the same lines, Barker describes her long-term struggle to find full-time employment as a journalist in the United States. Her career trajectory is typical for a creative-class professional in a late neoliberal economy defined by job scarcity and the prevalence of freelancing—precarious labor that carries no benefits. Barker's time in Afghanistan coincides, mostly, with the era of her being employed full-time by the *Chicago Tribune*, which makes her a member of a privileged class that Guy Standing calls "salariat." However, the memoir as a whole makes evident her continuous struggle to find and maintain steady employment, as well as the stress associated with labor precarity:

I studied journalism at Northwestern University outside of Chicago and slogged away on newspaper jobs in various meth-addled towns before landing my dream job at the *Seattle Times*, where for two years I wrote serious stories about the downtrodden and afflicted and won awards for investigative reporting. . . .

But then came the newspaper strike in Seattle and impending financial ruin. I cobbled together rent money by carrying a picket sign, dealing blackjack, and parking cars as a valet. . . .

I stuck with newspapers, all that I really knew, landing at *The Chicago Tribune* in early 2001, at age thirty. (17)

Thereby, the path to full employment, difficult to begin with, is riddled with further difficulties and setbacks: a period of stability (having a salaried job in *Seattle Times*) is then followed by a period of crisis (financial ruin) through no fault of her own, when she is, once again, reduced to temporary work and forced to take odd jobs outside her field. This backstory, which positions salaried full-time employment as a hard-won victory—an exception rather than the norm—foreshadows another crisis: During Barker's term in Afghanistan, the *Chicago Tribune* starts flailing, suffers a takeover, files for bankruptcy, and during the restructuring phase, eliminates thousands of jobs, including Barker's. By the end of the memoir, Barker is, once again, unemployed. Facing financial uncertainly and personal crisis, she has to reinvent herself and rebuild her life from ruins. Writing this memoir, it is implied, is a part of this self-reinvention.

Wild's and Barker's accounts, set in a war zone, bring into focus another war—an economic one that takes the form of flexibilization of labor power and the downgrading of full-time work to temporary and freelance jobs in the global North. As many have pointed out, twenty-first-century first-world economies are characterized by the dissolution of the wage relation that has been central to the Fordist economy—full-time salaried jobs with benefits are progressively replaced by a combination of "voluntary" unpaid effort, technology, and part-time labor. Jodi Dean notes that what was previously considered labor requiring wages now gets recast as a competition in a contest in hopes of winning a prize (139). Wendy Brown talks of the post-Fordist era as one where "responsibilized" individuals are "required to provide for themselves in the context of power and contingencies radically limiting their ability to do so" (134)—an exorbitant effort resulting in epidemiological rates of depression and generalized anxiety disorder. The withdrawal of state protection affects citizens of the world unevenly; however, the boundaries between the first world and the third world are no longer as clear-cut as they once were. In fact, they might be collapsing, as Gordon Lafer shows in his insightful article that details how the War on Terror not only opened up Iraq to neoliberal exploitation, but also enabled a full-frontal assault on labor unions and public sector employees in the post-9/11 United States. He calls the War on Terror "neoliberalism by other means" (325). "[I]f we continue to follow the logic of [neoliberal] capitalist globalization," Lafer writes, "the fate of most Americans is to become much poorer, until we balance out at the level of typical or middle- and working-class people in the rest of the world, i.e. the third world" (332).

Notably, in all three texts, reconstruction-era Kabul figures as an open playground for international corporations. It also figures as a zone of self-refashioning for enterprising individuals—a personal and a career opportunity. Neoliberalism, Brown observes, reconfigures individuals as private enterprises who are expected to continuously improve themselves by treating themselves as objects of investment and sites of capitalization: "Human capital's constant and ubiquitous aim, whether studying, intern-ing, working, planning retirement, or reinventing itself in a new life, is to enterpreneurialize its endeavors, appreciate its value, and increase its rating or ranking" (36). Brown explains that "actual or figurative credit rating" is assigned "across every sphere" of existence (33). In Fey's film, both implicit and overt ranking systems are deployed as a source of com-edy. To her amusement, Kim's rating literally goes up with her relocation to Afghanistan. Her attractiveness score increases from her usual six (in the United States) to nine or even nine-and-a-half in Kabul, due to the shortage of women in the expat community. As a result, she is able to capitalize on the increased attractiveness rating by having a selection of available sexual/romantic partners. The rating system, of course, applies also to the work the characters perform. Fey's protagonist has to participate in the cutthroat competition for the desirable jobs in the global North by putting herself, literally, in the line of fire. She captures her audience in the United States (thus increasing her company ratings) by capturing on camera the Taliban's attack on a military convoy, but later has to face the fact that "Afghanistan does not rate anymore." She loses this race, even-tually, to a more aggressively competitive Tanya who outranks her both in terms of her story ratings and in her attractiveness (she is considered "a fifteen" in Kabul). Tanya gets a coveted job in London after subjecting herself to extreme danger by traveling to meet with the Taliban in tribal areas. This encounter has massive human costs: Her cameraman loses an eye and her Afghan fixer gets killed. Tanya herself, remarkably, walks away with only minor bruises, and manages to sell the story well to negotiate a high-paying contract with the network. The film makes it clear: It is not enough to travel to the war zone—one has to travel further into the heart of darkness, chasing danger and bullets, and sacrificing other people's lives to deliver a good scoop.

Similarly, Barker focuses on corporeal injury as a mark of creative professionals' need to compete for airtime and funding. Her friend Sean, a freelance documentary film director, gets kidnapped as he travels to the tribal areas to meet with Taliban commanders in hope of making a movie. Having spent months in captivity, he is released after his government pays ransom money and returns to England. Sean himself, Barker reveals, suffers irreparable psychological damage; furthermore, the ransom money (paid by British taxpayers to the Taliban) will finance more violence and kidnappings. By forcing the properly interpellated enterprising individuals to take undue risks, Barker suggests, neoliberal economies set up structures that create a spiral of violence. Barker herself, in spite of relocating to a war zone, facing corporeal risks, and facing the psychological risks associated with addiction-prone expat culture, is not safe from failure, but has to continuously struggle for her ever-diminishing share of resources. In a race to compete for success and survival, she and other expats face what Brown calls, poignantly, "employment unto death" (218)—an unrelenting drive to produce more (more news, more clicks, higher ratings) while having to do so with fewer resources. By the end of her term in Kabul, Barker no longer has a place of her own but resorts to couch surfing, paying out-of-pocket for incidentals, and is unable to pay for her Afghan fixer's help. "I was a newspaper reporter working for a bankrupt company in the middle of a war on terror," she says. "I was standing in line like a dumb steer in a chute in Montana, and I didn't even know it" (256).

In the climate of austerity, unemployment, and recession in the global North, the famed dichotomy between first-world privilege and third-world destitution is no longer clear-cut. For instance, Barker's highly effective and in-demand Afghan contact, Farouq, by the end of her stay in Afghanistan, charges $300 per day (whereas she can afford to pay him only $125), owns a business (an internet café bringing in $1,500 per month), gets married, and has children, while Barker has to give up on relationships, never sees her family, and does not get vacation time, running a race for a job that will be cancelled in matter of months anyway. This situation is brought into comic relief as various Afghan and Pakistani officials (men who lust after Barker) keep offering her jobs: as a PR-consultant in Kabul with a $100,000/year salary, as a hospital manager in Pakistan, as a secretary for a major political figure. Even though these positions require having an affair with the men who offer them, Barker admits to considering the offers, because her employment prospects look so bleak.

The Ruins of Neoliberalism

In these texts, the ruins of Afghanistan are reconfigured, paradoxically, as the ruins of late neoliberalism—a baneful system that ruins human lives worldwide while enriching a select few. Many contemporary researchers criticize neoliberal development schemes for being grounded in what Astri Suhrke calls "destructive forms of development" (1293). Producing large-scale transnational corruption, "markets without investors" (Schwartz 256), and infrastructures with no purpose, these forms of development trigger progressive cycles of immiseration of the local population, and are seen by many as structural adjustments imposed via military conquest. Throughout her memoir, Barker picks apart the reconstruction process by offering snapshots of such destructive development and critiquing the inflated bubble economy that follows the US-led invasion. Reconstruction-era Kabul enjoys a construction boom—ornate narco-mansions, blast walls, barricaded-off international agencies' buildings, and overpriced venues catering to the international development-and-reconstruction crowd pop up everywhere. She is critical of the economic bubble created by the presence of foreign businesses and agencies in the Afghan capital—a bubble that distorts the local economy, impeding post-conflict recovery:

> [F]or an average Afghan, life still consisted of a mud hut, an outhouse, and a couple of hours of electricity a day. Renting a decent concrete house in Kabul now cost at least $1,500 a month. Afghan teachers and police officers made between $60 and $125 a month. The only changes most Afghans had seen in Kabul had been negative—higher rent and food costs, higher bribes, greater hassles. Traffic jams were regularly caused by convoys of Land Cruisers with dark windows and no license plates, by U.S. soldiers screaming out orders and pointing their guns, by concrete barriers set up by foreign aid groups and companies worried about suicide bombs. (92)

While in the early NATO years, she observes, Kabul still bore the mark of
the war-borne destruction—it "looked like someone had shaken a giant box of
crackers and dumped them out" (20)—the subsequent years produce ruins of a
new kind. These ruins are deteriorating shells of new buildings—unfinished or
made through corrupt development schemes that allow large companies from
the global North to pocket taxpayers' money by subcontracting to local businesses who employ cheap labor and use cheap materials. Barker thus recalls a
story of visiting a site of such neoliberal "reconstruction" that left behind a ruin:

> On one patrol, we visited a clinic built through the U.S. schools-and-
> clinics program. . . . The program was largely considered a debacle. The
> new buildings came in shoddy, late, and over budget. The lead USAID
> contractor, the Louis Berger Group of New Jersey, reportedly charged
> U.S. taxpayers an average of $226,000 for each building—almost five
> times as much as Afghans and European nonprofit groups had paid for
> similar buildings. . . . Corners were cut. Many buildings were already
> falling apart. Some roofs had caved in from heavy snow.
> We sat with elders at their new clinic.
> "Do you use it?" an American staff sergeant asked.
> "Well . . . we have no medicine," an Afghan answered, then added,
> almost as an afterthought, "And we have no doctor." (116)

Here, Barker shows how the neoliberal development economy, with its
intricate forms of transnational corruption and profiteering schemes is
flawed by design, out of touch with the real needs of the people, and leaves
behind new infrastructures that already are derelict. She recalls seeing such
new ruins everywhere in Afghanistan: "We drove south to Kandahar on
a highway that the Americans had built in 2003," she writes, "already, the
road was falling apart, and entire chunks had crumbled away, due to poor
design, poor execution, and really poor asphalt" (101).[15] In his "Military
Neoliberalism: Endless War and Humanitarian Crisis in the 21st Century,"
Schwartz argues that it was not the lack of funding, but the overall "neoliberal orientation" that was the cause of these massive failures. An opening
of Afghanistan to international markets involved dismantling repairable
existing infrastructures and replacing them with proprietary new technology installed by "imported, unsupervised, profit-seeking contractors"
(255) in a business climate where the only sanction for failure was "a small
monetary fine and the danger of losing the next contract" (254).

A 2015 BuzzFeed News investigation by Azmat Khan in Afghanistan found that "the overwhelming majority of the more than 50 US-funded schools it visited resemble abandoned buildings—marred by collapsing roofs, shattered glass, boarded-up windows, protruding electrical wires, decaying doors, or other structural defects" (par. 17). An image by Khan, "The ruins of Nahre Karez Primary School," shows an elder in front of a building that looks as if it has been abandoned for decades—except it is a new build. Such ruins continue to serve as instruments of profit extraction; a BuzzFeed correspondent found that such "ghost schools . . . are being used to embezzle teacher salaries" (par. 20).

It is significant, however, that Barker's book does not present the ruinous "development" in Afghanistan as an exception (related, one might assume, to endemic corruption), but contextualizes it by tying these processes to the concomitant crisis in the global North. As Barker travels back to Chicago for a weeklong visit in 2006, she finds evidence of an ongoing war—an economic one—in her own homeland. Her verdict—"I flew back to the States, where things would be even worse" (208)—reminds us of Christina Lamb's book subtitle, "From Afghanistan to a More Dangerous World." The processes of ruination and crisis have come home. While Barker was away, the company suffered a takeover and thousands of jobs were eliminated. "Walking into the newsroom," she writes, "now felt like walking into the newsroom during Christmas—it was depressing, and most of the desks were empty. Only it was June, and many desks were empty because of layoffs and buyouts" (211). The empty desks of her media company were as glaring as the emptiness of the ruined schools and clinics in Afghanistan. Barker's job would soon be eliminated as well, but not until the company launched its "Ultimate Fight Challenge" in which journalists have to compete with each other for the few jobs that were left. Barker thus writes of accepting the fight for her job:

> I focused on work, on cultivating new sources, on winning Ultimate
> Fight Challenge [to keep my job]. I vowed to do embeds, blogs, video,
> interviews, cartwheels, breaking news, long features, recipes, algebra.
> If there was going to be some kind of contest over my job, I was going
> to fight as hard as possible to win. I channeled the theme from *Rocky*. I
> would cancel all holidays, write at all hours, say yes to every editor. (262)

When her job was eliminated, Barker decided to stay in Afghanistan "to have a quiet place to figure out what [she] wanted to do next" (281).

Paradoxically, the United States and Afghanistan seemed to have switched places: Afghanistan here figured as a quiet place where Barker would have the time to think and plan her future, while the United States figured as an economic war zone and a site of ongoing destruction of people's livelihood. This, again, pushes back against the privilege hypothesis, suggesting that many expatriates flocked to Kabul in search of a break, a respite from the hyper-competition for diminishing resources in their home countries. While one can rightfully argue that their transnational mobility marks them as privileged, their lack of economic stability, entrapment in the downward cycle toward looming unemployment or part-time work, mental fatigue, and diminishing prospects continuously chip away at that privilege.

Through their comedic pedagogies, Barker, Wild, and Fey prompt us to ask new questions about the humanitarian efforts that take place as part of twenty-first-century NATO-led wars. They begin to develop a vocabulary for talking about the global precariat in a time of widespread economic and political crisis. The attempt at a new language starts by bringing into view these transnational workers as a group, thus making visible the structures underlying their individual choices. We can finally say what has shifted: These workers no longer think of themselves as saviors. Nor do they have what Heron describes as "a sense of obligation and entitlement to intervene so as to 'help' in the world—a scope of action sanctioned by the planetary consciousness of bourgeois subjectivity" (121). Development work, indeed, has become simply a job opportunity in a recession-era world where jobs are scarce. However, having lost the sense of moral righteousness that permeates early Afghanistan writing and film, these new texts have not yet developed a sense of class consciousness or a politics that would respond to the conditions they describe. While comprising a weak form of collectivity (party culture), the precarious humanitarians of these cultural texts do not coalesce into a political body that is able to advocate for itself (or for Afghanistan, for that matter). Transnational, and lacking a sense of home, belonging neither to Afghanistan nor fully to their own nations, they congregate without coalescing into a citizenry. They are a party without a Party. Seeming to accept their lot as inevitable, they also do not seem to have any beliefs or subscribe to any ideology. Unable to think of itself as a class, the expatriate community in Barker, Fey, and Wild's work is not able to think of the common good either; they congregate without being able to reflect on their own conditions, let alone devise alternatives to the destructive development they are unwittingly conscripted into. What is the alternative? There does not seem to be one. Theirs is an anemic collectivity that consists of individuals interpellated as entrepreneurs, as having their own economic interest, and survival, in mind.

As such, there is something incomplete about these critiques—these texts are diagnostic of the present moment but do not offer any solutions. They represent the no-alternative attitude of the "capitalist realism" generation described by Mark Fisher (*Capitalist Realism*). Many precarious laborers are either still invested in anti-socialism, as Wild's graphic novel series demonstrates, or lack real knowledge about socialist histories. In Afghanistan, they find the ruins of socialism and the ruins of neoliberalism side by side; they laugh at the sight of this proximity, yet no new vision manifests itself. At the same time, what becomes strikingly clear is that the very surfacing of these stories marks the end of an era—the NATO-led era in Afghanistan, and with it, the era of the humanitarian imaginary's dominance. The initial promise—that Afghan modernity would be restored through Afghanistan's integration into, and submission to, the neoliberal present, did not materialize. The US Afghan reconstruction project ended with the massive loss of faith in military-humanitarian interventions. Having begun with a call to liberate (by unveiling) Afghan women, it ended with another kind of unveiling—the unveiling of the dead-end of the late neoliberal moment.

Conclusion: The End of an Era

As we have seen throughout this book, Afghanistan serves as a mirror upon which contemporary cultural producers project their values and beliefs, as well as their presumptions and biases. The two decades of the 9/11 wars have seen a production of thousands of titles on Afghanistan, all of which tried to respond, make sense of, and provide a witness to the Afghan crisis. Some of them became purveyors of myths, while others sought to revise or dispute them. There is no single aesthetic that unites all of these works. They all seek to bring Afghanistan and its turbulent history into mainstream visibility. While doing so, they struggle with how to articulate various aspects of its past: its socialist history, the invasion by the Soviet Union, the role of the United States in the "Afghan" jihad, and the failures of the US-led intervention that followed the Taliban ouster. While early works deploy the humanitarian narrative to create a victim that needs saving (in particular, Afghan women), there is a clear shift away from this approach toward the end of the first decade of the war. This is partly due to the criticism that the discourse of saving Afghan women received in transnational feminist circles and partly due to the failures of the NATO-era Afghanistan that started to manifest since 2006—rapidly deteriorating security, the squandering of money that amounted to transnational corruption, and the overall lack of vision for the country's future. At the end of the second decade of the 9/11 wars, the global Afghanistan corpus of works is a case study in the humanitarian imaginary, but also, as I argued in this book, offers a way out of it.

As I demonstrate in chapters four through six, global Afghanistan writing and film cannot be captured through the framework of humanitarianism alone; while creating a witness to suffering and crisis, cultural texts discussed in these chapters work to decenter the human figure and seek to develop a vocabulary and an aesthetic alternative to the humanitarian imaginary. Qais Akbar Omar in his memoir creates the figure of a joyful survivor—a witness to unspeakable darkness that overwhelms Afghanistan after the defeat of the socialist state who nevertheless resists victimization and feels the joy of being an Afghan. Kamila Shamsie shifts focus away from the individual and makes visible the infrastructures—of jihad as well as of the War on Terror—both of which are racialized, reflecting colonial power structures. Zia Haider Rahman's epistemological novel decenters the human by imagining a nonhuman witness in mathematics. With its focus on deep time, Nadeem Aslam's aesthetics of the geologic turn situate the drama of human history between the microtemporal register (insect perception, flowers promptly recolonizing minefields) and the immemorial time of geology, further recontextualizing the human via multiscalar optics. To add, his works foreground two processes—excavation and burial as opposed to language-mediated testimony—as two modes of working through traumatic memory—memory that does not belong to a human alone. Finally, the texts discussed in chapter six shift focus from victims of the disaster to the humanitarian community that arrives to the zone of crisis. By making visible, and making fun of, in a comedic reversal, the infrastructures of humanitarian labor, these works dramatically change the way we see humanitarian work in the twenty-first century. Texts discussed in chapters four through six thus conjure powerful new vocabularies that, no doubt, will be useful for analyzing texts outside the global Afghanistan corpus as well.

When I started writing this book, many of the works I discuss in this book hadn't been published yet. It was the time prior to the creation, and the eventual, tentative defeat of the Islamic State in Syria and Iraq. The disastrous failures of the Iraq War weren't yet fully known. It was prior to the proxy war that tore apart Syria and that saw an uncanny repetition of some of the patterns of the Cold-War-era conflict in Afghanistan, with the United States, Russia, Saudi Arabia, and Iran's involvement (among other parties). The deployment of the humanitarian imaginary to frame the Syrian war to the US public bore an uncanny resemblance to the mythologies created in the Western press around the Afghan jihad, with images of suffering children used to stir up bipartisan support of the strikes against the Syrian state. I hope this book will provide an alternative to NATO-centric imaginaries that dominate, quite understandably, Western media and academic contexts. In these contexts, the bipartisan romanticization of anti-statist insurgency persists in spite of the fact that the echoes of Afghanistan's unraveling reached the United States and the world in the form of transnational terror, and in spite of the knowledge of the tremendous human costs of the state collapse in Iraq, Libya, and Syria that has reached Europe in the form of an unprecedented refugee crisis. Still, the deeply held suspicion, even disdain toward the third-world state, a perception of the third-world state as irredeemably totalitarian (engaged in wholesale oppression of its people and thus a legitimate target for insurgency), over and over again makes it easy for Western governments to use unverified stories of human rights abuses to gain the Western public's endorsement of invasions and bombing campaigns. A reader of this book should note, for instance, the conspicuous absence in NATO-centric media of voices of Iraqis, Libyans, or Syrians who were invested, for multiple reasons, in the preservation of their nation-states and opposed US-led attempts to weaken these states. This is not to mount a defense of particular regimes; it is, however, to remind readers of the paradoxes of humanitarian imaginary that Afghanistan's history teaches us. Given the tremendous human costs of a third-world state collapse, which are visible in the history of post-Cold War Afghanistan, one should weigh such costs against the costs of such state's *preservation*. Once again, we need more than one story, as there exists, in all these cases "the danger of a single story."[1]

Curiously, the last years of the second decade of the 9/11 wars also saw the return of virulent anti-Russian rhetoric in the American media. Suddenly, the anti-Russian tropes that I discussed by analyzing *The Photographer* or *The Kite Runner* became instantly recognizable to my undergraduate students who haven't live through the Cold War. Of course, this time around they are a result of a geopolitical rather than ideological rivalry; however, it is remarkable how easy it was to tap into this repertoire of tried and tired tropes, especially during the legitimacy crisis that followed the 2016 election in the United States. There are other shifts taking place. America's war in Afghanistan (the longest war in US history) did not end in victory, but in "a grinding stalemate" for which there is no end in sight.[2] The promise of complete withdrawal of US troops from Afghanistan by 2014 did not materialize. In 2017, President Donald Trump announced a reengagement in Afghanistan and promised to add thousands of American troops in an attempt to change the course of the war against the Taliban and other insurgents; in 2018, however, he reversed his decision and announced a withdrawal. Security in Afghanistan is at its worst. Aside from the Taliban, there is now a contingent of Islamic State insurgents in eastern Afghanistan, growing since the defeats that ISIS forces suffered in Syria and Iraq. The stakes are high and so is the death toll: May 2017 saw the deadliest terrorist attack in Kabul to date, where a truck bomb exploded in the middle of a busy intersection killing over 150 and injuring 413, mostly civilian, people. The attack is attributed to the Haqqani network—a successor to the CIA-funded, anti-Soviet guerilla network of the 1980s founded and led by mujahid Jalaluddin Haqqani in 1978. Echoes of the long 1979 are still heard around the planet, and will continue to be, for the foreseeable future.

As we consider, through texts conjured by contemporary authors, the fallout of Western policies and operations in 1980s Afghanistan, we also must begin taking stock of the legacies of the twenty-first-century US-led war. What will this recent war in Afghanistan bequeath to the world—the war that started in response to the attack on the Twin Towers and hasn't ended, trapped in an uncertainty of a seemingly perpetual cycle of withdrawal and return?[3] What problems became obvious, what paradoxes came to the surface, and what, if anything, was learned from this engagement? Journalist Jason Burke writes, in *The 9/11 Wars*, of his impressions during the first days of Operation Enduring Freedom. He recalls:

> Watching the aerial bombing of Tora Bora in the mountains of eastern Afghanistan in December 2001, with vapour trails from B-52s slicing across the pale sky above the snowy peaks and row upon row of rocky ridges successfully lit by the slanting rising sun, a fellow journalist commented as a scene of untold horror and violence and extraordinary aesthetic beauty unfolded before us that *only a vast novel could make sense of what was happening.* He was probably right. (xxi, emphasis my own)

Without doubt, it will take decades to understand this war fully, just as it is taking many decades to weigh the full impact of US involvement in the "Afghan" jihad of the 1980s. As this book shows, however, this process has begun, and new texts keep emerging that add more nuance and texture to that work. In 2019, as I am writing this conclusion, there is a vast corpus of texts that try to make sense of what happened. To comprehend this war, as Burke intuited, we need multi-scalar optics. Nadeem Aslam's geological imagery serves to capture precisely the violence and the beauty of warfare on the geological scale, as if answering Burke's call for an optics that can absorb something as tremendous as the bombing of Tora Bora—an event that seems to approximate a meteoric incursion, an extraterrestrial assault. Aslam's novels make audible the echoes of this geological warfare through his vision of planetary interconnection.

A commemoration, an epistemology, a political debate—the global Afghanistan corpus is still a work in progress, but some of its contours are already visible. In the 2018 Hollywood Afro-futuristic blockbuster *Black Panther*—a movie that takes place in Wakanda, a site of a prosperous and technologically advanced African civilization—the antagonist who challenges the king for the throne is an African American veteran of the Afghanistan and Iraq wars. Nicknamed "Killmonger," he defeats the king in ritual combat and assumes the throne. Allegorizing American-led "humanitarian" invasions of the twenty-first century (Killmonger wants to be a liberator of the oppressed), his immediate effect is the collapse of the Wakandan state; he divides the people, starts a civil war, and orders shipments of Wakanda's secret weapons to countries worldwide, thus exporting the crisis. It is explained (appropriately, by a white CIA agent) that Killmonger was trained as a black ops specialist to undermine governments, destroy nation-states, and start civil wars. He is not good at state governance, caring for citizens' needs, building consensus, or long-term planning—all hallmarks of a good statesman. The film's diagnosis of the 9/11 wars is this: Humanitarian interventions of the 9/11 war era were successful at destroying, dislodging, and dividing, but failed when it came to building a better, safer, more just world.

Exemplifying the anxieties about the long-term legacies of the US-led intervention, Donald Rumsfeld writes, in his 2011 memoir:

> the United States did not "break" . . . Afghanistan, a land that had been broken, at least by Western standards, for centuries. . . . Solving corruption in Afghanistan or building a secular democracy in the Middle East are not America's problems to tackle. They are not our broken societies to fix. (724)

This gesture of resignation—"they are not our societies to fix"—of course, contradicts the very ethos of humanitarian wars, one that takes for granted the right to intervene precisely because distant countries are brought into focus, via humanitarian imagery, as ours to fix. Rumsfeld's rhetoric indexes a sense of failure that is in stark contrast with the sense of triumph this former secretary of state felt when he first arrived to Kabul in 2001, firmly believing in the success of "American liberation" (see chapter 2). Fey, Wild, and Barker's accounts, among many others,[4] also register this sense that the US-led war and reconstruction in Afghanistan have ended in failure. While Rumsfeld's refusal to take responsibility for this failure obfuscates the processes that led to it, these other accounts seek to make them legible.

The era of optimistic belief in the moral rightness of humanitarian invasions seems to have ended.[5] As we transition, tentatively, out of the age of weaponized human rights into a new as yet undefined era, the case study in global NATO-centric Afghanistan writing and film allows us to decipher representational matrices that persist and still structure our perceptions. As the global Afghanistan corpus of works teaches us, sometimes we need to combat the deployment of humanitarian imaginary by inquiring about the ideology or dogma that structures such representations. At other times, we might need to respond to it, like Fey, Barker, and Wild, with laughter. My hope is that we can put the post-Cold War humanitarian imaginary to rest, and that Afghanistan and its history will no longer be sutured to a humanitarian image—a green-eyed refugee girl from a 1985 *National Geographic* cover. Afghanistan is not simply a defiant relic of socialist barbarity. We need to hear other stories—the story of the Afghan revolutionary subject, the story of Afghan modernity, of Afghan cosmopolitanism, the story of its people's desire for peaceful development, their long quest for political and economic justice. In spite of all its failures, and against all odds, "red Afghanistan" has to be inscribed as an important chapter in the global history of the struggle for women's rights and for economic justice. And it has to be done in a meaningful way, to sufficiently recognize the people (many of them revolutionary women) who held these dreams dear. The *National Geographic*'s Afghan girl, in the Western imaginary, has been asked to bear a burden that is too heavy for one child—to be a synecdoche for the nation at large, to be a cause for moral outrage, a reason for the increase of weapons being smuggled into her country, all of which brought additional suffering until her country was no more. With kindness and respect, we need to put this image to rest. We need other images and other stories—not of Afghan victimhood on behalf of which the global West has to interfere, again and again, against the Afghan state, but of Afghan revolutionary dreaming, self-determination, state-building, globalism, and the tragically interrupted, but not erased, Afghan modernity.

Notes

Introduction

1. Taylor, "These Are America's 9 Longest Foreign Wars Yet."
2. See Crews 269.
3. The United States alone allocated over $100 billion for the Afghan reconstruction project. Most of that money has been spent on training the Afghan military and police force, building government capacity, and on various reconstruction projects. For more detailed information, visit the official USAID site: https://explorer.usaid.gov/cd/AFG. See also Lutz and Desai, "US Reconstruction Aid for Afghanistan." The war itself is estimated to have cost American taxpayers over one trillion dollars (Amadeo).
4. *Empire Lite* 73–74, quoted in Douzinas 64.
5. The period of 2001–2014 is of particular significance as it is the era of the NATO-led military intervention on a large scale. The period beyond 2014 is an ambiguous era in which deteriorating security, the difficulty of negotiating with the Taliban, political rivalries, and the new threat of ISIS in Afghanistan trap the United States government in a political and military stalemate while other major actors (such as the United Kingdom) have withdrawn from the country. At the time when I am writing this (2019), President Trump had announced his plans for complete withdrawal; the exact contours of this plan remain uncertain, however.
6. In this project, I focus on works produced or circulating in the NATO-centric context, that is, works made for transnational yet mostly Western audiences. I deliberately excluded, for instance, written and visual texts produced in the Russophone world, although this corpus of works is vast and includes many informative, gripping memoirs by Soviet-Afghan War veterans from Russia, Ukraine, Tajikistan, and other post-Soviet states. Within the post-Soviet world, cultural texts on Afghanistan reflect the need to process the traumatic experience of the Soviet-Afghan War. By contrast, the NATO-centric corpus was spurred by the more recent US-led intervention in Afghanistan.

7. Consider, for instance, American writer James Currier, who set his novel *The Third Buddha* (2011) in Bamyan—the former site of the two colossal Buddhas dynamited by the Taliban regime. While never having traveled to Afghanistan, he imagines the country as a site of thriving gay male sexuality, thus inscribing it as an exotic locale where liberal, Western gay male desire is reaffirmed and reinvigorated.

8. See, for instance, Gray, *After the Fall: American Literature Since 9/11*; Keniston and Quinn, *Literature After 9/11*; Randall, *9/11 and the Literature of Terror*; or Banita, *Plotting Justice: Narrative Ethics and Literary Culture After 9/11*.

9. Burke writes: "[the 9/11 wars are] a matrix of ongoing, overlaid, interlinked and overlapping conflicts, some of which ended during the ten years since 9/11 and some of which started; some of which worsened and some of which died away; some of which have roots going back decades if not centuries and some of which are relatively recent in origin" (xix). These include US-led foreign wars and operations in Afghanistan, Iraq, Libya, and Syria as well as many executed or thwarted terrorist attacks and localized fighting between third parties.

10. See DeRosa and Peebles 211.

11. Quoted in Douzinas 267.

12. While Burke suggests that the 9/11 wars era has no defining end point, it is possible that the 9/11 wars might have ended in 2014. The advent of ISIS with its new strategy of territorial capture, state-building, and Russian involvement in Syria signal that we may be now facing something entirely new. However, the lack of transparency or governmental accountability, the privatization of warfare, and the prevalence of the humanitarian imagery used to legitimize invasions and strikes are features that define both decades.

13. See "Afghanistan: Human Development Indicators."

14. In his discussion of the country's fate during the Cold War and beyond, leading Afghanistan scholar Barnett Rubin calls Afghanistan "the mirror of the world" (*The Fragmentation of Afghanistan* 1). For an overview of Afghanistan's recent history, see Rubin's *Afghanistan from the Cold War to the War on Terror*.

15. To my knowledge, the term "global civil war" was first used in relation to Afghanistan by Oona Frawley in 2013. In 2002, Stein Tønnesson used the term to describe the US's war with Al-Qaeda. More recently, Franco (Bifo) Berardi used a modified term—"fragmentary global civil war"—in relation to the conflicts of the two first decades of the twenty-first century in "The Coming Global Civil War: Is There a Way Out?" Of the nature of this war, he writes: "no declarations of war are being issued, but innumerable combat zones are proliferating. No unified fronts are in sight, but fragmented micro-conflicts and uncanny alliances with no general strategic vision abound."

16. See Crews for a critique of this trope (3, 118, 310).

17. See "The Calm Before the Storm" in *The 9/11 Wars*.

18. See, for instance, Seth G. Jones, *In the Graveyard of Empires*.

19. Women's equality in Afghanistan was first established in the constitution of 1923 drawn by Amanullah Khan (the reformer king), but these advances

were then reversed in 1929 as the king himself was overthrown. Afghan women regained voting rights in 1964, during the rule of King Mohammed Zahir Shah.

20. The term "mujahideen" (plural) or "mujahid" (singular) refers to jihad fighters; in Afghanistan, mujahideen engaged in the jihad against Afghan communists and later against the Soviet contingent.

21. James Darmesteter, *Chants populaires des afghans,* Paris: Imprimerie nationale. 1888–1890, quoted in Crews 3.

22. In the post-9/11 context, Steve Coll's *Ghost Wars* made the facts related to the CIA's involvement in fueling the flames of the Afghan jihad available to popular audiences.

23. "Kabubble" is a common term in expat writing on Afghanistan connoting foreigners' Kabul. See, for instance, David Marshall Fox's "The K-Town 'Kabubble': Thoughts on Expat Security in Kabul." The term has been popularized via Tina Fey's comedy *Whiskey Tango Foxtrot.*

1   Humanitarian Sublime and the Politics of Pity

1. See Ryzik, "Q. and A. with Tina Fey: Live From Kabul, It's a Feminist Comedy."
2. I will discuss the film, as well as the memoir it is based on, in chapter six.
3. See Mitchell, "Film Review; Veils of Tears Frame Lives in Kandahar."
4. See Corliss, "All-Time 100 Movies."
5. See Román, *Performance in America: Contemporary U.S. Culture and the Performing Arts* 260.
6. Berson, "Prescient Tony Kushner Takes on Issues of Our Time in 'Homebody/Kabul.'"
7. See Jeffries, "Reader, I Am a He."
8. See Jeffries, "Reader, I Am a He."
9. "Tony's Eye on the Future."
10. Green, "His Very Own Scoop."
11. See Slaughter's *Human Rights Inc.* and Anker's *Fictions of Dignity* for in-depth analysis of the 1990s human rights novel and its conventions.
12. Graham further explains that "there was little subsequent criticism in Iran or in the world community itself over how Afghans were portrayed in the film. The only objections came from voices in the Afghan diaspora, which not surprisingly objected to *Kandahar*'s portrayal of 'a country full of grave robbers, con artists, and thieves'" (65). Graham's chapter provides an insightful critique of the film's pseudodocumentary aesthetics. While appearing to bring the "real" Afghanistan to the global audience, the film relies, instead, on Orientalist tropes of Afghanistan's changelessness, immutability, and depravity.
13. An anti-veiling narrative, *The Swallows of Kabul* is likely to have been written during the era of the hijab wars in France; it interpellates the European reader as a compassionate liberal subject who might be able to intervene on behalf of the women oppressed by fundamentalist regimes yet yearning to be free.

14. See Kushner's interview with Taft-Kaufman 45.
15. See Kolhatkar and Ingalls, *Bleeding Afghanistan* 169.
16. See Kolhatkar and Ingalls, *Bleeding Afghanistan;* Stabile and Kumar, "Unveiling Imperialism: Media, Gender, and the War on Afghanistan"; Schueller, "Cross-cultural Identification, Neoliberal Feminism, and Afghan Women"; Khan, "Afghan Women: The Limits of Colonial Rescue"; and Puar, "Feminists and Queers in the Service of Empire," among many others.
17. Douzinas 72.
18. Humanitarianism also has a prehistory—primarily, in the eighteenth-century narrative as well as in the imaginary associated with the abolitionist movement. See Baucom; Lacquer; and Slaughter, "Humanitarian Reading."
19. The book was first published in French in 1993; the English version, from which I am citing, came out in 1999.
20. For a critique of such hierarchies of humanity, see Butler, *Precarious Life: The Power of Mourning and Violence,* in which she introduces a distinction between grievable and ungrievable lives.
21. See Fisher, *Capitalist Realism.*
22. The failures of these wars are now acknowledged even by those on the more conservative end of the political spectrum. See, for instance, Zakaria's "The Long Road to Hell: America in Iraq." Aside from Fassin, Slaughter, and Douzinas, see also critiques of contemporary humanitarianism by Weizman, Ganguly, and Oliver, among others.
23. In his essay on making the film, Makhmalbaf says that "the Afghan woman [is] the most imprisoned woman in the world" ("Buddha").
24. The "doctor," self-admittedly, lacks medical education; he claims that most of the sick he tends to suffer from simple causes, such as poverty and starvation, thus not requiring specialized medical knowledge.
25. On humanitarianism as spectacle, see, for instance, Lacquer's analysis of the eighteenth-century anti-slavery narrative and Ganguly's discussion of the YouTube-mediated Kony campaign to raise awareness of violence in Uganda in 2012 ("The World Novel").
26. For a detailed account of how such humanitarian triangulation works, see Slaughter, "Humanitarian Reading."
27. See the discussion of ethics versus morality in Chaudhuri, "Documenting the Dark Side."
28. See Taylor, "'Kandahar' Actor Accused of Being Assassin."
29. Feehily, "Yasmina Khadra: Tools in the War for the Truth."
30. See Burke 82.
31. See Nunan 207.
32. "The Challenge of Afghanistan's House of Warlords," *The Scotsman.*
33. The fact that Atiq, the main character of the novel, is a mujahid, is symptomatic. Once again, he is a member of the group who emerged victorious at the end of the Soviet-Afghan War but is overcome by melancholy and a sense of meaninglessness.

34. While certainly a stylistic feature characteristic of Khadra's writing more generally, this mode of representing Afghanistan is typical of the early post-9/11 era. In her reading of post-9/11 media coverage of Afghanistan, Fowler demonstrates how the country's geographical features were used as symbols of cultural backwardness and danger. Fowler remarks on the similarity between post-9/11 journalist accounts and old British colonial tropes in which Afghanistan's landscape is personified as a devouring force: "The instant the protagonist crosses into Afghanistan, the landscape tends to assume a sinister aspect. In travel narratives, Afghanistan's mountain ranges frequently resemble implements of harm: they become saws, jagged blades and gaping jaws waiting to devour the unfortunate traveler. [. . .] Metaphors of teeth abound, particularly when the landscape is conflated with the fabled hostility of Afghans to the British" (33).

35. Jeffries, "Reader, I Am a He."

36. After 2005, it became widely known that Yasmina Chadra was a pen name for Mohammed Moulessehoul.

37. See, for instance, Marks, "For Tony Kushner, an Eerily Prescient Return" and Reston, "A Prophet in His Time: Premonition and Reality in Tony Kushner's *Homebody/Kabul*."

38. I disagree with Anker's suggestion that homebody's obsession with guidebooks "imaginatively relegates Afghanistan to a space outside modernity, or a condition of stasis and immaturity," drawing attention to the guidebooks as a kind of "false intelligence" ("The Spectacle of Our Suffering" 211). By contrast, the guides dated 1965 would be likely to present Afghanistan as a model image of successful modernization, heralding a possible future that was cancelled by the subsequent wars.

39. These old guidebooks are an intriguing image as they hold the potential to contest the tyranny of the present by projecting a ghost image of this present as it was imagined in 1965 (imagined, that is, as a future of 1965). Novak proposes the term "paleofuture" to designate a fantasy of the future as imagined in a certain moment in the past. Such paleofutures can open up the actual history for questioning and investigation, providing access to what no longer is, and more importantly, what can be no longer imagined. This potential, however, is not sufficiently explored by the play.

40. Out of the three works discussed in this chapter, Kushner's play received the most scholarly attention. See Phillips, Manis, Minwalla, and Anker, among others.

41. Here I refer to Butler's argument about the existing differential grievability of Western and non-Western lives.

42. Anker proposes a similar reading of homebody, suggesting that she allegorizes the multiple contradictions underpinning human rights rhetoric ("The Spectacle of Our Suffering"). I came across Anker's essay having already finished writing this chapter and discovered that our readings are similar in some ways, especially insofar as Anker, too, reads homebody as "an

armchair humanitarian" manifesting "a position of luxury with which the audience-reader is complicit" (211). The details, examples, and conclusions we draw from our critique are different, however, as Anker is primarily motivated by exploring the paradoxes of human rights rhetoric as imbricated with the liberal notions of embodiment and selfhood, following the trajectory outlined in her book-length project, *Fictions of Dignity: Embodying World Literature*.

43. The term "postcolonial exotic" was introduced by Huggan in *The Postcolonial Exotic: Marketing the Margins*.

44. "Gharbi" here most probably signifies "Western"; "Ferengi" are an alien race in *Star Trek* (from planet Ferenginar).

45. Phillips suggests that Kushner's play contains at its core an apocalyptic ideation: "we are left with an endless cycle, in which the present, seeming to be the horrific culmination of some ultimate event, is actually the latest in an ongoing cycle—an apocalyptic loop, an apocalyptic leveling without benefit of eschatological closure" (10).

46. For a detailed timeline of women's history in Afghanistan, see Ahmed-Ghosh, "A History of Women in Afghanistan."

47. For a distinction between ontic and ontological trauma, see Edkins, "Time, Personhood, Politics" 131.

48. For an in-depth discussion of the image of Cain's grave in the play, see Manis, "Cain's Grave."

49. In my reading of the play, I have benefited from a discussion with the participants in the Northeast Modern Language Association (NeMLA) seminar I organized in 2015, titled "Imagining Afghanistan," among them Derek Gingrich, Caitlin Forbes, Meryl Borato, Irene Martyniuk, and Tracy Dale. I also am grateful to the audience member whose name I do not know, who brought our attention to the fact that the last lines of the play were likely an allusion to T. S. Eliott's *The Waste Land*. Dale's discussion of the imagery related to Cain was instrumental in my thinking through the issues of ontological trauma in the play.

50. See Anker, "The Spectacle of Our Suffering" 219–224, for a discussion of the theme of European multiculturalism in the play.

51. Mirzoeff talks about weaponized images in his book on the US invasion of Iraq, *Watching Babylon*.

52. Weizman's term introduced in *The Least of All Possible Evils*.

53. Consequently, when *Kandahar* and *The Swallow* condemn the forces of fundamentalist repression represented by the Taliban, they have no other place to turn to for a solution, but an intervention from the West.

2   Imagining the Soviets

1. For an in-depth discussion of Brodsky's Afghanistan poems, "On the Winter Campaign of 1980" and his 1992 poem "On the Talks in Kabul," see Sandler, "The Poetry of Decline: On Joseph Brodsky, 'On the Talks in Kabul.'"

2. For a more in-depth discussion of the global leftist response, see Nunan 147.

3. As stated on the book's back cover, *Zinky Boys* "brings us the truth of the Soviet-Afghan war: the beauty of the country and the savage Army bullying." Characteristically, the blurb evokes Cold War-era anti-Soviet rhetoric as a marketing tactic.

4. See, for instance, Jones, *In the Graveyard of Empires: America's War in Afghanistan*.

5. See Starosta, "Perverse Tongues, Postsocialist Translations"; Suchland, "Is Postsocialism Transnational?"; Kovačević, *Narrating Post/Communism: Colonial Discourse and Europe's Borderline Civilization;* Nikolchina, "The Seminar: *Mode d'emploi* Impure Spaces in the Light of Late Totalitarianism"; and Tlostanova, "Postsocialist ≠ Postcolonial? On Post-Soviet Imaginary and Global Coloniality," among many others.

6. See Nowicha, "Statement from the Non-Region."

7. Trees in Afghanistan were among the many nonhuman casualties of war. See Rubin, "Severed Trees in Orchards Mirror Afghan History," and Pearce, "The Wasteland."

8. Other countries in the region watched the Afghan revolution carefully with an expectation that its outcomes would have transnational significance. "If the Khalqi [communist] regime succeeds in taming the mullahs, it will have repercussions in other Muslim countries. This logic is exercising the minds of conservative forces throughout the Islamic world," wrote Karadia in *India Today* in 1979.

9. In doing so, I do not seek to downplay the horrors of the Soviet-Afghan War. Memoirs of veterans of that war, from Russia, Ukraine, Belarus, Tajikistan, and other post-Soviet countries paint a chilling panorama of this war and do not gloss over the violence that all parties unleashed on each other. Seeing violence, however, is not the same as seeing an abstraction of barbarity—a specter of the Cold War propagandist apparatus that obscures more than it reveals.

10. See Gibbs, "Reassessing Soviet Motives for Invading Afghanistan." Also useful is Halliday's analysis of the events in his two articles, "Revolution in Afghanistan" (1978) and "War and Revolution in Afghanistan" (1980) both published in the *New Left Review*.

11. Quoted in Grigory, *Lenin's Brain and Other Tales from the Secret Soviet Archives* 121.

12. Quoted in Maley, *The Afghanistan Wars* 31.

13. The Soviets suspected that Amin might have started working with the CIA, effectively switching sides and betraying the revolution (Gibbs 256).

14. Since the CIA operation in Afghanistan was covert, the actual training of jihad soldiers was conducted via Inter-Services Intelligence (ISI)—Pakistan's intelligence agency that served as a proxy for the CIA throughout the entire war. As the Soviets suspected, CIA support of the mujahideen started before the Soviet intervention, as early as 1978 (Gibbs). At the time, Pakistan's spokesmen denied such allegations calling them "preposterous" (see Karadia).

15. Slaughter, *Human Rights Inc.* 321.
16. See, for instance, reviews by Taylor, "Grounded: Controversy Aside, This Just Won't Fly" and Miller, "'The Kite Runner' Critiqued: New Orientalism Goes to the Big Screen." Most literary scholars, among them Anker (*Fictions of Dignity*), Gray, Keshavarz, and Chan emphasized the novel's neo-imperial investments. Jefferess and Aubry provided nuanced readings of the text seeking to account for novel's unprecedented popularity with readers. Jefferess reads the novel as an allegory that is reflective of "contemporary discourses of humanitarianism" (394) as articulated in the liberal West, exemplifying both their ambition and their tensions (395). He notes that the novel reinforces the distinction between the "good" Muslim, with whom the reader identifies with, and the "bad" Muslim, whom the reader must reject—a binary that affirms the problematic "contemporary constructions of transnational humanity and benevolence" as they are articulated in the West (394). In turn, Aubry explores the avenues of reader-identifications with the novel's characters (as evidenced by Amazon reader-generated comments) that might explain the novel's unprecedented bipartisan success in the United States. Aubry points out that the novel appealed to American readers on both sides of the political spectrum (as well as to nonpartisan readers), allowing them to "feel right" in the midst of the War on Terror.
17. Muntz, "Front Porch Lessons"; Angelo and colleagues, "Afghanistan and Multiculturalism."
18. The novel's deployment of all-American imagery suggests that *The Kite Runner's* target audience was, initially, American. See note 19.
19. Hosseini's Afghanistan is created in America's image. Amir's father is a Mustang-driving, whiskey-drinking businessman who gives generously to local charities and loves sports competitions. The flaws of prewar Afghan society, the novel suggests, could have been addressed through a healthy dose of the culture of diversity and inclusion, US-style. Representations of race in *The Kite Runner* are more akin to the film *The Blind Side* (set in Mississippi) than to that in Hosseini's own subsequent works.
20. Kovačević in her book *Narrating Post/Communism* develops the notion of "nested orientalisms" (originally introduced by Bakić-Hayden) that, she argues, complicates Said's initial insight into how Orientalizing discourses work. For instance, nested Orientalism can be deployed strategically to simultaneously portray certain types of empires as either colonial or Oriental themselves. Specifically, her analyses of Cold War-era portrayals of the Soviet Union as an Oriental (despotic) aggressor are pertinent to my argument about Hosseini.
21. Consider, for instance, internet memes depicting President Donald Trump as Russian President Vladimir Putin's bride, among others. The meme can be seen at http://knowyourmeme.com/photos/1154781-trumpolympics.
22. Puar, "Queer Times, Queer Assemblages" 127.

23. Accounts of the exact role the CIA played in Afghan mujahideen training vary. Burke, for instance, asserts that while instruction manuals for mujahideen fighters were provided by the CIA, most of the training was done through the ISI: "any U.S. contact with *mujahideen* of any background was indirect, with the Pakistani ISI acting as intermediary" (514).

24. My search returned only one review of this 450-page novel and no critical commentary or analysis.

25. As of June 2018, Amazon lists 12 reader reviews of *Kabul* and 5,988 reviews of *The Kite Runner*. Goodreads contains 21 reviews (and 163 ratings) of *Kabul* and 63,122 reviews (and over two million ratings) of *The Kite Runner*.

26. Benjamin, "On the Concept of History."

27. Söderbäck, "Revolutionary Time: Revolt as Temporal Return" 311.

28. The notion of "a revolutionary situation" is discussed by Lenin in his 1913 "May Day Action by the Revolutionary Proletariat" and is defined as twofold: The lower classes no longer want the old ways and the ruling class is no longer able to rule as it used to. Lenin writes: "Oppression alone, no matter how great, does not always give rise to a revolutionary situation in a country. In most cases it is not enough for revolution that *the lower classes should not want* to live in the old way. It is also necessary that *the upper classes should be unable* to rule and govern in the old way" (par. 13, emphasis in original).

29. While there is no evidence that the USSR was involved in the coup in any direct manner, the presence of Soviet advisers in Kabul was considerable at the time immediately preceding the coup. While Taraki and Amin insisted on the Afghan Revolution being homegrown, it is clear that they also expected to be backed by the USSR (Gibbs). Nevertheless, Crews insists, the revolutionaries who seized power in 1978 were "staunch nationalists, [who] resisted the accusation that they were merely Trojan horses for the USSR" (232–233). Crews demonstrates that Afghan revolutionaries were influenced not just by the USSR, but by multiple movements—by Soviet and Cuban socialists as well as by Iranian Tudeh Party, whose texts were circulated widely. Stories of Algerian revolutionaries, as well as nineteenth-century French literature (such as Victor Hugo), were formative for the generation of Afghan revolutionaries. Taraki, the first socialist head of state, for instance, had lived in Washington, as well in India and in China.

30. "President George W. Bush Press Conference on 11 October 2001," *Johnston's Archive*.

31. See Halliday, "Revolution in Afghanistan" 21.

32. "Interview with a RAWA activist on Afghanistan," *ZNet*.

33. See Kushner's interview with Taft-Kaufman 45.

34. Nunan 202.

35. See Jefferess and Slaughter (*Human Rights, Inc.*).

3   Humanitarian Jihad

1. See Reagan, "Proclamation 5033—Afghanistan Day, 1983."
2. See Gibbs. This fact is important: During the 1980s, the West's support for the jihad was framed as a response to the Soviet intervention; documents show, however, that US involvement, having predated the dispatch of Soviet troops, was an attempt to undermine and halt the socialist revolution.
3. I use the concept of multidirectional memory as introduced by Rothberg in his eponymous book.
4. See Horn and Kenney, *Transnational Moments of Change: Europe 1945, 1968, 1989.*
5. See Horn and Kenney or Cohen and Frazer ("Scale: Exploring the Global 1968"). See also Badiou, *The Communist Hypothesis.*
6. See Horn and Kenney.
7. See Lawson, "Introduction."
8. See Rorty, "Human Rights, Rationality, and Sentimentality"; Fukuyama, "The End of History?"
9. See Dubmadze and Hudson, *Contemporary Art: 1989 to the Present.*
10. See Eshel; Ganguly, *This Thing Called the World.*
11. Rabinow, in *Marking Time,* provides a non-epochal definition of the contemporary as a shifting point of view that allows for the construction of different genealogies from various continuously morphing moments in the present (2).
12. In *The Fragmentation of Afghanistan,* Barnett Rubin talks about his inability to participate in the triumphalism of the 1989 moment during a celebration of the fall of the Berlin Wall with his colleagues (278–279).
13. For a discussion of humanitarian violence, see Weizman, *The Least of All Possible Evils.*
14. Caruth writes: "history, like trauma, is never simply one's own, . . . history is precisely the way we are implicated in each other's traumas" (24).
15. As Mamdani shows, these are the terms frequently found in the documents from that period.
16. Aslam writes: "By the time he came to Peshawar as an employee of the CIA, his opposition to Communism was the result of study and contemplation. Not something that grew out of a personal wound. He was in Peshawar as a believer" (112).
17. Nunan 221–233.
18. Emmanuel Guibert and Juliette Fournot were interviewed on *The Rachel Maddow Show,* June 12, 2009. The interview can be viewed at https://www.youtube.com/watch?v=eSK_zN-Ne8Y.
19. Omar, whose gripping memoir I discussed in chapter four, narrates the horrors of the collapse of the state that followed the end of the Soviet presence in Afghanistan.
20. For an analysis of the memoir's hybrid form, see Daniel Lawson.
21. Jamila was the name Juliette Fournot used in Afghanistan.

22. See Nunan's discussion of the funding structure, as well as his discussion of how the MSF's mission was reframed with the focus changing from treating patients to serving as a witness (221–233).

23. Barnes writes, in 1988 *Reader's Digest:* "the Soviets began to withdraw, their war machine defeated by a peasant army, their dreams of a new colony shattered" (88).

24. See, for instance, soldier memoirs by Bobrov and by Usolcev.

25. Badakhshan and Panjshir Valley were mujahideen strongholds throughout the entire Soviet-Afghan War. After Taliban forces captured Kabul in 1996, the allied mujahideen forces (a.k.a. the Northern Alliance) retreated to these provinces with Fayzabad becoming the informal capital of the mujahideen-controlled areas (see Anderson, "In the Court of the Pretender").

26. Girardet (*Killing the Cranes*) writes that Massoud's fighters reminded him of Cuban revolutionaries. However, ideologically, these two group could not be further apart from one another. Massoud espoused a patriarchal-conservative, Islamist, anticommunist point of view; when his faction came to power in Kabul in 1992, veil laws were reinstituted and a religious curriculum was adopted in the school system.

4   Witness

1. See, for instance, Rothberg, "Decolonizing Trauma Studies."

2. For a discussion of the experience of terror from the subaltern perspective, see, for instance, Boehmer and Morton. In a similar vein, Westad writes: "the crime against the people in the Twin Towers of New York City was no bigger, or smaller, than those committed against the people of Luanda or Kabul during the Cold War. In light of the history of the recent past, the greatest shock of 11 September 2001 was certainly where it happened, not the murderous act itself" (406).

3. These texts are, to use O'Gorman's phrase, "not only global but self-consciously *globalized*: working within—while at the same time challenging—a lucrative global market for Anglophone fiction by South Asian authors" (*Fictions* 112, emphasis in original).

4. See *This Thing Called the World*. While I agree with Ganguly's assessment, the capacity to produce legibility is not limited, in my view, to the novel form, as evidenced by Omar's memoir.

5. Consider, for instance, such titles as *Out of the Blue: September 11 and the Novel* by Versluys.

6. See Shamsie, "The Missing Picture."

7. As Bowers points out, the name "Kim Burton carries associations with the Irish-Indian character Kim from Kipling's eponymous novel set in the North-West Frontier region, as well as remind us of Richard Burton, the 19th-century orientalist explorer, and translator of *Arabian Nights*" (194).

8. He also reminds of Rushdie's Max Ophuls (*Shalimar the Clown*).

9. In the Epilogue, Omar briefly discusses the American invasion of 2001, similarly suspending judgment about the possible long-term effects of the American chapter in Afghanistan's history.

10. See Ross, "Qais Akbar Omar: Boston's Afghan Writer Who Cannot Return Home."

11. See my discussion of Khadra in chapter one.

12. See Rubin, *The Fragmentation of Afghanistan* 2.

13. Brzezinski's 1998 interview with *Le Nouvel Observateur*, quoted in Gibbs 242.

14. See note prefacing the book, no page number.

15. Many textbooks used in mujahideen-run schools during the Soviet-Afghan War, such as the one that Omar describes as being adopted by his school after the mujahideen capture of Kabul, were paid for by US taxpayers; some of them were printed in the United States as well. These books promoted jihad and violence more generally, espoused an Islamist worldview, and taught hatred of communism. These books were later used in Taliban-run schools as well. See, for instance, Stephens and Ottaway. The US Agency for International Development at the University of Nebraska Omaha played a key role in developing, printing, and shipping such textbooks to Afghan refugee communities and into Afghanistan.

16. Mamdani writes: "State-centered Islamist political movements should not be equated with terrorism. As long as authoritarian movements remain confined within national borders and adhere to even a semblance of rule of law—as with the Zia dictatorship in Pakistan, the House of Saud in Saudi Arabia, and the Taliban in Afghanistan—the potential for terror remains sheathed. The emergence of terror goes along with the erosion of the rule of law. The distinction between a lawful dictatorship and terror outside the law will help us distinguish between the Taliban, on the one hand, and the mujahideen, on the other. In Afghanistan, after the Soviet Union was defeated, terror was unleashed on the Afghani people in the name of liberation" (176).

17. See Dearden.

18. Borradori 28; quoted in Gray 7.

19. Quoted in Boehmer and Morton 6.

5   The Deep Time of War

1. Aslam's essay "Where to Begin" speaks directly to his interest in the geological aspect of human history.

2. For a discussion on the short- and long-term effects of Afghanistan's protracted war on the environment, see Schultheis and Pearce.

3. A decade later, the US military also considered using crows in its search for Osama bin Laden. See Neurophilosophy, "US Military Planned on Using Spy Crows to Find Osama bin Laden."

4. As I mentioned earlier, trees are among many nonhuman casualties of war in Afghanistan. See Rubin (A6).

5. Ellsworth and Kruse's edited collection *Making the Geologic Now* is one example of a productive infusion of geological thought into the field of cultural studies.

6. As Lee explains: the *longue durée*, as "the time of the long-term structures of social reality, was privileged [by Braudel] over the time of events (only 'dust' for Braudel)" (2).

7. Cited in Mitchell, *Cloning Terror* 3.

8. On the Bamyan Buddhas as negative heritage, see Meskell 561–566. Negative heritage, according to Meskell, preserves the memory of violence inflicted on the site through a conspicuous absence.

9. The Durand Line is a border established in 1896 between Afghanistan and British India (now Pakistan). It was drawn by British diplomat Sir Henry Mortimer Durand when Afghanistan was an area effectively controlled by the British; it has been contested since then as it cuts through tribal Pashtun territories. It is not recognized by the government of Afghanistan as a legitimate international border.

10. For an in-depth discussion of the Islamic world system, see Irwin.

11. For the importance of Eurasia as a framework for thinking recent postsocialist histories, see Suchland. Additionally, a collection of essays edited by Lieberman provides useful insights on the limitations of binary divisions (such as the East-West dichotomy and other, similar historiographic divisions based on geographic region), proposing Eurasia as a framework for discussing such regional histories as interconnected.

12. For a discussion of Aslam's memory as palimpsestic, see Frawley 439–443.

13. Emeralds and rubies emerge in hyperthermal veins formed when hydrothermal fluids escape the magma or in pegmatite deposits. A granitic magma serves as a source of beryllium, a rare element that is necessary for emerald formation.

14. On the war-financing gem trade in Afghanistan, see Adnan Khan.

15. On the history of Koh-i-Noor, see Streeter and Hatten 63–78.

16. For a discussion of contemporary warfare as demodernization, see Graham, "Urban Metabolism."

17. In *Creating the Witness*, Torchin offers the term "media witnessing" to capture a mode of witness brought into existence by the presence of the camera: witness via imaging (7).

18. Spanning four decades, the conflict in Afghanistan is now known to have affected multiple species of migratory birds, among them pelicans and several species of cranes (such as the demoiselle crane and the endangered Siberian crane). Migratory birds travel from Siberia across eastern Afghanistan, an area deeply impacted by military operations (especially aerial warfare). Smith reports that the number of birds safely surviving winter migration to the south fell by 85% in 2001–2002, with the birds likely affected by coalition bombing. See also "Afghan Danger for Migrating Birds." For discussions of environmental damage and the issues of wildlife preservation

in Afghanistan, see also Kanderian et al., Simms et al., Smallwood et al., Welsh, and Schultheis. "Kabul's Lion King" offers a view of the fate of captive nonhumans (Kabul Zoo animals) during the protracted crisis.

19. I borrow the term "machinic sensorium" from Hansen, who introduces it to capture the specificity of machine-mediated perception as a "technical distribution of sensibility rooted in an expansion of perception beyond [human] consciousness and bodily self-perception" (128).

20. Swarming as a form of collective action has been adopted in military strategy, as Kosek demonstrates. Kosek brings into focus "emerging insectoid forms of warfare" that involve not only modeling swarmic behavior, but also integrating live bees and other insects into the military-industrial complex; live bees have become a key component of chemical-detection cartridges (653).

6   The Kabubble

1. Lamb writes: "Some of the drug lords [in Kabul] had invested in building large houses in wedding-confection style known as 'narcitecture' or 'bling houses,' and these were perfect for parties" (400).

2. "Kabubble" is a term frequently used in expat writing in relation to foreigners' Kabul. It is used by Lamb and Barker in their memoirs and by Fey in her film. Lamb writes: "throughout the war, Kabul had always been a safe haven. People called it 'Kabubble.' As often among expat communities on the edge of a war zone there is a raucous social life fueled by illicit alcohol, cheap hash and the adrenalin of fear" (399).

3. I borrow the idea of international development as a carnivalesque space from Heron 112.

4. See Hornaday, "'Whiskey Tango Foxtrot' and Hollywood's enduring problem with whitewashing" and Rosen, "Tina Fey: Whiskey Tango Foxtrot Casting Controversy Addressed."

5. See, as an example, Seierstad's chapter "Billowing, Fluttering, Winding" in her 2002 *The Bookseller of Kabul*.

6. Liu, "Now I See the Sunlight."

7. See chapters one and two for additional sources.

8. It is estimated that as much as 40 percent of funds pledged for Afghan development returned to originating countries in the form of contract payments, consultant salaries, and so on (see Lutz and Desai). What is more, a significant portion of the money that stayed in the country enriched powerful local strongmen or was spent on projects that remain unfinished or were not functional to begin with—ghost infrastructures. See, for instance, Rose, "Afghanistan Waste Exhibit A: Kajaki Dam, More Than $300M Spent and Still Not Done" and Khan, "Ghost Students, Ghost Teachers, Ghost Schools."

9. Eton is one of the most prestigious private boarding schools in England. Tuition is about USD $51,452 per year.

10. See Al Yafai, "The Ruling against *Bookseller of Kabul* Author Asne Seierstad."
11. Burke further recalls: "for eighteen months it was possible to travel anywhere without concern for anything except the appalling state of the roads" (78).
12. See Fluri 998.
13. The Democratic Republic of Afghanistan was not anti-Islamic even at its inception (see Halliday, "War and Revolution in Afghanistan" 31). Throughout the 1980s, the moderate socialist government of Babrak Karmal tried to incorporate Islamic worldview as part of the socialist worldview. This can be clearly observed in the evolution of the flag of the Democratic Republic of Afghanistan from its inception in 1978 to its end in 1992. The early version is red, and includes no Islamic elements. In subsequent years, Islamic colors (green and black) and symbols are incorporated into the flag and the socialist elements recede into the background. Halliday writes: "the Soviet position on Islam was that it was, if not inherently progressive, then at least capable of socialist interpretation. On visits in the 1980s to the then two communist Muslim states—the now equally-forgotten Democratic Republic of Afghanistan and the People's Democratic Republic of Yemen—I was able to study the way in which secondary school textbooks, taught by lay teachers rather than clerics, treated Islam as a form of early socialism. A verse in the Qur'an stating that 'water, grass and fire are common among the people' was interpreted as an early nomadic form of collective production; while Muslim concepts of ijma' (consensus), zakat (charitable donation) and 'adala (justice) were interpreted in line with the dictates of the noncapitalist road" (79).
14. Wild's graphic novels overlapped with the economic slowdown and the subsequent austerity period in France. Following the global financial crisis of 2008, France implemented austerity measures by raising taxes, raising the retirement age from sixty to sixty-two, and cutting into multiple social programs and benefits (see Nicola Clark).
15. The failures of most infrastructure improvement projects were immediately visible to both residents and foreign observers. Chandrasekaran in his memoir *Little America* recalls: "Another prized project was a highway from Kabul to Kandahar. President Bush demanded that it be completed in less than a year. USAID met this goal, but in order to do so, it allowed contractors to deposit such a thin layer of asphalt that in some areas it washed away when the snow melted the following spring" (103).

Conclusion

1. Adichie's phrase; see chapter two.
2. "After 16 Years, Afghanistan War Is 'At Best a Grinding Stalemate,' Journalist Says," *Fresh Air* from NPR, 6 Feb. 2018.
3. Zakaria voiced his critique of President Trump's plan for reengagement in Afghanistan, stating that it locks the nation into "its forever war" ("Trump Locks America into its Forever War").

4. See, for instance, Bolger, *Why We Lost: A General's Inside Account of the Iraq and Afghanistan Wars;* Gall, *The Wrong Enemy: America in Afghanistan 2001–2014;* and Chandrasekaran, *Little America: The War Within the War in Afghanistan.*

5. See Hogood, *The Endtimes of Human Rights.*

Works Cited

Abraham, Stephanie. "The Orientalist Narrative and Erasure in 'Whiskey Tango Foxtrot.'" *BitchMedia*, 11 Mar. 2016, https://www.bitchmedia.org/article/wtf-tina-fey-orientalist-narrative-and-erasure-whiskey-tango-foxtrot.

Abu-Lughod, Lila. "Do Muslim Women Really Need Saving? Anthropological Reflections on Cultural Relativism and Its Others." *American Anthropologist*, vol. 104, no. 3, 2002, pp. 783–790.

Addario, Lynsey. *It's What I Do: A Photographer's Life of Love and War.* New York, Penguin Press, 2015.

Adichie, Chimamanda Ngozi. "The Danger of a Single Story." *TED*, July 2009, https://www.ted.com/talks/chimamanda_adichie_the_danger_of_a_single_story.

"Afghan Danger for Migrating Birds." BBC News, *BBC*, 1 Oct. 2001.

"Afghanistan: Human Development Indicators." *United Nations Development Programme/ Human Development Reports*, http://hdr.undp.org/en/countries/profiles/AFG.

"After 16 Years, Afghanistan War Is 'At Best a Grinding Stalemate,' Journalist Says." *Fresh Air* from NPR, 6 Feb. 2018, https://www.npr.org/2018/02/06/583625482/after-16-years-afghanistan-war-is-at-best-a-grinding-stalemate-journalist-says.

Ahmed-Ghosh, Huma. "A History of Women in Afghanistan." *Journal of International Women's Studies*, vol. 4, no. 3, 2003, pp. 1–14.

Al Yafai, Faisal. "The Ruling against *Bookseller of Kabul* Author Asne Seierstad." *The National*, 20 Aug. 2010, https://www.thenational.ae/arts-culture/the-ruling-against-bookseller-of-kabul-author-asne-seierstad-1.518300.

Alexander, Jeffrey C. *Trauma: A Social Theory.* Maiden, Polity Press, 2012.

Alexievich, Svetlana. *Zinky Boys: Soviet Voices from the Afghanistan War,* W. W. Norton & Company, 1992.

Altaf, Hasan. "Induced Nostalgia." *Three Quarks Daily*, 5 Sept. 2011, https://www.3quarksdaily.com/3quarksdaily/2011/09/induced-nostalgia.html.

Amadeo, Kimberly. "Afghanistan War Cost, Timeline and Economic Impact: The Ongoing Costs of the Afghanistan War." *The Balance*, 15 Mar. 2019, https://www.thebalance.com/cost-of-afghanistan-war-timeline-economic-impact-4122493.

Anderson, Jon Lee. "In the Court of the Pretender: Who Has the Right to Rule Afghanistan?" *New Yorker*, 5 Nov. 2001.

---. "The Warlord." *New Yorker*, 14 Oct. 2001, https://www.newyorker.com /magazine/2001/10/22/the-warlord.

Angelo, Mary F., et al. "Afghanistan and Multiculturalism in Khaled Hosseini's Novels: Study of Place and Diversity." *Multicultural Education and Technology Journal*, vol. 3, no. 2, 2009, pp. 96–111.

Anker, Elizabeth S. *Fictions of Dignity: Embodying Human Rights in World Literature*. Cornell UP, 2012.

---. "The Spectacle of Our Suffering: Staging the International Human Rights Imaginary in Tony Kushner's *Homebody/Kabul*." *Imagining Human Rights in Twenty-First Century Theater: Global Perspectives*, Palgrave Macmillan, 2013.

Argo. Directed by Ben Affleck, performances by Ben Affleck and John Goodman, GK Films, 2012.

Aslam, Nadeem. *The Blind Man's Garden*. New York, Vintage, 2013.

---. *Maps for Lost Lovers*. New York, Vintage, 2004.

---. *Season of the Rainbirds*. New York, Vintage, 1993.

---. *The Wasted Vigil*. New York, Vintage, 2008.

---. "Where to Begin." *Granta: The Magazine of New Writing*, no. 112: Pakistan, 2010.

Aslam, Nadeem, and Terry Hong. "An Interview with Nadeem Aslam." *Bookslut*, July 2013, http://www.bookslut.com/features/2013_07_020162.php.

Aubry, Timothy. "Afghanistan Meets the *Amazon*: Reading *The Kite Runner* in America." *PMLA*, vol. 124, no. 1, 2009, pp. 25–43.

Badiou, Alain. *The Communist Hypothesis*. Verso, 2015.

Bakić-Hayden, Milica. "Nesting Orientalisms: The Case of Former Yugoslavia." *Slavic Review*, vol. 54, no. 4, 1995, pp. 917–931.

Banita, Georgiana. *Plotting Justice: Narrative Ethics and Literary Culture After 9/11*. U of Nebraska P, 2012.

Barker, Kim. "My Kabubble, Starring Tina Fey." *New York Times*, 26 Feb. 2016, https://www.nytimes.com/2016/02/28/books/review/my-kabubble-starring -tina-fey.html.

---. *The Taliban Shuffle: Strange Days in Afghanistan and Pakistan*. New York, Anchor Books, 2011.

Barnes, Fred. "Victory in Afghanistan: The Inside Story." *Readers' Digest*, vol. 132, 1988, pp. 87–93.

Baucom, Ian. *Specters of the Atlantic: Finance Capital, Slavery, and the Philosophy of History*. Duke UP, 2005.

Baudrillard, Jean. *The Spirit of Terrorism and Requiem for the Twin Towers*. Translated by Chris Turner, London, Verso, 2002.

Benjamin, Walter. "On the Concept of History." *Marxists Internet Archive*. Translated by Dennis Redmond, 2005, https://www.marxists.org/reference/archive /benjamin/1940/history.htm.

Berardi, Franco (Bifo). "The Coming Global Civil War: Is There a Way Out?" *e-flux*, vol. 69, 2016.

Bergson, Henri. *Laughter: An Essay on the Meaning of the Comic*. New York, Macmillan Company, 1914.

Berlant, Lauren, and Sianne Ngai. "Comedy Has Issues." *Critical Inquiry*, vol. 43, Winter 2017, pp. 233–249.

Berson, Misha. "Prescient Tony Kushner Takes on Issues of Our Time in 'Homebody/Kabul.'" *Seattle Times*, 14 Sep. 2003.

Black Panther. Directed by Brian Coogler, performances by Chadwick Boseman, Michael B. Jordan, and Lupita Nyong'o, Marvel Studios, 2018.

Blanchot, Maurice. *The Writing of the Disaster*. U of Nebraska P, 1995.

Bobrov, Gleb. *Fayzabad* [Файзабад]. 2013, http://booksonline.com.ua/view.php?book=26327&page=19.

Boehmer, Elleke, and Stephen Morton. "Introduction: Terror and the Postcolonial." *Terror and the Postcolonial*, edited by Elleke Boehmer and Stephen Morton, Oxford, Wiley Blackwell, 2010, pp. 11–24 .

Boes, Tobias, and Kate Marshall. "Writing the Anthropocene: An Introduction." *Minnesota Review*, vol. 83, 2014, p. 6072.

Bolger, Daniel. *Why We Lost: A General's Inside Account of the Iraq and Afghanistan Wars*. 1st ed., New York, Eamon Dolan/Houghton Mifflin Harcourt, 2014.

Boltanski, Luc. *Distant Suffering: Morality, Media, and Politics*. Cambridge UP, 1999.

Borradori, Giovanna, editor. *Philosophy at the Time of Terror: Dialogues with Jurgen Habermas and Jacques Derrida*. U of Chicago P, 2003.

Bowers, Maggie Ann. "Asia's Europe: Anti-Colonial Attitudes in the Novels of Ondaatje and Shamsie." *Journal of Postcolonial Writing*, vol. 51, no. 2, 2015, pp. 184–195.

Boym, Svetlana. *The Future of Nostalgia*. New York, Basic Books, 2001.

Braudel, Fernand. "History and the Social Sciences: The *Longue Durée*." *Review*. Translated by Immanuel Wallerstein, vol. 32, no. 2, 2009, pp. 171–203.

Brodsky, Joseph. "Lines on the Winter Campaign 1980." *Poetry Foundation*. https://www.poetryfoundation.org/poems/57941/lines-on-the-winter-campaign-1980

Brown, Wendy. *Undoing the Demos: Neoliberalism's Stealth Revolution*. New York, Zone Books, 2015.

Bryant, Levi. R. "Five Types of Objects: Gravity and Onto-Cartography." *Larval Subjects*, 17 June 2012, https://larvalsubjects.wordpress.com/2012/06/17/five-types-of-objects-gravity-and-onto-cartography/.

Burke, Jason. *The 9/11 Wars*. London, Penguin, 2011.

Butler, Judith. *Precarious Life: The Power of Mourning and Violence*. New York, Verso, 2004.

Caillois, Roger. *The Writing of Stones*. UP of Virginia, 1985.

Caruth, Cathy. *Trauma: Explorations in Memory*. Johns Hopkins UP, 1995.

Chakrabarty, Dipesh. "The Climate of History: Four Theses." *Critical Inquiry*, vol. 35, 2009, pp. 197–222.

"The Challenge of Afghanistan's House of Warlords." *The Scotsman*, 3 July 2004.

Chan, Steven. "The Bitterness of the Islamic Hero in Three Recent Western Works of Fiction." *Third World Quarterly*, vol. 31, no. 5, 2010, pp. 829–832.

Chandrasekaran, Rajiv. *Little America: The War Within the War in Afghanistan.* Vintage, 2013.

Chaudhuri, Shohini. "Documenting the Dark Side: Fictional and Documentary Treatments of Torture and the 'War on Terror.'" *Cinema of the Dark Side: Atrocity and the Ethics of Film Spectatorship.* Edinburgh UP, 2014.

Chiu, Monica. "Graphic Self-Consciousness, Travel Narratives, and the Asian-American Studies Classroom: Delisle's *Burma Chronicles* and Guibert, Lefèvre, and Lemercier's *The Photographer.*" *Asian-American Literature: Discourses and Pedagogies*, vol. 5, 2014, pp. 23–44.

Clark, Nicola. "Government of France Proposes Austerity Cuts." *New York Times*, 7 Nov. 2011, https://www.nytimes.com/2011/11/08/world/europe/french -austerity-measures-aimed-at-new-reality.html.

Cohen, Deborah, and Lessie Jo Frazer. "Scale: Exploring the Global 1968." *Framing the Global: Entry Points for Research*, edited by Hilary E. Kahn, Indiana UP, 2014, pp. 253–275.

Cohen, Jeffrey Jerome. *Stone: An Ecology of the Inhuman.* U of Minnesota P, 2015.

Coll, Steve. *Ghost Wars: The Secret History of the CIA, Afghanistan, and Bin Laden, from the Soviet Invasion to September 10, 2001.* New York, Penguin Books, 2004.

Corliss, Richard. "All-Time 100 Movies." *Time Magazine*, 14 Jan. 2010, http:// entertainment.time.com/2005/02/12/all-time-100-movies/slide/kandahar -2001/.

Crews, Robert D. *Afghan Modern: The History of a Global Nation.* Cambridge, Harvard UP, 2015.

"Crocodile." *Black Mirror,* season 4, episode 3, 29 Dec. 2017. *Netflix*, https://www .netflix.com/title/70264888.

Crutzen, Paul, and Eugene F. Stoermer. "The 'Anthropocene.'" *IGBP Newsletter*, no. 41, 2000, pp. 17–18.

Currier, James. *The Third Buddha.* New York, Chelsea Station Editions, 2011.

Dean, Jodi. *The Communist Horizon.* New York, Verso, 2012.

Dearden, Lizzie. "Isis in Fallujah: Starving families forced to eat pet food to survive during brutal siege of Iraqi city." *Independent*, 9 Jun. 2016, https://www .independent.co.uk/news/world/middle-east/isis-in-fallujah-starving-families -forced-to-eat-pet-food-to-survive-during-brutal-siege-of-iraqi-a7073211.html.

DeLanda, Manuel. *A Thousand Years of Nonlinear History.* Brooklyn, Zone Books, 1997.

DeLillo, Don. "In the Ruins of the Future." *Harper's Magazine*, Dec. 2001, pp. 33–40.

Denker, Debra. "Along Afghanistan's War-torn Frontier." *National Geographic*, vol. 167, no. 6, June 1985, pp. 772–797.

DeRosa, Aaron, and Stacey Peebles. "Enduring Operations: Narratives of the Contemporary Wars." *Modern Fiction Studies*, vol. 63, no. 2, 2017, pp. 203–224.

Dimock, Wai Chee. *Through Other Continents: American Literature across Deep Time.* Princeton UP, 2008.

Douzinas, Costas. *Human Rights and Empire: The Political History of Cosmopolitanism.* Abingdon, Oxford, Routledge-Cavendish, 2007.

Dubord, Guy. *Society of the Spectacle.* Black and Red, 2000.

Dumbadze, Alexander, and Suzanne Hudson, editors. *Contemporary Art: 1989 to the Present.* West Sussex, Wiley-Blackwell, 2013.

Dunks, Glenn. "'Whiskey Tango Foxtrot' Would Be Better If It Wasn't All About White Lady Empowerment." *Junkee,* 13 May 2016, https://junkee .com/whiskey-tango-foxtrot-better-wasnt-white-lady-empowerment/78148.

Edkins, Jenny. "Time, Personhood, Politics." *The Future of Trauma Theory: Contemporary Literary and Cultural Criticism,* edited by Gert Buelens, Sam Durrant, and Robert Eaglestone, New York, Routledge, 2014, pp. 127–139.

Ekman, Ulrich. "Addressing the Witness." *Witness: Memory, Representation, and the Media in Question,* edited by Eivind Røssaak, U of Chicago P, 2008, pp. 15–38.

Ellsworth, Elizabeth, and Jamie Kruse. *Making the Geologic Now: Responses to Material Conditions of Contemporary Life.* New York, Punctum Books, 2013.

Ensler, Eve. *Insecure at Last.* New York, Villard, 2006.

Eshel, Amir. *Futurity: Contemporary Literature and the Quest for the Past.* Chicago UP, 2013.

Fassin, Didier. *Humanitarian Reason: A Moral History of the Present.* Berkeley, U of California P, 2012.

Feehily, Gerry. "Yasmina Khadra: Tools in the War for the Truth." *Independent,* 6 July 2006, https://www.independent.co.uk/arts-entertainment/books/features /yasmina-khadra-tools-in-the-war-for-truth-406905.html.

Fisher, Mark. *Capitalist Realism: Is There No Alternative?* Washington, Zero Books, 2009.

---. *Ghosts of My Life: Writings on Depression, Hauntology, and Lost Futures.* Zero Books, 2014.

Fluri, Jennifer. "'Foreign Passports Only': Geographies of (Post)Conflict Work in Kabul, Afghanistan." *Annals of the Association of American Geographers,* vol. 99, no. 5, Dec. 2009, pp. 986–994.

Fowler, Corinne. *Chasing Tales: Travel Writing, Journalism and the History of British Ideas about Afghanistan.* Amsterdam: Rodopi, 2007.

Fox, David Marshall. "The K-Town 'Kabubble': Thoughts on Expat Security in Kabul." 3 Apr. 2014, https://davidmarshallfox.wordpress.com/2014/04/03 /the-k-town-kabubble-my-thoughts-on-expat-security-in-kabul/.

Frawley, Oona. "Global Civil War and Post-9/11 Discourse in *The Wasted Vigil.*" *Textual Practice,* vol. 27, no. 3, 2013, pp. 439–457.

Fuery, Patrick. "Afterword: Afterwards." *Terror and the Cinematic Sublime: Essays on Violence and the Unrepresentable in Post-9/11 Films,* edited by Comer Todd A. and Lloyd Isaac Vayo. Jefferson, McFarland & Company, 2013, pp. 181–185.

Fukuyama, Francis. "The End of History?" *The National Interest*, vol. 16, 1989, pp. 3–18.

Gall, Carlotta. *The Wrong Enemy: America in Afghanistan 2001–2014*. Houghton Mifflin Harcourt, 2014.

Ganguly, Debjani. *This Thing Called the World: The Contemporary Novel as Global Form*. Duke UP, 2016.

---. "The World Novel, Mediated Wars, and Exorbitant Witnessing." *Cambridge Journal of Postcolonial Inquiry*, vol. 1, no. 1, 2014, pp. 11–31.

Gibbs, David N. "Reassessing Soviet Motives for Invading Afghanistan: A Declassified History." *Critical Asian Studies*, vol. 38, no. 2, 2006, pp. 239–263.

Ginsberg, Robert. *The Aesthetics of Ruins*. Amsterdam: Rodopi, 2004.

Girardet, Edward. *Killing the Cranes: A Reporter's Journey Through Three Decades of War in Afghanistan*. White River Junction, Chelsea Green Publishing, 2011.

---. "A New Day in Kabul." *National Geographic*, December 2003.

Girardet, Edward, and Jonathan Walter. *The Essential Field Guide to Afghanistan*. Crosslines Communications, 1998.

Godrillo, Gastón R. *Rubble: The Afterlife of Destruction*. Duke UP, 2014.

Graham, Mark. *Afghanistan in the Cinema*. U of Illinois P, 2010.

Graham, Stephen. "Urban Metabolism as Target: Contemporary War as Forced Demodernization." *In the Nature of Cities: Urban Political Ecology and the Politics of Urban Metabolism*, edited by Nik Heynen, Maria Kaika, and Erik Swynge-douw. London, Routledge, 2006, pp. 245–265.

Gray, Richard. *After the Fall: American Literature Since 9/11*. Malden, Wiley-Blackwell, 2011.

Green, Blake. "His Very Own Scoop." *Los Angeles Times*, 16 Dec. 2001.

Green, Nile, and Nushin Arbabzadah, editors. *Afghanistan in Ink: Literature Between Diaspora and Nation*. Oxford UP, 2012.

Grigory, Paul. *Lenin's Brain and Other Tales from the Secret Soviet Archives*. Stanford, Hoover Press, 2008.

Grosz, Elizabeth. "Time Matters: On Temporality in the Anthropocene." *Architecture in the Anthropocene*, edited by Etienne Turpin, Open Humanities Press, 2013, pp. 129–138.

Guibert, Emmanuel, Didier Lefèvre, and Frédéric Lemercier. *The Photographer: Into War-Torn Afghanistan with Doctors Without Borders*. First Second Books, 2009.

Halliday, Fred. *Political Journeys: The Open Democracy Essays*. Yale UP, 2012.

---. "Revolution in Afghanistan." *New Left Review*, no. 112, Nov.–Dec. 1978, pp. 3–44.

---. "War and Revolution in Afghanistan." *New Left Review*, no. 119, Jan. 1980, pp. 20–41.

Hansen, Mark. "Our Predictive Condition; or, Prediction in the Wild." *The Nonhuman Turn*, edited by Richard Grusin, U of Minnesota P, 2015, pp. 101–138.

Heron, Barbara. *Desire for Development: Whiteness, Gender, and the Helping Imperative*. Wilfrid Laurier UP, 2007.

Hirsh, M. E. *Kabul*. New York, Thomas Dunne Books, 1986.

The Global 1989: Continuity and Change in World Politics, edited by George Lawson, Chris Armbruster, and Michael Cox, Cambridge UP, 2010, pp. 23–50.

Hogood, Stephen. *The Endtimes of Human Rights*. Cornell UP, 2013.

Horn, Gerd-Rainer, and Padraic Kenney. *Transnational Moments of Change: Europe 1945, 1968, 1989*. New York, Rowman & Littlefield Publishers, 2004.

Hornaday, Ann. "'Whiskey Tango Foxtrot' and Hollywood's Enduring Problem with Whitewashing." *Washington Post*, 4 Mar. 2016, https://www .washingtonpost.com/lifestyle/style/whiskey-tango-foxtrot-and-hollywoods -enduring-problem-with-whitewashing/2016/03/03/f33153ea-e16f-11e5 -8d98-4b3d9215ade1_story.html?noredirect=on.

Hosseini, Khaled. *And the Mountains Echoed*. New York, Riverhead Books, 2013.

---. *The Kite Runner*. New York, Riverhead Books, 2003.

---. *A Thousand Splendid Suns*. New York, Riverhead Books, 2007.

Huggan, Graham. *The Postcolonial Exotic: Marketing the Margins*. Routledge, 2001.

Huntington, Samuel. "The Clash of Civilizations." *Foreign Affairs*, vol. 72, no. 3, Summer 1993, pp. 22–49.

Hussain, Zahid. "No Future—And No Past." *Newsweek*, vol. 137, no. 14, 2 Apr. 2001, p. 38.

"Interview with a RAWA activist on Afghanistan." *ZNet*, 24 May 2009.

Irwin, Robert. "The Emergence of the Islamic World System, 1000–1500." *The Cambridge Illustrated History of the Islamic World*, edited by Francis Robinson, Cambridge UP, 1996, pp. 32–61.

Jefferess, David. "To be Good (Again): *The Kite Runner* as Allegory of Global Ethics." *Journal of Postcolonial Writing*, vol. 45, no. 4, 2009, pp. 389–400.

Jeffries, Stuart. "Reader, I Am a He." *The Guardian*, 22 June 2005.

Joes, Anthony James. *Victorious Insurgencies: Four Rebellions that Shaped Our World*. UP of Kentucky, 2010.

Jones, Seth G. *In the Graveyard of Empires: America's War in Afghanistan*. W. W. Norton & Company, 2010.

Kabir, Ananya Jahanara. *Partition's Post-Amnesias: 1947, 1971 and Modern South Asia*. New Delhi, Women Unlimited, 2013.

"*Kabul Disco* by Nicolas Wild." *Indiequill*, 2 Mar. 2010, https://indiequill.word press.com/2010/03/02/kabul-disco-nicolas-wild/.

"Kabul's Lion King." *The Economist*, 10 Jan. 2002, https://www.economist.com /asia/2002/01/10/kabuls-lion-king.

Kandahar. Directed by Mohsen Makhmalbaf, performance by Nelofer Pazira, Avatar Films, 2001.

Kanderian, Nina, David Lawson, and Peter Zahler. "Current Status of Wildlife and Conservation in Afghanistan." *International Journal of Environmental Studies*, vol. 68, no. 3, 2011, pp. 281–298.

Karadia, Chhotu. "Afghanistan President Noor Mohammad Taraki Fights Islamic Forces Led by Mullahs." *India Today*, 15 June 1979.

Keen, Judy. "First Lady and Her Favorite Books." *USA Today,* 13 Jan. 2005.

Keniston, Ann, and Jeanne Follansbee Quinn. *Literature After 9/11.* Routledge Studies in Contemporary Literature, 2008.

Keshavarz, Fatemeh. *Jasmine and Stars: Reading More Than Reading Lolita in Tehran.* U of North Carolina P, 2007.

Khadra, Yasmina. *The Swallows of Kabul.* New York, Anchor, 2002.

Khan, Adnan. "Blood Stones." *Maclean's,* vol. 127, no. 21, 2 June 2014, pp. 30–32.

Khan, Azmat. "Ghost Students, Ghost Teachers, Ghost Schools." *BuzzFeed News,* 9 July 2015, https://www.buzzfeed.com/azmatkhan/the-big-lie-that-helped -justify-americas-war-in-afghanistan?utm_term=.kpea8PYaA#.onxqRGEqm.

Khan, Douglas. *Earth Sound, Earth Signal: Energies and Earth Magnitude in the Arts.* Berkeley, U of California P, 2013.

Khan, Shahnaz. "Afghan Women: The Limits of Colonial Rescue." *Feminism and War: Confronting U.S. Imperialism,* edited by Robin L. Riley, Chandra Talpade Mohanty, and Minnie Bruce Pratt, New York, Zed Books, 2008, pp. 161–178.

Khan, Sorayya. *City of Spies.* New York, Aleph Book Company, 2015.

Kirksey, Eben S., and Stefan Helmreich. "The Emergence of Multispecies Ethnography." *Cultural Anthropology,* vol. 25, no. 4, 2010, pp. 545–576.

The Kite Runner. Directed by Marc Forster, performances by Khalid Abdalla and Zekeria Ebrahimi, DreamWorks Pictures, 2007.

Klein, Adam. *The Gifts of the State and Other Stories: New Writing from Afghanistan.* Disquiet, 2013.

Kolhatkar, Sonali. "'Saving' Afghan Women." *Revolutionary Association of Women in Afghanistan (RAWA),* 2002, http://www.rawa.org/znet.htm.

Kolhatkar, Sonali, and James Ingalls. *Bleeding Afghanistan: Washington, Warlords, and the Propaganda of Silence.* New York, Seven Stories Press, 2006.

Kollin, Susan. *Nature's State: Imagining Alaska as the Last Frontier.* U of North Carolina P, 2001.

Kosek, Jake. "Ecologies of Empire: On the New Uses of the Honeybee." *Cultural Anthropology* vol. 25, no. 4, 2010, pp. 650–678.

Kovačević, Nataša. *Narrating Post/Communism: Colonial Discourse and Europe's Borderline Civilization.* Abingdon, Oxon, Routledge, 2008.

Kushner, Tony. *Homebody/Kabul.* New York, Theatre Communications Group, 2002.

Lacquer, Thomas M. "Mourning, Pity, and the Work of Narrative in the Making of Humanity." *Humanitarianism and Suffering: The Mobilization of Empathy,* edited by Richard Ashby Wilson and Richard D. Brown, Cambridge UP, 2009, pp. 31–57.

Lafer, Gordon. "Neoliberalism by Other Means: The 'War on Terror' at Home and Abroad." *New Political Science,* vol. 26, no. 3, 2004, pp. 323–346.

Lamb, Christina. *Farewell, Kabul: From Afghanistan to a More Dangerous World.* London, William Collins Books, 2016.

Laub, Dori. "Truth and Testimony: The Process and the Struggle." *Trauma: Explorations in Memory,* edited by Cathy Caruth, Johns Hopkins UP, 1995, pp. 61–75.

Lauzen, Martha. "The Funny Business of Being Tina Fey: Constructing a (Feminist) Comedy Icon." *Feminist Media Studies*, vol. 14, no. 1, 2014, pp. 106–117.

Lawson, Daniel. "The Rhetorical Work of Remediation in *The Photographer*." *Studies in Comics*, vol. 5, no. 2, 2014, pp. 319–336.

Lawson, George. "Introduction: the 'What,' 'When,' and 'Where' of the Global 1989." *The Global 1989: Continuity and Change in World Politics*, edited by George Lawson, Chris Armbruster, and Michael Cox, Cambridge UP, 2010, pp. 1–20.

---, et al. *The Global 1989: Continuity and Change in World Politics*. Cambridge UP, 2010.

Lee, Richard E., editor. *The Longue Durée and World-Systems Analysis*. Albany, SUNY P, 2012.

Lenin, Vladimir. "May Day Action by the Revolutionary Proletariat." *Sotsial-Demokrat. Translated by George Hanna, Marxist Internet Archive*. https://www.marxists.org/archive/lenin/works/1913/jun/15.htm.

Lieberman, Victor, editor. *Beyond Binary Histories: Re-imagining Eurasia to c. 1830*. U of Michigan P, 1999.

Liu, Melinda. "Now I See the Sunlight." *Newsweek*, 26 Nov. 2001, https://www.newsweek.com/now-i-see-sunlight-149777.

Lutz, Catherine, and Sujaya Desai. "US Reconstruction Aid for Afghanistan: The Dollars and Sense." Watson Institute for International Studies, 5 Jan. 2015, http://watson.brown.edu/costsofwar/files/cow/imce/papers/2015/US%20 Reconstruction%20Aid%20for%20Afghanistan.pdf.

Magnus, Ralph H., and Eden Naby. *Afghanistan: Mullah, Marx, and Mujahid*. Boulder, Colorado, Westview Press, 1998.

Makhmalbaf, Mohsen. "Buddha Was Not Demolished in Afghanistan; It Collapsed out of Shame." *MFH Makhmalbaf Film House: Makhmalbaf Family Official Website*, 1 Mar. 2001, http://makhmalbaf.com/?q=article /text-book-buddha-was-not-demolished-afghanistan-it-collapsed-out-shame.

Maley, William. *The Afghanistan Wars*. New York, Palgrave, 2002.

Mamdani, Mahmood. *Good Muslim, Bad Muslim: America, Cold War and the Roots of Terror*. New York, Doubleday, 2005.

Manis, Shelley. "Cain's Grave, Ground Zero, and 'History Unmarked Grave of Discarded Lies': The Question of Hospitality to the Other in *Homebody/Kabul*." *Journal of American Drama and Theater*, vol. 24, no. 3, 2012, pp. 23–43.

Marks, Peter. "For Tony Kushner, an Eerily Prescient Return." *New York Times*, 25 Nov. 2001, https://www.nytimes.com/2001/11/25/theater/for-tony-kushner -an-eerily-prescient-return.html.

Meskell, Lynn. "Negative Heritage and Past Mastering in Archeology." *Anthropological Quarterly*, vol. 75, no. 3, Summer 2002, pp. 557–574.

Miller, Matthew Thomas. "'The Kite Runner' Critiqued: New Orientalism Goes to the Big Screen." *Common Dreams*, 5 Jan. 2008, https://www.commondreams.org /views/2008/01/05/kite-runner-critiqued-new-orientalism-goes-big-screen.

Minwalla, Framji. "Tony Kushner's Homebody/Kabul: Staging History in a Post-Colonial World." *Theater*, vol. 33, no. 1, Winter 2003, pp. 29–43.

Mirzoeff, Nicholas. *Watching Babylon: The War in Iraq and Global Visual Culture.* Routledge, 2005.

Mitchell, Elvis. "Film Review; Veils of Tears Frame Lives in Kandahar." *New York Times,* 14 Dec. 2001, https://www.nytimes.com/2001/12/14/movies/film-review-veils-of-tears-frame-lives-in-kandahar.html.

Mitchell, W. J. T. *Cloning Terror: The War of Images, 9/11 to the Present.* U of Chicago P, 2011.

Mulvey, Laura. "Visual Pleasure and Narrative Cinema." *Screen,* vol. 16, no. 3, 1975, pp. 6–18.

Muntz, Lori. "Front Porch Lessons: 'The Kite Runner,' 'Kabul Transit,' and Required First-Year Writing." *The Journal of the Midwest Modern Language Association,* vol. 41, no. 1, 2008, pp. 111–120.

Neurophilosophy. "US Military Planned on Using Spy Crows to Find Osama bin Laden." *Science Blogs,* 8 May 2011, http://scienceblogs.com/neurophilosophy/2011/05/08/us-military-spy-crows-binladen/.

Nikolchina, Miglena. "The Seminar: *Mode d'emploi* Impure Spaces in the Light of Late Totalitarianism." *Differences: A Journal of Feminist Cultural Studies,* vol. 13, no. 1, 2002, pp. 96–127.

Nixon, Rob. *Slow Violence and the Environmentalism of the Poor.* Harvard UP, 2011.

Norland, Rob. "Portrait of Pain Ignites Debate over Afghan War." *New York Times,* 5 Aug. 2010, https://www.nytimes.com/2010/08/05/world/asia/05afghan.html.

Novak, Matt. *Paleofuture.* https://www.paleofuture.com.

Nowicha, Wanda. "Statement from the Non-Region." *Statement Made at the Fourth World Conference on Women,* Beijing, 1995, http://www.astra.org.pl/?statement-from-the-non-region.

Nunan, Timothy. *Humanitarian Invasion: Global Development in Cold War Afghanistan.* Cambridge UP, 2016.

O'Gorman, Daniel. *Fictions of the War on Terror: Difference and the Transnational 9/11 Novel.* London, Palgrave Macmillan, 2015.

---."'Planetarity' and Pakistani Post-9/11 Fiction." *Alluvium,* vol. 1, no. 7, 2012.

Oliver, Kelly. *Carceral Humanitarianism: Logics of Refugee Detention.* U of Minnesota P, 2017.

Omar, Qais Akbar. *A Fort of Nine Towers: An Afghan Family Story.* New York, Picador, 2013.

---. Interview with Anna Maria Tremonti. *The Current with Anna Maria Tremonti,* 30 Apr. 2013, https://www.cbc.ca/radio/thecurrent/qais-akbar-omar-a-fort-of-nine-towers-1.1539633.

Parikka, Jussi. *A Geology of Media.* U of Minnesota P, 2015.

Pazira, Nelofer. *A Bed of Red Flowers: In Search of My Afghanistan.* New York, Free Press, 2005.

Pearce, Fred. "The Wasteland." *New Scientist,* vol. 173, no. 2324, 5 Jan. 2002, p. 4.

Petersen, Anne Helen. "It's Time to Stop Apologizing for Tina Fey." *BuzzFeed,* 4 Mar. 2016, https://www.buzzfeednews.com/article/annehelenpetersen/the-dangerous-privilege-of-tina-fey.

Phillips, M. Scott. "The Failure of History: Kushner's *Homebody/Kabul* and the Apocalyptic Context." *Modern Drama,* vol. 47, no. 1, Spring 2004, pp. 1–20.

"The Photographer." *The Rachel Maddow Show.* MSNBC, 12 Jun. 2009.

"President George W. Bush Press Conference on 11 October 2001." *Johnston's Archive,* http://www.johnstonsarchive.net/terrorism/bush911e.html.

Puar, Jasbir K. "Queer Times, Queer Assemblages." *Social Text,* vol. 23, no. 3–4, 2005, pp. 121–139.

Puar, Jasbir. "Feminists and Queers in the Service of Empire." *Feminism and War: Confronting U.S. Imperialism,* edited by Robin L. Riley, Chandra Talpade Mohanty, and Minnie Bruce Pratt, New York, Zed Books, 2008, pp. 47–55.

Rabinow, Paul. *Marking Time: On the Anthropology of the Contemporary.* Princeton UP, 2008.

Rahimi, Atiq. *A Thousand Rooms of Dreams and Fear.* Other Press, 2007.

---. *Earth and Ashes.* Other Press, 2010.

Rahman, Zia Haider. *In the Light of What We Know.* New York, Farrar, Straus, and Giroux, 2014.

Randall, Martin. *9/11 and the Literature of Terror.* Edinburgh UP, 2011.

Reagan, Ronald. "Proclamation 5033—Afghanistan Day, 1983." *The American Presidency Project,* 21 Mar. 1983, http://www.presidency.ucsb.edu/ws/index.php?pid=41077.

Reston, James. "A Prophet in His Time: Premonition and Reality in Tony Kushner's *Homebody/Kabul.*" *American Theater,* vol. 9, no. 3, Mar. 2002, pp. 28–30, 50–53.

Román, David. *Performance in America: Contemporary U.S. Culture and the Performing Arts.* Duke UP, 2006.

Rorty, Richard. "Human Rights, Rationality, and Sentimentality." *On Human Rights: The Oxford Amnesty Lectures,* edited by Stephen Shute and Susan Hurley, New York, Basic Books, 1993, pp. 111–134.

Rose, Megan. "Afghanistan Waste Exhibit A: Kajaki Dam, More Than $300M Spent and Still Not Done." *ProPublica,* 19 Jan. 2016, https://www.propublica.org/article/afghanistan-waste-kajaki-dam-more-than-300-million-spent-still-not-done.

Rosen, Christopher. "Tina Fey: Whiskey Tango Foxtrot Casting Controversy Addressed." *Entertainment,* 4 Mar. 2016, https://ew.com/article/2016/03/04/tina-fey-whiskey-tango-foxtrot-casting-controversy.

Ross, Elizabeth. "Qais Akbar Omar: Boston's Afghan Writer Who Cannot Return Home." *WGBH News,* 9 June 2015, http://news.wgbh.org/post/qais-akbar-omar-boston-s-afghan-writer-who-can-t-return-home.

Røssaak, Eivind. "The Unseen of the Real: Or, Evidential Efficacy from Muybridge to 'The Matrix.'" *Witness: Memory, Representation, and the Media in Question,* edited by Eivind Røssaak, U of Chicago P, 2008, pp. 224–232.

Rothberg, Michael. "Decolonizing Trauma Studies: A Response." *Studies in the Novel,* vol. 40, no. 1–2, Spring and Summer 2008, pp. 224–234.

---. *Multidirectional Memory: Remembering the Holocaust in the Age of Decolonization.* Stanford UP, 2009.

Rubin, Alissa J. "Severed Trees in Orchards Mirror Afghan History." *New York Times*, 10 July 2010, https://www.nytimes.com/2010/07/11/world/asia/11 afghan.html.

Rubin, Barnett. *Afghanistan from the Cold War to the War on Terror*. Oxford UP, 2013.

---. *The Fragmentation of Afghanistan: State Formation and Collapse in the International System*. Yale UP, 1995.

Rumsfeld, Donald. *Known and Unknown: A Memoir*. New York, Sentinel, 2011.

Rushdie, Salman. *Shalimar the Clown*. Random House, 2006.

Ryzik, Melena. "Q and A. with Tina Fey: Live From Kabul, It's a Feminist Comedy." *New York Times*, 4 Mar. 2016, https://www.nytimes.com/2016/03/06 /arts/television/q-and-a-with-tina-fey-live-from-kabul-its-a-feminist-comedy .html.

Sandler, Stephanie. "The Poetry of Decline: On Joseph Brodsky, 'On the Talks in Kabul.'" *Russian Review*, vol. 61, no. 2, 2002, pp. 204–207.

Saull, Richard. "One World, Many Cold Wars: 1989 in the Middle East." *The Global 1989: Continuity and Change in World Politics*, edited by George Lawson, Chris Armbruster, and Michael Cox, Cambridge UP, 2010, pp. 179–197.

Scherr, Rebecca. "Framing Human Rights: Comics Form and the Politics of Recognition in Joe Sacco's Footnotes in Gaza." *Textual Practice*, vol. 21, no. 1, 2015, pp. 111–131.

Schueller, Malini Johar. "Cross-cultural Identification, Neoliberal Feminism, and Afghan Women." *Genders*, vol. 53, 2011.

Schultheis, Rob. "Perilous Gardens, Persistent Dreams: Healing the Wounds of War and Nature in Afghanistan." *Sierra Magazine*, May–June 2003, pp. 24–33.

Schuster, Joshua. "How to Write the Disaster." *Minnesota Review*, vol. 83, 2014, pp. 163–171.

Schwartz, Michael. "Military Neoliberalism: Endless War and Humanitarian Crisis in the 21st Century." *Societies Without Borders*, vol. 6, no. 3, 2011, pp. 190–303.

Seierstad, Åsne. *The Bookseller of Kabul*. New York, Back Bay Books, 2002.

Shamsie, Kamila. *Burnt Shadows*. New York, Picador, 2009.

---. *A God in Every Stone*. Atavist Books, 2014.

---. "The Missing Picture." *World Literature Today*, Mar.–Apr. 2013, pp. 10–13.

Sharp, Joanne P. "'The Russians Acted Like the Russians': The 'Othering' of the Soviet Union in the *Reader's Digest*, 1980–90." *DisClosure: A Journal of Social Theory*, vol. 1, 1992, pp. 58–73.

Shryock, Andrew, and Daniel Lord Smail. *Deep History: The Architecture of Past and Present*. Berkeley, U of California P, 2011.

Shryock, Andrew, Thomas Trautmann, and Clive Gamble, "Imagining the Human in Deep Time." *Deep History: The Architecture of Past and Present*, edited by Andrew Shryock and Daniel Lord Smail, Berkeley, U of California P, 2011, pp. 55–77.

Simms, Anthony, et al. "Saving Threatened Species in Afghanistan: Snow Leopards in the Wakhan Corridor." *International Journal of Environmental Studies*, vol. 68, no. 3, 2011, pp. 299–312.

Singh, Harleen. "Insurgent Metaphors: Decentering 9/11 in Mohsin Hamid's *The Reluctant Fundamentalist* and Kamila Shamsie's *Burnt Shadows*." *Ariel: A Review of International English Literature*, vol. 43, no. 1, 2012, pp. 23–44.

---. "A Legacy of Violence: Interview with Kamila Shamsie about *Burnt Shadows* (2009)." *Ariel: A Review of International English Literature*, vol. 42, no. 2, 2012, pp. 157–162.

Slaughter, Joseph R. *Human Rights, Inc.: The World Novel, Narrative Form, and International Law*. Fordham UP, 2007.

---. "Humanitarian Reading." *Humanitarianism and Suffering: The Mobilization of Empathy*, edited by Richard Ashby Wilson and Richard D. Brown, Cambridge UP, 2009, pp. 88–107.

Smallwood, Peter, et al. "Wildlife Conservation . . . in Afghanistan?" *BioScience*, vol. 61, no. 7, 2011, pp. 506–511.

Söderbäck, Fanny. "Revolutionary Time: Revolt as Temporal Return." *Signs: Journal of Women in Culture and Society*, vol. 37, no. 2, 2012, pp. 301–324.

Spiegelman, Art. *In the Shadow of No Towers*. Viking Press, 2004.

Spitzer, Kirk. "U.S. Using Mammoth 'Daisy Cutter' Bomb." *USA Today*, 6 Nov. 2001.

Stabile, Carol A., and Deepa Kumar. "Unveiling Imperialism: Media, Gender, and the War on Afghanistan." *Media, Culture & Society*, vol. 27, no. 5, 2005, pp. 765–782.

Standing, Guy. *Precariat: The New Dangerous Class*. Bloomsbury Academic, 2011.

Starosta, Anita. "Perverse Tongues, Postsocialist Translations." *Boundary 2*, vol. 41, no. 1, 2014, pp. 203–227.

Stephens, Joe, and David B. Ottaway. "From U.S., the ABC's of Jihad." *Washington Post*, 23 Mar. 2002, https://www.washingtonpost.com/archive/politics/2002/03/23/from-us-the-abcs-of-jihad/d079075a-3ed3-4030-9a96-0d48f6355e54/?utm_term=.7c2c35babadf.

Stewart, Rory. *The Places In Between*. London, Picador, 2004.

Streeter, Edwin William, and Joseph Hatten. *The Great Diamonds in the World. Their History and Romance*. London, George Bell and Sons, 1882.

Suchland, Jennifer. "Is Postsocialism Transnational?" *Signs: Journal of Women in Culture and Society*, vol. 36, no. 4, 2011, pp. 837–862.

Suhrke, Astri. "Reconstruction as Modernisation: The 'Post-Conflict' Project in Afghanistan." *Third World Quarterly*, vol. 28, no. 7, 2007, pp. 1291–1308.

Taft-Kaufman, Jill. "A *TPQ* Interview: Tony Kushner on Theatre, Politics, and Culture." *Text and Performance Quarterly*, vol. 21, no. 1, 2004, pp. 38–54.

Taylor, Adam. "These Are America's 9 Longest Foreign Wars Yet." *Washington Post*, 29 May 2014, https://www.washingtonpost.com/news/worldviews/wp/2014/05/29/these-are-americas-9-longest-foreign-wars/?utm_term=.8ed050dfce16.

Taylor, Ella. "Grounded: Controversy Aside, This Just Won't Fly." *Phoenix New Times,* 20 Dec. 2007.

Taylor, Michael. "'Kandahar' Actor Accused of Being Assassin/Tantai Said to Have Killed Diplomat." *San Francisco Gate,* 4 Jan. 2002, https://www .sfgate.com/entertainment/article/Kandahar-actor-accused-of-being-assassin -2885807.php.

Tlostanova, Madina. "Postsocialist ≠ Postcolonial? On Post-Soviet Imaginary and Global Coloniality." *Journal of Postcolonial Writing,* vol. 48, no. 2, 2012, pp. 130–142.

Tønnesson, Stein. "Global Civil War?" *Security Dialogue,* vol. 33, no. 3, 2002, https://www.prio.org/Publications/Publication/?x=2800.

"Tony's Eye on the Future." *Evening Standard: Go London,* 21 May 2002, http:// www.standard.co.uk/goingout/theatre/tonys-eye-on-the-future-7434281 .html.

Torchin, Leshu. *Creating the Witness: Documenting Genocide on Film, Video, and the Internet.* U of Minnesota P, 2012.

Trautmann, Thomas R., Gillian Feeley-Harnik, and John C. Mitani. "Deep Kinship." *Deep History: The Architecture of Past and Present,* edited by Andrew Shryock and Daniel Lord Smail, Berkeley: U of California P, 2011, pp. 160–189.

Traverso, Enzo. *Left-Wing Melancholia: Marxism, History, and Memory.* Columbia UP, 2017.

Trexler, Adam. *Anthropocene Fictions: The Novel in a Time of Climate Change.* U of Virginia P, 2015.

Usolcev, Pavel. "People's Diplomacy's Successes in the Argu Valley." ["Успехи «народной дипломатии» в долине Аргу"]. *From Soldier to General: Memories of War* [От солдата до генерала. Воспоминания о войне]. Moscow, Academy of Historical Sciences, 2005, http://www.ainros.ru/postat.htm?kn_id=35.

Versluys, Kristaan. *Out of the Blue: September 11 and the Novel.* Columbia UP, 2009.

Wiezman, Eyal. *The Least of All Possible Evils: Humanitarian Violence from Arendt to Gaza.* New York, Verso, 2012.

---. "Matters of Calculation: The Evidence of the Anthropocene." *Architecture in the Anthropocene,* edited by Etienne Turpin, Open Humanities Press, 2013, pp. 63–81.

Welsh, William M. "Dog Teams Seek a Hidden Enemy." *USA Today,* 7 July 2010.

Westad, Odd Arne. *The Global Cold War.* Cambridge UP, 2005.

Whiskey Tango Foxtrot. Directed by Glenn Ficarra and John Requa, performance by Tina Fey, Paramount Pictures, 2016.

Wild, Nicolas. *Kabul Disco.* Noida, HarperCollins Publishers India, 2009.

---. *Kabul Disco, Book 2: How I Did Not Become an Opium Addict in Afghanistan.* Noida, HarperCollins Publishers India, 2013.

Wood, Ellen Meiskins. "A Manifesto for Global Capital?" *Debating Empire,* edited by Gopal Blakrishnan, London, Verso, 2013.

Zakaria, Fareed. "The Long Road to Hell: America in Iraq." *CNN*, 26 Oct. 2015.

---. "Trump Locks America into its Forever War." *Washington Post*, 24 Aug. 2017, https://www.washingtonpost.com/opinions/trump-signs-on-to-the-forever -war-in-afghanistan/2017/08/24/64684004-890e-11e7-a94f-3139abce39f5 _story.html?utm_term=.85b713b59bcb.

Zielinski, Siegfried. *The Deep Time of the Media: Toward and Archeology of Seeing and Hearing by Technical Means.* Cambridge, MIT P, 2006.

Zinck, Pascal. "Eyeless in Guantanamo: Vanishing Horizons in Kamila Sham-sie's *Burnt Shadows.*" *Commonwealth Essays and Studies*, vol. 33, no. 1, 2010, pp. 45–54.

Žižek, Slavoj. *Violence.* Picador, 2008.

Index

About the Author

Alla Ivanchikova holds a PhD from the University at Buffalo and is an associate professor of English and comparative literature at Hobart and William Smith Colleges in Geneva, New York.